Get the eBook FREE!
(PDF, ePub, Kindle, and liveBook all included)

We believe that once you buy a book from us, you should be able to read it in any format we have available. To get electronic versions of this book at no additional cost to you, purchase and then register this book at the Manning website.

Go to https://www.manning.com/freebook and follow the instructions to complete your pBook registration.

That's it!
Thanks from Manning!

D1294289

Knative in Action

Knative in Action

JACQUES CHESTER

FOREWORD BY VILLE AIKAS

MANNING

SHELTER ISLAND

For online information and ordering of this and other Manning books, please visit
www.manning.com. The publisher offers discounts on this book when ordered in quantity.
For more information, please contact

> Special Sales Department
> Manning Publications Co.
> 20 Baldwin Road
> PO Box 761
> Shelter Island, NY 11964
> Email: orders@manning.com

Manning Publications Co.
20 Baldwin Road
PO Box 761
Shelter Island, NY 11964

Development editor:	Jenny Stout
Technical development editor:	John Guthrie
Review editor:	Mihaela Batinic
Production editor:	Deirdre S. Hiam
Copy editor:	Frances Buran
Proofreader:	Jason Everett
Technical proofreader:	Kelvin Johnson
Typesetter:	Dennis Dalinnik
Cover designer:	Marija Tudor

ISBN: 9781617296642
Printed in the United States of America

Pour la petite maman.

brief contents

contents

foreword

Over the last couple of years, Knative has seen rapid growth in adoption and maturity, with a flourishing ecosystem that's building around and on top of it. *Knative in Action* by Jacques Chester is a long overdue book, giving the user a well-structured, easy approach, and a clearly written grounds-up explanation on what Knative is, what kinds of problems it helps the user tackle, and how to best utilize Knative to solve those problems.

The examples in this book are super easy to follow, cleverly written (many lols were had while reading the pre-release version of the book), and build up the material in easy to approach piece-meal chunks. In particular, I liked the real-world examples and great illustrations. I also enjoyed following along, as it was easy to re-create the examples and to gain an understanding of the various components, resources, and trade-offs.

As Knative is still seeing rapid development, Jacques also provides a balanced viewpoint for things that still need to be worked on (for example, a richer filtering model). He also discusses ways to work around those limitations.

Jacques is one of the longest serving members of the Knative community. We're lucky to have him in the community.

VILLE AIKAS
SOFTWARE ENGINEER & CO-CREATOR OF KNATIVE EVENTING

preface

I was working for Pivotal when I was approached to write this book. At the time, we were in the early stages of our partnership with Google and the community. At Pivotal, I had (through the Project riff team) been one of the early chosen to learn about it before it became a public project.

My original plan for this book was, in retrospect, absurdly overambitious. Instead of the medium-sized book you're now holding, there would have been a slab of words worthy of industrial use. Primarily, the evolution of the book has been from my urge to talk about many different things, including Knative, to just talk about Knative. This is an improvement all round. While I like to talk about related topics, these aren't what is needed right at the outset. This book is *Knative in Action*, not *Grand Unified Theory of Knative*.

That said, I like writing, and I am, perhaps, too proud of mine, so at times I take the scenic routes. If English is not your first language, it might be slow going. One thing I can offer is that any unfamiliar words can usually be skipped; it's just me showing off.

acknowledgements

I could thank a thousand people and still not scratch the surface. But here are some of them.

Thanks to Eleonor Gardner for scouting some random person from the Internet, so that Michael Stephens could greenlight the project. Thanks to Jennifer Stout, my endlessly cheerful editor and John Guthrie, my suitably grizzled tech editor. Frances Buran tolerated my endless blizzard of commas. Thank you, all. You made the book better.

Thanks also to other Manning folks who have (so far!) been involved: Nicole Butterfield, Kristen Watterson, Rebecca Rinehart, Rejhana Markanovic, Matko Hrvatin, Sam Wood, Radmila Ercegovac, Cody Tankersley, Troy Dreier, Candace Gillhoolley, Branko Latincic, Mehmed Pasic, Jennifer Houle, Stjepan Jureković, Deirdre Hiam, Jason Everett, and Mihaela Batinic.

As well as the staff at Manning, I am grateful to the anonymous reviewers who ploughed through earlier drafts—some of them three times! The book was greatly improved by their honesty and attention to detail. I know I didn't act on every suggestion, but thank you, thank you, thank you.

I owe the subject matter to the Knative community. I have enjoyed talking to and learning from Matt Moore, Ville Aikas, Evan Anderson, Joe Burnett, Scott Nichols, Jason Hall, Markus Thömmes, Nghia Tran, Julian Friedman, Carlos Santana, Nima Kaviani, Michael Maximilien, Doug Davis, Ben Browning, Grant Rodgers, Paul Morie, Brenda Chan, Donna Malayeri, Mark Kropf, and Mark Chmarny. Also in the community are many folks I know from Pivotal or VMware, including the unflappable Dave Protasowski, Mark Fisher, Scott Andrews, Glynn Normington, Sukhil Suresh, Tanzeeb

Khalili (who I will probably meet some day), David Turanski, Thomas Risberg, Dmitriy Kalinin, Jurgen Leschner, and the tireless Shash Reddy.

Continuing with the Pivotal/VMware theme, there are the folks who made it possible for me to focus on writing this book. I already owed Mike Dalessio and Catherine McGarvey for giving me an opportunity to work for Pivotal; they just doubled down on helping me. Graham Siener listened to my venting, despite having actually important things to do. Ian Andrews and Richard Seroter smoothed the path for marketing, while Cyrus Wadia, Dave Schachner, and Heidi Hischmann made sure all the formalities were formed correctly. I also owe my managers during the process, Edie Beer and Ben Moss.

Plus *all* the folks at Pivotal NYC (and SF! and Toronto! and London! and Santa Monica! and everywhere!), past and present. I have loved, sincerely *loved*, my time with each and every one of you. The worst part of writing this book was that I spent all my time working solo. The best part is knowing that I still belonged to a kind, smart, and capable fellowship. Once a Pivot, always a Pivot.

I'm grateful to the podcasters who spoke with me while I was writing the book. W. Curtis Preston and Prasana from "Backup Central: Restore it All," Tim Berglund of "Streaming Audio: A Confluent Podcast" (with assistance by Victoria Yu), Jomiro Eming of "OfferZen Podcast," and Jonathan Baker and Justin Brodley of "The Cloud Pod." I thoroughly enjoyed every one of our discussions.

To all the reviewers: Alessandro Campeis, Alex Lucas, Andres Sacco, Bojan Djurkovic, Clifford Thurber, Conor Redmond, Eddú Meléndez Gonzales, Ezra Simeloff, Geert Van Laethem, George Haines, Guy Ndjeng, Jeffrey Chu, Jerome Meyer, Julien Pohie, Karthikeyarajan Rajendran, Kelum Prabath Senanayake, Kelvin Johnson, Luke Kupka, Matt Welke, Michael Bright, Miguel Cavaco Coquet, Pethuru Raj, Raffaella Ventaglio, Richard Vaughan, Rob Pacheco, Satadru Roy, Taylor Dolezal, Tim Langford, and Zorodzayi Mukuya—thank you for your hard work!

Everything I've done that's ever impressed anyone is actually just my pale imitation of my parents, Barry and Juliette. Whenever I begin to bore people, I just tell the story of their lives. They have roamed so widely, done so much, overcome such obstacles; this book is as substantial as a shadow next to them.

And, of course, Renée, who is the best stroke of luck I've ever had. I couldn't have made it to the end without you.

about this book

Who should read this book?

This book is intended for folks who want to learn the fundamental components and capabilities of Knative Serving and Knative Eventing. I describe Kubernetes concepts when I absolutely need to, but otherwise, I have aimed to talk exclusively about Knative.

My goal while writing was that someone with no Kubernetes experience would be able to make practical day-to-day use of Knative. I don't know if I truly succeeded, because I came to writing with a fair amount of background knowledge about containers, Cloud Native architecture, and Kubernetes. It's hard to know what "obvious" facts get left out. Not too many, I hope.

The book does not aim to teach you about the questions that will follow from learning the basic mechanics. It is one thing for me to show you how to build a web of interacting functions, but another thing to talk about the trade-offs of doing so. I hint briefly at topics I think are related (such as queuing theory), but in the interests of space and time, it wasn't possible to go into any depth.

How this book is organized: A roadmap

Chapter 1 introduces Knative and positions it in the big wide world. Chapters 2 through 5 deal with Knative Serving. I begin with a survey of Serving in chapter 2. In chapter 3, I perform a deep dive on Services and Configurations, followed by a discussion of routing in chapter 4. Chapter 5, on Autoscaling, is a little bit of dessert.

Then I turn to Knative Eventing. In chapter 6, I introduce Eventing and Cloud-Events. Chapter 7 hits Sources and Sinks, the main concepts of Eventing. Chapter 8 builds on chapter 7, introducing Brokers, Filters, Sequences, and Parallels.

To wrap things up, in chapter 9, I focus on the basic questions of "How does my software get to production?" and "Is my software producing?"

The book is not designed for reading out of order; it will be easiest to read straight through. That said, you may be able to read Eventing before Serving and still get some value.

Conspicuously absent is a running example. I did consider this and did draft some code. I decided against it to mitigate risk. While writing this book, I was also learning about parts of Knative that I had not yet used. Some of these were evolving quickly as I went. I felt that building a full example would have run the risk that I'd need to throw it out and redo it at least once. Instead, examples are created or described within the context of individual chapters.

About the code

Most of the code in this book is a mix of CLI commands and YAML. Actual *code* code is in Golang.

liveBook discussion forum

Purchase of *Knative in Action* includes free access to a private web forum run by Manning Publications where you can make comments about the book, ask technical questions, and receive help from the author and from other users. To access the forum, go to https://livebook.manning.com/book/knative-in-action/discussion. You can also learn more about Manning's forums and the rules of conduct at https://livebook .manning.com/#!/discussion.

Manning's commitment to our readers is to provide a venue where a meaningful dialogue between individual readers and between readers and the author can take place. It is not a commitment to any specific amount of participation on the part of the author, whose contribution to the forum remains voluntary (and unpaid). We suggest you try asking the author some challenging questions lest his interest stray! The forum and the archives of previous discussions will be accessible from the publisher's website as long as the book is in print.

Other online resources

First, Knative's own documentation (https://knative.dev/docs/) is improving all the time. This book is written as an introduction for a general technical audience. But, sometimes, you need a task-oriented reference material. The Knative docs are the place to go.

The Knative community is open and welcoming to newcomers (https://knative
.dev/community/). The best place to start is joining the Knative Slack instance (https://
knative.slack.com/) and joining the `knative-users` (https://groups.google.com/g/
knative-users) group. Joining the group gives you more than a mailing list member-
ship—you also get access to a shared community calendar and working documents.

Meetings of working groups happen throughout the week on a variety of topics,
from the Serving API to Autoscaling to operations to documentation. Also each week,
the project's Technical Oversight Committee receives an update from one working
group describing their previous few months of work. All meetings are noted and
recorded, so you can look up previous conversations easily.

about the author

JACQUES CHESTER is an engineer at VMware, via the Pivotal acquisition. He has worked in R&D since 2015, contributing to several projects, including Knative. Before R&D, Jacques worked for Pivotal Labs as a consulting software engineer.

about the cover illustration

The figure on the cover of *Knative in Action* is captioned "Français," or Frenchman. The illustration is taken from a collection of dress costumes from various countries by Jacques Grasset de Saint-Sauveur (1757–1810), titled *Costumes de Différents Pays*, published in France in 1797. Each illustration is finely drawn and colored by hand. The rich variety of Grasset de Saint-Sauveur's collection reminds us vividly of how culturally apart the world's towns and regions were just 200 years ago. Isolated from each other, people spoke different dialects and languages. In the streets or in the countryside, it was easy to identify where they lived and what their trade or station in life was just by their dress.

The way we dress has changed since then and the diversity by region, so rich at the time, has faded away. It is now hard to tell apart the inhabitants of different continents, let alone different towns, regions, or countries. Perhaps we have traded cultural diversity for a more varied personal life—certainly for a more varied and fast-paced technological life.

At a time when it is hard to tell one computer book from another, Manning celebrates the inventiveness and initiative of the computer business with book covers based on the rich diversity of regional life of two centuries ago, brought back to life by Grasset de Saint-Sauveur's pictures.

Introduction 1

This chapter covers

- What Knative is and why you should use it
- The places where Knative shines (and doesn't)
- The basics of Serving and Eventing
- Where to get started

One of my north stars is the Onsi Haiku Test:

```
Here is my source code.
Run it on the cloud for me.
I do not care how.
```

This is actually a radical notion of how software can best be developed, deployed, upgraded, observed, managed, and improved. It must be, because so often it emerges long after we've tried everything else first. The Onsi Haiku Test implies

- That a fast, reliable path to production is a shared goal for everyone
- That there is a crisp, contractual boundary between folks who provide platforms and folks whose work will consume the platform
- That building software that handles other software is, for most developers, not the most urgent, most valuable work they could be doing

1

Kubernetes, by itself, does not pass the Onsi Haiku Test. The boundary between development and operation is unclear. Developers can't walk up to a vanilla Kubernetes cluster, hand it raw source code, and get all the basic amenities of routing, logging, service injection, and so on. Kubernetes gives you a rich toolbox for solving the Test in your own particular way. But a toolbox is not a machine. It is a toolbox.

This book is not about Kubernetes, it's about Knative. Knative builds on the toolbox Kubernetes provides, but it also sets out to achieve a level of consistency, simplicity, and ease of use that brings Kubernetes much closer to meeting the Test's high standard. Knative is a machine.

While it has something to offer many different professional specialties, Knative is primarily focused on the needs and pains of developers, to elevate them to the heights of "I do not care how." Kubernetes is amazing, but it never strongly demarcated what is meant to be changed or managed by whom. That's a strength: you can do anything! And a weakness: you could, and did, do anything! Knative provides crisp abstractions that, by design, don't refer to the grungy physical business of nodes and containers and virtual machines (VMs). In this book, I'll also focus on developers, referring to or explaining Kubernetes only when necessary to understand Knative.

1.1 *What is Knative?*

There are several ways to answer this question. To begin with, the *purpose* of Knative is to provide a simple, consistent layer over Kubernetes that solves common problems of deploying software, connecting disparate systems together, upgrading software, observing software, routing traffic, and scaling automatically. This layer creates a firmer boundary between the developer and the platform, allowing the developer to concentrate on the software they are directly responsible for.

The *major subprojects* of Knative are Serving and Eventing.[1] Serving is responsible for deploying, upgrading, routing, and scaling. Eventing is responsible for connecting disparate systems. Dividing responsibilities this way allows each to be developed more independently and rapidly by the Knative community.

The *software artifacts* of Knative are a collection of software processes, packaged into containers, that run on a Kubernetes cluster. In addition, Knative installs additional customizations into Kubernetes itself to achieve its ends. This is true of both Serving and Eventing, each of which installs its own components and customizations. While this might interest a platform engineer or platform operator, it shouldn't matter to a developer. You should only care *that* it is installed, not where or how.

The *API* or *surface area* of Knative is primarily YAML documents that declaratively convey your intention as a developer. These are CRDs (Custom Resource Definitions),

---

[1] If you look at early talks and blog posts about Knative, you'll see references to a third subproject, Build. Build has since evolved and spun out into Tekton, an independent project. This decision moved Knative *away* from the Onsi Haiku Test, but it also resolved a number of architectural tensions in Serving. Overall, it was the right decision, but it leaves you with the responsibility of deciding how to convert source code into containers. Happily, there are many ways to do this, and I'll be introducing some later in the book.

which are, essentially, plugins or extensions for Kubernetes that look and feel like vanilla Kubernetes.

You can also work in a more imperative style using the Knative kn command-line client, which is useful for tinkering and rapid iteration. I'll show both of these approaches throughout the book. But first, let's take a quick motivational tour of Knative's capabilities.

1.1.1 Deploying, upgrading, and routing

Deployment has evolved. What used to be a process of manually promoting software artifacts through environments (with scheduled downtime, 200 people on a bridge call all weekend …) becomes continuous delivery and Blue/Green deploys.

Should deployment be all or nothing? Knative enables progressive delivery: instead of requests arriving at a production system that is entirely one version of the software, these arrive at a system where multiple versions can be running together with traffic split among these. This means that deployments can proceed at the granularity of *requests*, rather than *instances*. "Send 10% of traffic to v2" is different from "10% of instances are v2." I'll talk more about this in chapter 9.

1.1.2 Autoscaling

Sometimes there *is* no traffic. Sometimes there is *too much* traffic. One of these is wasteful; the other is stressful. Knative is ready with the Knative Pod Autoscaler (KPA), a request-centric autoscaler that's deeply integrated with Knative's routing, buffering, and metrics components. The autoscaler can't solve all your problems, but it will solve enough so that you can focus on more important problems. I'll discuss autoscaling in chapter 5.

1.1.3 Eventing

Easy management of HTTP requests will take you a long way, but not everything looks like a POST. Sometimes we want to react to events instead of responding to requests. Events might come from your software or external services, but these can arrive without anyone *requesting* something. That's where Knative Eventing for events comes into play. It enables you to compose small pieces of software into flexible processing pipelines, connected through events. You can even prepare to process things that don't exist yet (really). I'll discuss these topics in chapters 6, 7, and 8.

1.2 So what?

I know your secret. Somewhere in your repo is deploy.sh. It's a grungy bash script that does some grep-and-sed and calls kubectl a bunch of times. It probably also has some sleeps, and maybe you got ambitious and so there's a wget floating around in it too. You wrote it in a hurry and, of course, of course, *of course*, you're going to do a better job, but right now you're busy working to get this thing done before Q3 and you need to implement floozlebit support and refactor the twizzleflorp, and ... deploy.sh works well enough.

But this is always true for everything: there's never enough *time*. Why, really, didn't you make that change yet?[2] Easy—it's too hard. It's too much work when you already have enough.

Kubernetes *itself* is great, once you set it up. It absolutely shines at its core purpose in life: reconcile the differences between the desired state of the system and the actual state of the system on a continuous basis. If all you ever need is to deploy your system once and let it run forever without changing it, then you're good to go and lucky you. The rest of us, however, are on the hedonic treadmill. We have desired worlds that *change*. We ship bugs that need to be fixed, our users think of new features they want, and our competitors make us scramble to address new services.

And that's how you wound up with the script. And doing a better job of deployment doesn't seem urgent. After all, it works, right? Yes ... if and *only* if your goal is to be afraid to upgrade anything or to have umpteen slightly different versions of deploy.sh floating around company repos or to write your own CD system without intending to. Why bother? Let Knative toil for you instead.

Actually, I know two of your secrets. Your code knows a lot about all your other code. The Login Service knows about the User Service and the Are-You-A-Robot? Service. It tells these what it wants and it waits for their answer. This is the imperative style, and with it, we as a profession have built incredible monuments to human genius. But we've also built some incredible bowls of spaghetti and warm droppings.

It would be nice to decouple your services a bit, so that software responds to reports of stuff happening and, in turn, reports stuff that it did. This is not a novel concept: the idea of software connected through pipes of events or data has sailed under various flags and in various fleets for decades now. There are deep, important, and profound differences between all of these historical schools of thought. I will, in an act of mercy, spare you any meaningful discussion of these. Before you learn how to chisel apart the monolith, you need a chisel and a hammer.

1.3 *Where Knative shines*

Knative's focus on event-driven, progressively-delivered, autoscaling architectures lends itself to some particular sweet spots. Let's look at a few of these.

1.3.1 *Workloads with unpredictable, latency-insensitive demand*

Variability is a fact of life: nothing repeats perfectly. Nothing can be perfectly predicted or optimized. Many workloads face *demand* variability: it is not always clear from

---

[2] Those of you in the class who are pointing at their Spinnaker instances can lower your hands.

moment to moment what demand to expect. The Law of Variability Buffering says that you can deal with demand variability by buffering it in one of three ways:

- *With inventory*—Something you produced earlier and have at hand (for example, caching)
- *With capacity*—Unused reserve capacity that can absorb more demand without meaningful effect (for example, idle instances)
- *With time*—Making the demand wait longer

These are all costly. Inventory costs money to hold (RAM and disk space aren't free), capacity costs money to reserve (an idle CPU still uses electricity), and famously, "time is money" and nobody likes to wait.

> **NOTE** Inventory, capacity, and time really are the *only* options for buffering variability. It's basic calculus. Inventory is an integral, a sum of previous capacity utilization and demand. Capacity is a derivative, a rate of change of inventory. And time is time. You can rearrange the terms, and you can change their values, but you can't escape the boundaries of mathematics. The only alternative is to reduce variability so that you need less buffering in the first place.

Knative's default strategy for buffering is *time*. If demand shows up, but capacity is low or even zero, Knative reacts by raising capacity and holding your request until it can be served. That's well and good, but it takes time to bring capacity online. This is the famous "cold start" problem.

Does this matter? It depends on the nature of the demand. If the demand is latency-sensitive, then maybe scaling to zero is not for you. You can tell Knative to keep a minimum number of instances alive (no more pinging your function). On the other hand, if it's a batch job or background process that can wait a while to kick off, buffering by time is sensible and efficient. Let that thing drop to zero. Spend the savings on ice cream.

Regardless of sensitivity to latency, the other consideration is: how predictable is the demand? Highly variable demands require larger buffers. Either you hold more inventory, or more reserve capacity, or you make folks wait longer. There are no alternatives. If you don't know how you want to make trade-offs, the autoscaler can relieve you of dealing with common cases (figure 1.1). In cases of extreme latency sensitivity and highly predictable demand (e.g., a Netflix or YouTube video server), Knative might not actually be a good fit. In those cases, you are probably already doing some kind of capacity planning.

One thing Knative can't do much to save you from is *supply* variability. That is, it can't make

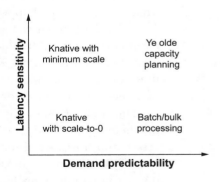

Figure 1.1 Knative's sweetspots in terms of latency sensitivity and demand predictability

variability due to your software vanish, or magic away variability due to upstream systems you rely on. But how long your software takes to become live and how responsive it is is largely in your court.

1.3.2 *Stitching together events from multiple sources*

Sometimes you have a square peg, a round hole, and a deadline. Knative won't shave the peg or hammer it into the hole, but Knative Eventing lets you glue things together so that you will be able to achieve your original purpose. By design, Eventing receives events from heterogenous sources and conveys these to heterogenous consumers. Webhook from Github? Yes. Pub/Sub message from Google? Yes. File uploaded? Yes.

Some combination of these? Also yes, which is the interesting part. Relatively small, consistent, standards-based interfaces allow many combinations of elements. To this, Knative adds some simple abstractions to enable you to go from dabs of glue to relatively sophisticated event flows. So long as some event or message can be expressed as a CloudEvent, which is pretty much anything ever, Knative Eventing can be used to do something smart with it.

Of course, the flipside of generality is that it can't be everything to everyone. Should you use it for CI/CD? Maybe. For streaming data analysis? Perhaps. Business workflow processing? Reply hazy, try again.

The key is that for all of these, there exist more specialized tools that may be a better fit. For example, you can build a MapReduce pattern using Knative. But realistically, you won't get anywhere near the kind of performance and scale of a dedicated MapReduce system. You can build CI/CD with Knative, but now you have to do a lot of homework to implement all the inflows and outflows.

Where Knative can shine is when you want to connect a variety of tools and systems in simple ways, in small increments. We all do this in our work, but typically, it gets jammed into whatever system that happens to have room for boarders. And so our web apps sprout obscure endpoints or our CI/CD accumulates increasingly hairy Bash scripts. Knative lets us pull these out into the open so that these can be more easily tested, monitored, and reused.

The trade-off here (figure 1.2) is between the heterogeneity of event types to be processed and how specialized the processing system will be. Knative is flexible and general, so that it can handle many kinds of events. At the

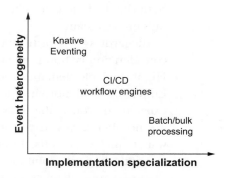

Figure 1.2 Knative's sweetspots in terms of event heterogeneity and implementation specialization

other end of the curve lie batch processing and bulk analytical systems that handle few kinds of events, usually known in advance, in a uniform way. By giving up flexibility, these can focus on raw throughput. By no means is Knative *incapable* of doing that work. In fact, you might prefer to use it first in most cases. But bear in mind that sometimes, specialization pays.

1.3.3 *Decomposing monoliths in small increments*

Microservices as a term describes a family of powerful architectural patterns. But getting to a microservices architecture isn't easy because most existing systems aren't designed for it. For better or worse, these are monoliths.

Easy, you say, use the strangler pattern. Add microservices incrementally, route requests to these so that the original code path goes cold, then repeat until you're done.[3]

Knative makes this easier in two ways. The first is that it's good at the routing thing. The concept of routing portions of traffic is key to its design. This matters because the strangler pattern tends to falter once you strangle the less scary bits (look boss, we broke out the cat gif subsystem!) and move on to the parts where the big money lives. Suddenly, it's a bit scarier because (1) a cutover is a cutover, (2) a big-bang cutover is a bet-your-job event, and (3) Knative makes it easier to stop believing in (1) and (2).

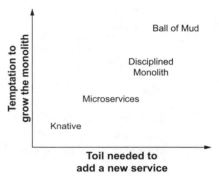

Figure 1.3   Knative's sweetspots in terms of resisting temptation to grow a monolith

The second way Knative makes strangulation easier is that you can deploy small units easily. Knative has a deep design assumption that you'll have a bunch of little functions that will come and go. A function takes less to recreate than a Service. The smaller you can start, the easier it is to start.

1.4   *It's a hit*

So far I have promised a lot: easier deployments, easier event systems, incremental development, Martian unicorns—the usual stuff that everyone promises to developers. But I haven't given you any concrete details. In order to support my pitch that we can start in small increments, I'll begin with one of the oldest, simplest examples of the dynamic web and show how Knative makes it faster, smarter, and easier. Remember hit counters?[4]

---

[3]   Of course, nothing is actually easy. One manuscript reviewer pointed out that success will rely on having a comprehensive test suite to prevent regressions. The same reviewer noted that APIs that are relatively rarely used (such as key rotations) are more difficult to safely strangle. My own corollary would be: infrequent exercise breeds frailty. Quiet, rarely-used code is a risk that needs to be managed. Extensive testing is necessary, but you should also consider changing your systems to use the infrequent code more frequently (e.g., setting a policy of rotating keys every week, or perhaps rotating some fraction daily).

[4]   If you don't remember hit counters, think of these as a likes or followers count.

Figure 1.4   The late 1990s were truly a golden era.

I sure do. The first time I saw one, it *blew my mind*. It changed! By itself! Magic!

Not magic, of course, it was a CGI program, probably some Perl.[5] CGI is one of the spiritual parents of Knative, so in its honor, we are going a make a hit counter for MY AWESOME HOMEPAGE.[6]

Listing 1.1   The awesome home page HTML

```html
<html>
<body>
  <style>body { font-family: "awesomefont" }</style>
  <center>
    <b>MY AWESOME HOMEPAGE</b><br />
    <img src="//hits.png" />
  </center>
</body>
</html>
```

First, let's talk about the basic flow of requests and responses. A visitor to the home page will GET an HTML document from the web server. The document contains some style and, most importantly, the hit counter.

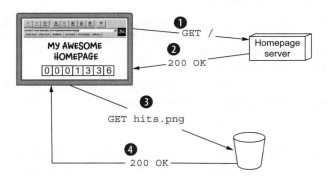

Figure 1.5   The flow of requests and responses

Specifically, as figure 1.5 shows

  1   The browser issues a GET request for the home page.

  2   The home page service returns the HTML of the home page.

  3   The browser finds an img tag for hits.png and issues a GET for hits.png.

  4   A file bucket returns hits.png.

---

[5]   OK, using ImageMagick, but not *magic* magic.

[6]   Two other spiritual parents are inetd and stored procedures.

In the old world, all of the processing needed to generate the hit counter would block the web server response. You'd submit your request, the web server would bestir the elder gods of Cämelbuk, and then /CGI-BIN/hitctr.pl would render the image. It might take a second or two, but nobody could tell, unless they were using one of those blazing 28.8 K modems.

But now, everyone is impatient: spending a few seconds to render an image that could otherwise be served from a fast data path isn't going to be acceptable. Instead, we'll break that responsibility out and do it asynchronously. That way, the web server can immediately respond with HTML and leave the creation of hit counter images to something else.

How will the web server signal that intention? Actually … it won't. Instead, it simply signals that a hit occurred. Remember, the web server wants to serve web pages, not orchestrate image rendering. So instead of blocking, it emits a new_hit CloudEvent.

Emits to *where?* To a Broker, a central meeting point for systems in Knative Eventing. The Broker has no particular interest in the new_hit event. It merely receives and forwards events. The exact details of who gets what is defined with triggers. Each Trigger represents an interest in some set of events and where to forward these. When events arrive at the Broker, it applies each Trigger's filter and, if it matches, forwards the event to the subscriber (figure 1.6).

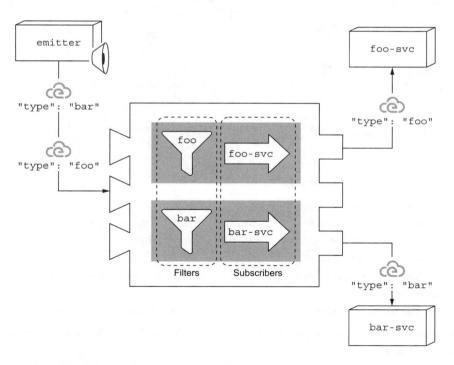

Figure 1.6   Broker applying triggers to CloudEvents.

Triggers enable the incremental composition of event flows. The web server doesn't know where new_hit will wind up and doesn't care. Given our new_hit, we can start to tally up the count of hits. Already, we're ahead of the 1999 status quo. We can take our original Perl script and have it react to the new_hit event instead of blocking the main web response.

But since we're here, let's go a step further. After all, is rendering images the actual proper concern of a tallying service? When I perform a SQL UPDATE, I don't get back JPEG files. Instead, I will have the tally service consume the new_hit and emit a new count, which can then wing its way to other subscribers.

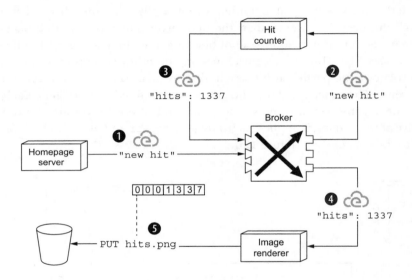

Figure 1.7   The flow of events

Putting it together (figure 1.7)

1 The homepage service emits a new_hit event.
2 A Trigger matches new_hit, and the Broker forwards it to the hit counter.
3 The hit counter updates its internal counter, then emits a hits event with the value of that counter.
4 Another Trigger matches for hits, so the Broker forwards it to the image renderer.
5 The image renderer renders a new image and replaces hits.png in the file bucket.

And now, if the visitor reloads their browser, they will see that the hit counter has incremented.

1.4.1 Trouble in paradise

Except, maybe, they don't. To see why, let's put the diagrams together (figure 1.8).

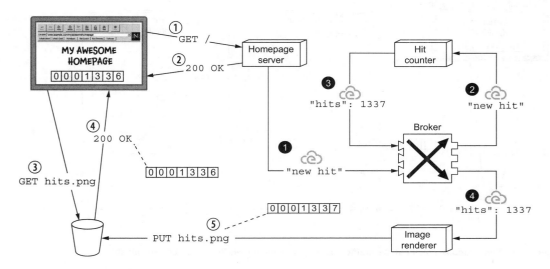

Figure 1.8 Combining the flows in one diagram

Note that I'm showing two sets of numbers: one for a web request/response (on the left side of the diagram) and another for the event flow (on the right side of the diagram). This illuminates an important point—the web flow is *synchronous* and the event flow is *asynchronous*. You knew that, but I handwaved away the consequences, and now I need to slap my wrist. The distinction matters (figure 1.9).

Because the event flow is asynchronous, there's no guarantee that hits.png will have been updated before the next visitor arrives. I might see 0001336, reload, and then see 0001336 again.[7] And that's not all: where one visitor might see no change, another visitor might observe that the hit counter jumps forward, because later renderings can overwrite earlier renderings before they're served. And *that's* not all! An observer might see the count go *backward*, because the rendering that increased the number to 0001338 might have finished before the rendering for 0001337. Or it might be that the events arrived out of order. Or some events never even arrived!

I'm not done. Remember how I said that a hit counter was keeping a tally of the hits? I didn't say *where*. If it's just keeping a value in memory, then you have new problems. For example, if Knative's autoscaler decides that things are too quiet lately, it reduces that number of hit counters to zero, and pow, your tally is gone. Next time it spins up, your hit count will be reset to zero. But on the other hand, if you have more

---

[7] Assuming that I used cache-disabling headers to force the browser to refetch each time!

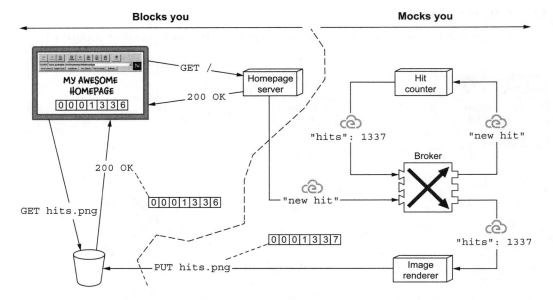

Figure 1.9 Synchronous flows can be inefficient. Asynchronous workloads can be inexplicable.

than one hit counter, those are keeping separate tallies. The exact hit count image at any moment will depend on traffic, but not in the way you might expect.

I'm describing stateless systems, of course. The answer is to keep state in a shared location, separately from the logic that operates on it. For example, each hit counter might be using Redis to increment a common value. Or you might get super fancy and have each instance listen for hits events.[8] If the incoming event represents a hit count higher than the hit counter's own tally, it can change its own tally to the incoming value. All that's left is to hope that you're not participating in an infinite event loop.

1.5   *Changing things*

You've probably noticed that my focus has been on an already deployed system. That's the bad news. The good news is that you can fix a key bug I introduced in the previous section. Can you guess what it is?

Correct. The font sucks.

You'll quickly learn that Knative prizes *immutability*. This has a lot of implications. For now, it means that we can't just SSH into homepage, open vi, and do it live.[9] But it does raise the question of how changes get moved from your workstation to the cloud.

---

[8] Please don't.
[9] And certainly I do not, for the purposes of law, recall ever doing so myself.

Knative encapsulates "run the thing" and "change the thing" into Services.[10] When the Service is changed, Knative acts to bring the world into sync with the change.

You can see how this looks in figure 1.10:

1 A user who arrives before the update sees the existing HTML as served by the homepage server v1.
2 The developer uses kn to update the Service.
3 Knative starts the homepage server v2.
4 The v2 server passes its readiness check.
5 Knative stops the v1 server.
6 A second user arrives after the update and sees a more professional font.

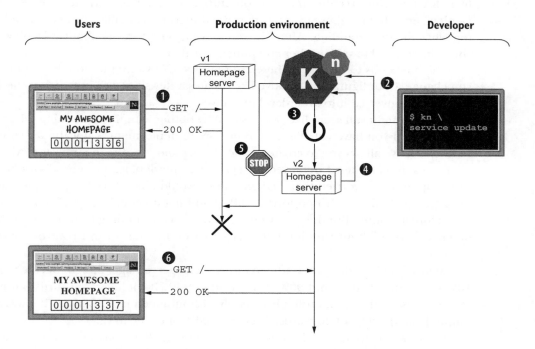

Figure 1.10 Updating the home page

This Blue/Green deployment behavior is Knative's default. When updating Services, it ensures that no traffic is lost and that load is only switched when it's safe to do so.

---

[10] Not to be confused with Kubernetes Services. More on that later.

1.6   *What's in the Knative box?*

Let's break this down into subprojects: Serving and Eventing.

1.6.1   *Serving*

Serving is the first and most well-known part of Knative. It encompasses the logic needed to run your software, manage request traffic, keep your software running while you need it, and stop it running when you don't need it. As a developer, Knative gives you three basic types of document you can use to express your desires: Configuration, Revision, and Route.

Configuration is your statement of what your running system should look like. You provide details about the desired container image, environment variables, and the like. Knative converts this information into lower-level Kubernetes concepts like Deployments. In fact, those of you with some Kubernetes familiarity might be wondering what Knative is adding. After all, you can just create and submit a Deployment yourself, no need to use another component for that.

Which takes us to *Revisions*. These are *snapshots* of a Configuration. Each time that you change a Configuration, Knative first creates a Revision, and in fact, it is the *Revision* that is converted into lower-level primitives.

But this might still seem like overhead. Why bother with this versioning scheme in Knative when you have Git? Because Blue/Green deployment is not the *only* option. In fact, Knative allows you to create nuanced rules about traffic to multiple Revisions.

For example, when I deployed homepage v2, the deployment was all-or-nothing. But suppose I was worried that changing fonts would affect how long people stay on my page (an A/B test). If I perform an all-or-nothing update, I will get lots of data for the before and after. But there may be a number of confounding factors, such as time-of-day effects. Without running both versions side by side, I can't control for those variables.

Knative is able to divvy up traffic to Revisions by percentage. I might decide to send 10% of my traffic to v2 and 90% of my traffic to v1. If the new font turns out to be worse for users, then I can roll it back easily without much fuss. If, instead, it was a triumph, I can quickly roll forwards, directing 100% of traffic to v2.

It's this ability to selectively target traffic that makes Revisions a necessity. In vanilla Kubernetes, I can roll forward and I can roll back, but I can't do so with *traffic*; I can only do it with *instances of the Service*.

Perhaps you wondered what happened to the Services I was talking about in the walkthrough. Well, these are essentially a one-stop shop for all things Serving. Each Service combines a Configuration and a Route. This compounding makes common cases easier because everything you will need to know is in one place.

But these concepts aren't necessarily what get listed on the marketing flyer. Many of you have come to hear about autoscaling, including scale-to-zero. For many folks, it's the ability for the platform to scale all the way to zero that captures their imagination: no more wasting money on instances that are mostly idle. And, similarly, the ability to scale up: no more getting paged at absurd o'clock in the morning in New York because something huge happened in Sydney (or vice versa). Instead, you delegate the business of balancing demand and supply to Knative. Because sometimes you will want to understand what the heck it's doing, I'll spend some time delving into the surprisingly difficult world of autoscaling in chapter 5.

1.6.2 Eventing

Eventing is the second, less well-known part of Knative. It provides ways to express connections between different pieces of software through events. In practical terms, "this is my software" is simpler to describe than "here is how all my software connects together." Eventing consequently has a larger surface area, with more document types, than does Serving.

Earlier in the chapter, you learned that in the middle of the Eventing world is where Triggers and Brokers live. The Trigger exists to map from an event filter to a target. The Broker exists to manage the flow of events based on Triggers.

But that's just the headline description. It's light on detail. For example, how does a CloudEvent actually get into the Broker? It turns out, there are multiple possibilities. The most powerful and idiomatic of these is a *Source*. This represents configuration information about some kind of emitter of events and a Broker to which these should be sent. A Source can be more or less anything: GitHub webhooks, direct HTTP requests, you name it. So long as it emits CloudEvents to a Broker, it can be a Source.

Great! You are probably already composing event-processing graphs in your head, and it won't be long before you get tired of writing Trigger upon Trigger. It would be handy if you had a simple way to do things in order. This is what Sequences can express for you—that A runs before B. Or, maybe, you want to do more than one thing at a time. That's what Parallel does, allowing you to express that A and B can run independently.

Analogous to how Serving provides the convenience of Service, Sequence and Parallel are constructed from the same concepts that you can use directly. They're a convenience, not a constraint. They'll enable you to assemble event flows with much less YAML than handwiring equivalent Triggers would.

1.6.3 Serving and Eventing

By design, you don't need Serving to use Eventing, and you don't need Eventing to use Serving. But these do mesh pretty well together. For example, if you have long processing pipelines, it's nice if idle instances don't sit around burning money waiting on upstream work to finish. Or, if there's a bottleneck, it's helpful if that part of the pipeline is scaled up. That's Eventing gaining a superpower from Serving.

And it works the other way. Serving's focus is on request/reply designs—the simple, robust, but sometimes slow-blocking approach. By itself, this favors adding functionality to existing Services instead of creating new ones. Blocking is still blocking, but blocking on threads is faster than blocking on HTTP. You can easily drift back from microservices to monoliths in costume.

Eventing relieves some of that design pressure. You can now offload a lot of work that doesn't need to block, or that should react to events instead of following commands. Encouraging smaller units of logic and behavior allows Serving to really shine: autoscaling the GigantoServ™ is better than nothing. But it's wasteful to burn 100 GB of RAM on a system with 300 endpoints when only 2 of those are seeing any kind of traffic surge.

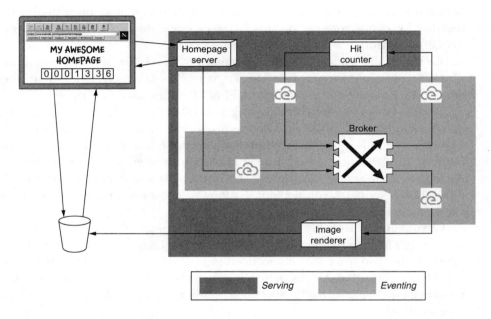

Figure 1.11   Serving runs the Services; Eventing wires those together.

In the hit counter system previously mentioned, I put both Serving and Eventing to work. Serving handles the business of the home page, hit counter, and image renderer. Eventing handles the Broker so that Services will receive and emit events without direct coordination. In this book, I'll describe these individually so that I can go into some depth. But these are intended to work well together. Ultimately, I want you to be able to do that.

1.7   *Keeping things under control*

And now a digression into software philosophy. "Knative" is a clever name. First, everyone gets to practice pronouncing it a few times ("KAY-nay-tiv"). From personal experience, I know that if folks are struggling to pronounce your name, they will *really* concentrate on it.

Second, it encompasses some of the design vision. Knative is native to Kubernetes both in spirit and implementation. In a kind of judo throw, it uses the extensibility of Kubernetes to conceal the complexity of Kubernetes. But every throw needs a little leverage to make it work. To give you that leverage, I need to step back a bit from Knative and give you a basic level of familiarity with a core organizing concept in Kubernetes and Knative: the feedback control loop.

1.7.1 Loops

As a profession, we use terms like *feedback loop* pretty loosely. Strictly speaking, feedback loops are any circular causality that amplifies or dampens itself. (I use the word "strictly" informally.)

For example, compound interest is a feedback loop. No humans are involved, just computers multiplying numbers. But the amount of interest paid is a function of the accumulated principal, which is itself a function of previous interest paid. After each period, the effect is amplified. Each payment feeds back into the system.

Or consider an avalanche after heavy snow. A small amount of snow slips further down, making the next spot down slightly heavier. More snow slips further down, making the next spot even heavier again. Within seconds, what starts as a few grams of attractive light fluff transforms into thousands of tons of mindless destruction.

The nature of pure feedback loops is that these require no intelligence or logic. These can be composed of pure causality. This is why both compound interest and an avalanche are of the same species. Whether the structure of the system was set by humans or by nature is unimportant to how it will behave.

We often *assume* that intelligence is involved in feedback loops, because pure circular causality is rarely apprehended and understood: purely damping loops disappear and purely amplifying loops fly apart. At a human level, the universe *appears* to be composed of linear causality, but beneath most of it lies a seething world of loops, shoving and pushing each other around an equilibrium.

Because purely causal circularity is rarely apprehended, we attribute intelligence to those things that we do observe. In our experience, humans are necessary to create a special case: *control loops*.[11]

Control loops are a special case because these add a controller to the loop. A controller observes the *actual* world, compares it to some reference of the *desired* world, then acts upon the actual world to make it look more like the desired world. This simple description disguises centuries of work and generations of engineering students being unceremoniously doused with calculus. But, at its heart, the idea of control loops is simple—make what we have look more like what we want.

---

[11] Attributing intelligence to causality is human. Lightning isn't due to angry super-beings, but if you've ever been near a lightning strike, you can understand why "static electricity" wasn't the first thing people thought of to explain such a phenomenon.

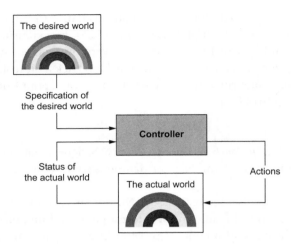

Figure 1.12   The basic structure of a control loop

Controllers vs. controllers

"Controller" in this context is not referring to the Model-View-Controller (MVC) pattern you might recognize from software frameworks. Trygve Reenskaug is typically credited with inventing the MVC pattern, initially using the name "Editor." In a different universe, we'd be talking about the "MVE" pattern. The name MVC came about because: "After long discussions, particularly with Adele Goldberg, we ended with the terms Model-View-Controller."

The Controller, or Editor, was meant to "… bridge the gap between the human user's mental model and the digital model that exists in the computer. The ideal MVC solution supports the user illusion of seeing and manipulating the domain information directly."

This is not what Kubernetes, and by extension Knative, mean by "controller." Instead, the meaning is taken by analogy from control theory, which deals with how dynamic systems can be made to behave more predictably and reliably. It's widely applied by engineers in fields like electrical and electronic systems, aerodynamics, chemical plant design, manufacturing systems, mining, refineries, and many others. You will avoid confusion by pretending you've never heard of MVC.

The key is that the loop runs repeatedly. The controller is regularly taking in information about the desired and actual worlds, comparing these, then deciding whether to take action in the actual world (figure 1.13). The repeated observations of the world are "fed back" to the controller, which is why this is a feedback controller.[12]

---

[12] When you design systems without the loop, the controller is using "feed forward." The designer usually takes advantage of some property of the controlled system to make feedback unnecessary. For example, you don't see many feedback controllers governing the position of concrete slabs because these typically stay put on their own. Feed forward control is a useful, legitimate design technique for many kinds of systems. For highly dynamic systems like software, though, feedback control is well suited to maintaining some amount of stability and reliability.

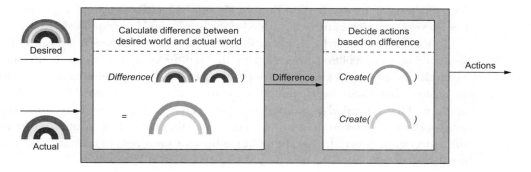

Figure 1.13   The internal structure of a controller

From my description so far, it's easy to form the impression that control loops are all about counteracting unwanted changes in the actual world; that the desired world is immutable, fixed, so that bursts of activity are only signalled by the controller when the actual world shifts out of alignment with the desired world.

This isn't really true. The controller does not "see" a change in the actual world, in contrast to an immutable desired world. What it sees is a difference between one input and another input.[13] On each pass around the loop, the controller sees the two inputs afresh, as if for the first time.[14] It doesn't need to know that the actual world changed since "last time." It doesn't know that the desired world changed since "last time." It doesn't care. It just knows that these aren't the same.

This leads to a simple conclusion: the controller can act due to changes in *either* of the actual world or the desired world because it's reacting to the emergence of the difference, not to the worlds *per se*. Something or someone outside the control loop can change the desired world in order to prompt activity.

1.7.2   *Loops within loops*

Who changes the desired world? Most of us assume that a human does it at first. Something like: push some YAML to update the desired world, knock off, and go home early.

This works, but it has at least one problem. The actual world is complex. Often, obnoxiously so. As a profession, we've tackled this complexity using abstraction (name things to banish their complexity) and composition (combine things to amplify their power). If I could not use abstraction and composition, if I had to define every detail

---

[13] That difference isn't commutative, so the order of inputs still matters. What comes through the "desired" door needs to be the desired state, and what comes through the "actual" door needs to be the actual state.

[14] This is not universally true of controllers in control theory. These can have many kinds of "memory" to carry information forward in time. In the most common approach to control theory, what I am describing is a purely proportional controller. Adding some averaging over previous states would add integral control. Adjusting the forcefulness of actions based on how quickly the two worlds are diverging would add derivative control.

for every part of my world, then I would (1) send a lot of worlds over the wire, and (2) need a very complex controller indeed—about as complex as the world itself.[15]

In the industrial world, this is dealt with by *hierarchical control.* That is, the desired world of one controller is modified by the actions of a supervising controller. For example, an industrial kiln will have controllers for managing individual gas burners to ensure that these burn the right amount of flammable gas. What's the right amount? That's decided by a supervising controller that's interested in controlling the temperature of the kiln. Instead of a controller that runs all the way from "maintain the right temperature" to "set the right gas flow for hundreds of burners," we have two feedback control loops that are nested (figure 1.14).

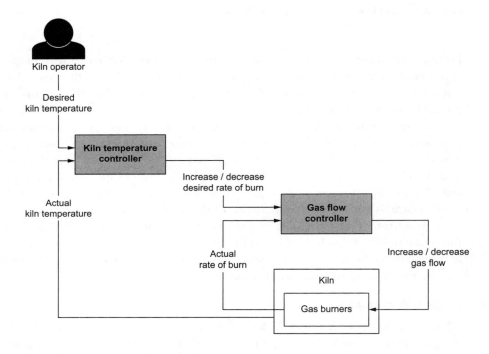

Figure 1.14   A hierarchical kiln controller

This should be recognizable as architectural layering according to the Single Responsibility Principle. Temperature control is a different concern from gas flow control. And so it is with software systems: the business of shipping photons over fiber-optic

---

[15] Ross Ashby, an early cyberneticist, called this the "Law of Requisite Variety": any *perfect* controller of a system must be as complex as the system. Of course, "perfect" is impossible in practice, and in fact, we don't need it (do you really think the kiln controller should include a weather forecaster and an ability to tell if the site foreperson is angry today?). The tactic of breaking control problems into hierarchies makes each level much more tractable to solve to a satisfactory standard.

cable is distinct from the business of forming frames, which is different from sending packets, that don't at all resemble a GET request. Developing optical control algorithms is not a precondition for using JavaScript. Some might think that's a pity, but that's besides my point.

Ultimately, this hierarchy of feedback control loops reaches up to you. You have a desired world of "software that achieves such-and-such purpose." Your desired world changes, creating a cascade of other worlds that change. Soon a deployment is setting new targets for lower-level controllers to react to. Most of the time, we are focused solely on the actions we are taking, but we (hopefully) don't act like pure noise. We are purposeful.

Kubernetes explicitly models its architecture on feedback control loops and provides infrastructure to enable the easy development of a variety of controllers for different purposes. Kubernetes then uses hierarchical control to layer responsibilities: Pods can be supervised by ReplicaSets that are supervised by Deployments.

Knative Serving builds on this infrastructure and adopts its norms (figure 1.15). It presents the surface interface of Services, Configurations, Revisions, and Routes. These are handled by first-level controllers, which break these into targets for other controllers, and so on, until code lands on a VM you don't care about and runs code

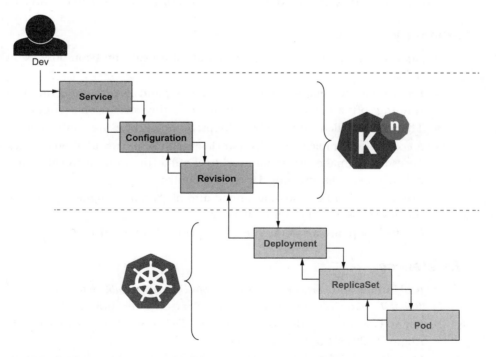

Figure 1.15 Some of the hierarchy of Knative and Kubernetes controllers involved in running a Service

that you care about very much. Your role is to be the highest-level controller in the hierarchy. Knative is meant to see to the rest.

1.8   Are you ready?

Before we dive in, let me tell you my assumptions about you. The first is that you've done some programming and can get the gist of code examples in Go. The second is that you are comfortable with installing and using CLI tools. Basically, I'm assuming that you're in Knative's primary audience: developers.

I don't assume that you know anything about Kubernetes or service meshes. I don't assume that you have used a serverless platform before. When I need to introduce necessary information I will, but my goal throughout is that Knative should live up to its vision of enabling you to ignore Kubernetes altogether.

In the next chapter, I will need you to have set up some tools. Most importantly, I'm guessing that you've installed Knative or someone is providing it for you. I'm also assuming that you've installed the kn tool, which I will focus on throughout. See appendix A for an installation guide for Knative and kn.

If you want to run the samples, you'll need to have installed Go. Take a moment to set up YAML support in your favorite editor. Some editor YAML extensions also include specialized Kubernetes support, which is nice to have but not essential.

Most of all, I just want you to have fun. Grab a drink of your choice and let's begin.

Summary

- Knative makes it easier to deploy, update, autoscale, and compose event-driven software.
- Knative has two major components: Serving and Eventing. Serving focuses on running software, scaling, and routing. Eventing focuses on event flows.
- The world is filled with feedback loops. Some of these are controlled.
- A controller compares a desired world and an actual world, then decides what is necessary to make the actual world resemble the desired world. This process occurs repeatedly, creating a feedback control loop.
- Controllers can be nested, arranged into hierarchies. Higher controllers adjust the desired world of lower controllers.
- Control loops are a core architectural principle of Knative.

References

- Jez Humble and David Farley, *Continuous Delivery: Reliable Software Releases Through Build, Test, and Deployment Automation* (Pearson Education, 2010)
- James Governor, "Towards Progressive Delivery," *James Governor's Monkchips*, August 6, 2018, http://mng.bz/j4Px
- Onsi Fakhouri, Keynote speech at CF Summit 2016, http://mng.bz/Wdz0

- Wallace J. Hopp and Mark L. Spearman, *Factory Physics*, 3rd ed., (Waveland Press, 2011), page 309
- Martin Fowler, "StranglerFigApplication," (MartinFowler.com, June 29, 2004), http://mng.bz/8NrP
- Trygve Reenskaug, "MVC Xerox Parc 1978-79," http://mng.bz/E2QJ

Introducing
Knative Serving

2

This chapter covers

- Deploying a new Service with Knative Serving
- Updating the Service with Revisions
- Splitting traffic between Revisions
- The major components of Serving and what
  they do

Serving is where I'm going to start you off in Knative, and the coming chapters will take you into a deeper dive on the major concepts and mechanisms. To begin with, I'll spend this chapter getting you warmed up in two ways.

First, I'm going to actually *use* Knative. You'll notice that I ducked and weaved around this in chapter 1. I did walk you through an example and that example *was* realistic. But it was also intended to whet your appetite for the whole book, and so necessarily, it needed to touch on a lot of points. A hypothetical example with diagrams and narrative is a quick way to do so.

But now, I'm going to put your fingers on a keyboard. We will use the kn CLI tool to deploy some software, change its settings, change its software, and finally, configure traffic. I won't be doing any YAMLeering. We'll be trying a purely interactive approach to Knative.

In the second part of the chapter, I will take a whistlestop tour of Serving's key software components. I'm doing this now because I would like to introduce these in one easy-to-find place. The following chapters are all structured around the concepts that Knative exposes to developers. I could introduce components as I go, but it would mean that you might need to hunt through the book to find component information.

This too will tie back to chapter 1. There I introduced you to the basic concept of control loops. In this chapter, I will get to apply that basic concept to explain the high-level architecture of Serving, which is one based on hierarchical control loops.

By the end of the chapter, my goal is that (1) you will be able to start poking around kn with your own example apps, and (2) you will have a nodding acquaintance with Knative Serving's runtime components. These will set up our progress into the following chapters, where we'll go into greater depth on concepts like Configurations, Routes, and the Knative Pod Autoscaler.

2.1 A walkthrough

In this section, I'll use kn exclusively to demonstrate some Knative Serving capabilities. I assume you've installed it, following the directions in appendix A.

kn is the "official" CLI for Knative, but it wasn't the first. Before it came along there were a number of alternatives, such as knctl. These tools helped to explore different approaches to a CLI experience for Knative.

kn serves two purposes. The first is a CLI in itself, specifically intended for Knative rather than requiring users to anxiously skitter around kubectl, pretending that Kubernetes isn't *right there*. The secondary purpose is to drive out Golang APIs for Knative, which can be used by other tools to interact with Knative from within Go programs.

2.1.1 Your first deployment

Let's first use kn service list to ensure you're in a clean state. You should see No Services Found as the response. Now we can create a Service using kn service create. The listing shows the basics of how to use kn to create Services.

Listing 2.1 Using kn to create our first Service

Names the service

References the container image. In this case, we use a sample app image provided by Knative.

```
$ kn service create hello-example \
    --image gcr.io/knative-samples/helloworld-go \
    --env TARGET="First"

Creating service 'hello-example' in namespace 'default':

  0.084s The Route is still working to reflect the latest desired
    ⮕ specification.
  0.260s Configuration "hello-example" is waiting for a Revision to
    ⮕ become ready.
```

Injects an environment variable that's consumed by the sample app

Monitors the deployment process and emits logs

```
  4.356s ...
  4.762s Ingress has not yet been reconciled.
  6.104s Ready to serve.

Service 'hello-example' created with latest revision 'hello-example-pjyvr-1'
➥ and URL: http://hello-example.example.com
```

**Returns the URL for the
newly deployed software**

The logs emitted by kn refer to concepts I discussed in chapter 1. The Service you provide is split into a Configuration and a Route. The Configuration creates a Revision. The Revision needs to be ready before the Route can attach Ingress to it, and Ingress needs to be ready before traffic can be served at the URL.

This dance illustrates how hierarchical control breaks your high-level intentions into particular software to be configured and run. At the end of the process, Knative has launched the container you nominated and configured, routing it so that it's listening at the given URL.

What's at the URL we were given in listing 1.2? Let's see what the following listing shows.

Listing 2.2   The first hello

```
$ curl http://hello-example.example.com
Hello First!
```

Very cheerful.

2.1.2   *Your second deployment*

Mind you, perhaps you don't like First. Maybe you like Second better. Easily fixed, as the following listing shows.

Listing 2.3   Updating hello-example

```
$ kn service update hello-example \
  --env TARGET=Second

Updating Service 'hello-example' in namespace 'default':

  3.418s Traffic is not yet migrated to the latest revision.
  3.466s Ingress has not yet been reconciled.
  4.823s Ready to serve.

Service 'hello-example' updated with latest revision 'hello-example-bqbbr-2'
➥ and URL: http://hello-example.example.com

$ curl http://hello-example.example.com
Hello Second!
```

What happened is that I changed the TARGET environment variable that the example application interpolates into a simple template. The next listing shows this.

Listing 2.4 How a hello sausage gets made

```
func handler(w http.ResponseWriter, r *http.Request) {
  target := os.Getenv("TARGET")
  fmt.Fprintf(w, "Hello %s!\n", target)
}
```

You may have noticed that the revision name changed. `First` was `hello-example-pjyvr-1`, and `Second` was `hello-example-bqbbr-2`. Yours will look slightly different because part of the name is randomly generated: `hello-example` comes from the name of the Service, and the 1 and 2 suffixes indicate the *generation* of the Service (more on that in a second). But the bit in the middle is randomized to prevent accidental name collisions.

Did `Second` replace `First`? The answer is—it depends who you ask. If you're an end user sending HTTP requests to the URL, yes, it appears as though a total replacement took place. But from the point of view of a developer, both Revisions still exist, as shown in the following listing.

Listing 2.5 Both revisions still exist

```
$ kn revision list
NAME                    SERVICE         GENERATION  AGE    CONDITIONS  READY
hello-example-bqbbr-2   hello-example   2           2m3s   4 OK / 4    True
hello-example-pjyvr-1   hello-example   1           3m15s  3 OK / 4    True
```

I can look more closely at each of these with `kn revision describe`. The following listing shows this.

Listing 2.6 Looking at the first revision

```
$ kn revision describe hello-example-pjyvr-1
Name:       hello-example-pjyvr-1
Namespace:  default
Age:        5m15s
Image:      gcr.io/knative-samples/helloworld-go (pinned to 5ea96b)
Env:        TARGET=First
Service:    hello-example

Conditions:
  OK TYPE                 AGE REASON
  ++ Ready                3h
  ++ ContainerHealthy     3h
  ++ ResourcesAvailable   3h
   I Active               3h NoTraffic
```

2.1.3 Conditions

It's worth taking a slightly closer look at the Conditions table (listing 2.6). Software can be in any number of states, and it can be useful to know what these are. A smoke test or external monitoring service can detect that you have a problem, but it may not be able to tell you *why* you have a problem. What this table gives you is four pieces of information:

- OK *gives the quick summary about whether the news is good or bad.* The ++ signals that everything is fine. The I signals an informational condition. It's not bad, but it's not as unambiguously positive as ++. If things were going badly, you'd see !!. If things are bad but not, like, *bad* bad, kn signals a warning condition with W. And if Knative just doesn't know what's happening, you'll see ??.
- TYPE *is the unique condition being described.* In this table, we can see four types reported. The Ready condition, for example, surfaces the result of an underlying Kubernetes readiness probe. Of greater interest to us is the Active condition, which tells us whether there is an instance of the Revision running.
- AGE *reports on when this condition was last observed to have changed.* In the example, these are all three hours, but they don't have to be.
- REASON *allows a condition to provide a clue as to deeper causes.* For example, our Active condition shows NoTraffic as its reason.

So this line

```
I Active 3h NoTraffic
```

Can be read as

"As of 3 hours ago, the Active condition has an Informational status due to NoTraffic."

Suppose we get this line:

```
!! Ready 1h AliensAttackedTooSoon
```

We could read it as

"As of an hour ago, the Ready condition became not OK because the AliensAttacked-TooSoon."

2.1.4   *What does Active mean?*

When the Active condition gives NoTraffic as a reason, that means there are no active instances of the Revision running. Suppose we poke it with curl as in the following listing.

Listing 2.7   Poking with curl

```
$ kn revision describe hello-example-bqbbr-2
Name:       hello-example-bqbbr-2
Namespace:  default
Age:        7d
Image:      gcr.io/knative-samples/helloworld-go (pinned to 5ea96b)
Env:        TARGET=Second
Service:    hello-example
```

```
Conditions:
  OK TYPE                   AGE REASON
  ++ Ready                  4h
  ++ ContainerHealthy       4h
  ++ ResourcesAvailable     4h
   I Active                 4h NoTraffic

$ curl http://hello-example.example.com
# ... a pause while the container launches
Hello Second!

$ kn revision describe hello-example-bqbbr-2
Name:       hello-example-bqbbr-2
Namespace:  default
Age:        7d
Image:      gcr.io/knative-samples/helloworld-go (pinned to 5ea96b)
Env:        TARGET=Second
Service:    hello-example

Conditions:
  OK TYPE                   AGE REASON
  ++ Ready                  4h
  ++ ContainerHealthy       4h
  ++ ResourcesAvailable     4h
  ++ Active                 2s
```

Note that we now see ++ Active *without* the NoTraffic reason. Knative is saying that a running process was created and is active. If you leave it for a minute, the process will shut down again and the Active Condition will return to complaining about a lack of traffic.

2.1.5 Changing the image

The Go programming language, aka Golang to its friends and "erhrhfjahaahh" to its enemies, is the Old Hotness. The New Hotness is Rust, which I have so far been able to evade forming an opinion about. All I know is that it's the New Hotness and that, therefore, as a responsible engineer, I know that it is "Better."

This means that helloworld-go no longer excites me. I would like to use helloworld-rust, instead. The following listing shows how this is easily done.

> Listing 2.8 Updating the container image

```
$ kn service update hello-example \
  --image gcr.io/knative-samples/helloworld-rust
Updating Service 'hello-example' in namespace 'default':

 49.523s Traffic is not yet migrated to the latest revision.
 49.648s Ingress has not yet been reconciled.
 49.725s Ready to serve.

Service 'hello-example' updated with latest revision 'hello-example-nfwgx-3'
 ➥ and URL: http://hello-example.example.com
```

And then I poke it (as in the next listing).

Listing 2.9   The New Hotness says Hello

```
curl http://hello-example.example.com
Hello world: Second
```

Note that the message is slightly different: "Hello world: Second" instead of "Hello Second!" Not being deeply familiar with Rust, I can only suppose that it forbids excessive informality when greeting people it has never met. But it does at least prove that I didn't cheat and just change the `TARGET` environment variable.

There's an important point to remember here: changing the environment variable caused the second Revision to come into being. Changing the image caused a third Revision to be created. But because I didn't change the variable, the third Revision *also* says "Hello world: Second." In fact, almost any update I make to a Service causes a new Revision to be stamped out.

Almost any? What's the exception? It's Routes. Updating these as part of a Service won't create a new Revision.

2.1.6   *Splitting traffic*

I'm going to prove that Route updates don't create new Revisions by splitting traffic evenly between the last two Revisions. The next listing shows this split.

Listing 2.10   Splitting traffic 50/50

```
$ kn service update hello-example \
  --traffic hello-example-bqbbr-2=50 \
  --traffic hello-example-nfwgx-3=50

Updating Service 'hello-example' in namespace 'default':

  0.057s The Route is still working to reflect the latest
  ➥ desired specification.
  0.072s Ingress has not yet been reconciled.
  1.476s Ready to serve.

Service 'hello-example' updated with latest revision 'hello-example-nfwgx-3'
➥ (unchanged) and URL: http://hello-example.example.com
```

The `--traffic` parameter shown in listing 2.10 allows us to assign percentages to each Revision. The key is that the percentages must all add up to 100. If I give 50 and 60, I'm told that "given traffic percents sum to 110, want 100." Likewise, if I try to cut some corners by giving 50 and 40, I get "given traffic percents sum to 90, want 100." It's my responsibility to ensure that the numbers add up correctly.

Does it work? Let's see what the following listing does.

Listing 2.11 Totally not a perfect made-up sequence of events

```
$ curl http://hello-example.example.com
Hello Second!

$ curl http://hello-example.example.com
Hello world: Second
```

It works! Half your traffic will now be allocated to each Revision.

50/50 is just one split; you can split the traffic however you please. Suppose you had Revisions called un, deux, trois, and quatre. You might split it evenly, as the next listing shows.

Listing 2.12 Even four-way split

```
$ kn service update french-flashbacks-example \
  --traffic un=25 \
  --traffic deux=25 \
  --traffic trois=25 \
  --traffic quatre=25
```

Or, you can split it so that quatre is getting a tiny sliver to prove itself, while the bulk of the work lands on trois. Let's look at the next listing to see this.

Listing 2.13 Production and next versions

```
$ kn service update french-flashbacks-example \
  --traffic un=0 \
  --traffic deux=0 \
  --traffic trois=98 \
  --traffic quatre=2
```

You don't explicitly need to set traffic to 0%. You can achieve the same by leaving out Revisions from the list as shown in this listing.

Listing 2.14 Implicit zero traffic level

```
$ kn service update french-flashbacks-example \
  --traffic trois=98 \
  --traffic quatre=2
```

Finally, if I am satisfied that quatre is ready, I can switch over all the traffic using @latest as my target. The following listing shows this switch.

Listing 2.15 Targeting @latest

```
$ kn service update french-flashbacks-example \
  --traffic @latest=100
```

2.2 Serving components

As promised, I'm going to spend some time looking at some Knative Serving internals. In chapter 1, I explained that Knative and Kubernetes are built on the concept of control loops. A *control loop* involves a mechanism for comparing a desired world and an actual world, then taking action to close the gap between these.

But that's the boxes-and-lines explanation. The concept of a control loop needs to be embodied as actual software processes. Knative Serving has several of these, falling broadly into four groups:

- *Reconcilers*—Act on both user-facing concepts like Services, Revisions, Configurations, and Routes, as well as lower-level housekeeping
- *The Webhook*—Validates and enriches the Services, Configurations, and Routes that users provide
- *Networking controllers*—Configure TLS certificates and HTTP Ingress routing
- *The Autoscaler/Activator/Queue-Proxy triad*—Manages the business of comprehending and reacting to changes on traffic

2.2.1 The controller and reconcilers

Let's talk about names for a second. Knative has a component named `controller`, which is really a bundle of individual "reconcilers." Reconcilers are controllers in the sense that I discussed in chapter 1: a system that reacts to changes in the difference between desired and actual worlds. So reconcilers are controllers, but the controller isn't really a controller. Got it?

No? You're wondering why the names are different? The simplest answer is: to avoid confusion about what's what. That may sound silly. Bear with me, I promise it will make sense soon.

At the top, in terms of actual running processes managed directly by Kubernetes, Knative Serving only has one controller. But in terms of logical processes, Knative Serving has several controllers running in Goroutines inside the single physical `controller` process (figure 2.1). Moreover, the Reconciler is a Golang interface that implementations of the controller pattern are expected to implement.

So that we don't wind up saying "the controller controller" and "the controllers that run on the controller" or other less-than-illuminating naming schemes, there are instead two names: controller and reconciler.

Each reconciler is responsible for some aspect of Knative Serving's work, which falls into two categories. The first category is simple to understand—it's the reconcilers responsible for managing the developer-facing resources. Hence, there are reconcilers called `configuration`, `revision`, `route`, and `service`.

For example, when you use `kn service create`, the first port of call will be for a Service record to be picked up by the service controller. When you used `kn service update` to create a traffic split, you actually get the route controller to do some work for you. I'll touch on some of these controllers in coming chapters.

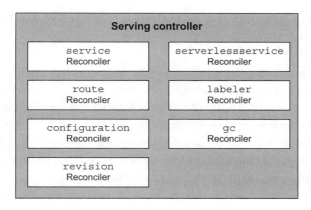

Figure 2.1 The Serving controller and its reconcilers

Reconcilers in the second category work behind the scenes to carry out essential lower-level tasks. These are `labeler`, `serverlessservice`, and `gc`. The labeler is part of how networking works; it essentially sets and maintains labels on Kubernetes objects that networking systems can use to target those for traffic.

The serverlessservice (that *is* the name) reconciler is part of how the Activator works. It reacts to and updates serverlessservice records (say that 5 times fast!). These are also mostly about networking in Kubernetes-land.

Lastly, the gc reconciler performs garbage-collection duties. Hopefully, you will never need to think about it again.

2.2.2 *The Webhook*

Things go wrong. A great deal of software engineering is centered on ensuring that when things *do* go wrong, they at least choose to go wrong at the least painful and/or least Tweetable moment. Type systems, static analysis, unit test harnesses, linters, fuzzers, the list goes on and on. We submit to their nagging because solving the mysteries of fatal errors in production is less fun than Agatha Christie made it out to be.

At runtime, Serving relies on the completeness and validity of information provided about things you want to manage (e.g., Services) and how you want Serving to behave generally (e.g., Autoscaler configurations). This brings us to the Webhook, which validates and augments your submissions. Like the controller, it's actually a group of logical processes that are collected together into a single physical process for ease of deployment.

The name "Webhook" is a little deceptive because it's describing the implementation rather than its actual purpose. If you're familiar with webhooks, you might have thought that its purpose was to dial out to an endpoint that you provide. Not so. Or perhaps it was an endpoint that you could ping yourself. Closer, but still incorrect. Instead, the name comes from its role as a Kubernetes "admissions webhook." When processing API submissions, the Knative Webhook is registered as the delegated authority to inspect and modify Knative Serving resources. A better name might be

"Validation and Annotation Clearing House" or perhaps the "Ditch-It or Fix-It Emporium." But "Webhook" is what we have.

The Webhook's principal roles include

- Setting default configurations, including values for timeouts, concurrency limits, container resources limits, and garbage collection timing. This means that you only need to set values you want to override. I'll touch on these as needed.
- Injecting routing and networking information into Kubernetes.
- Validating that users didn't ask for impossible configurations. For example, the Webhook will reject negative concurrency limits. I'll refer to these when needed.
- Resolving partial container image references to include the digest. For example, `example/example:latest` would be resolved to include the digest, so it looks like `example/example@sha256:1a4bccf2…`. I'm going to revisit this topic a few times, but generally, this is one of the best things Knative can do for you, and the Webhook deserves the credit for it.

2.2.3   *Networking controllers*

Early versions of Knative relied directly on Istio, the widely known service mesh founded by Google, Lyft, and IBM for core networking capabilities. That hasn't entirely changed. In the default installation provided by the Knative project, Istio is installed as a component and Knative will make use of some of its capabilities.

However, as it has evolved, more of Knative's networking logic has been abstracted up from Istio. Doing so allows some swappability of components. Istio might make sense for your case, but it's featuresome and might be overkill. On the other hand, you might have Istio provided as part of your standard Kubernetes environment. Knative extends to either approach.

Knative Serving requires that networking controllers answer for two basic record types: Certificate and Ingress.

CERTIFICATES

TLS is essential to the safety and performance of the modern internet, but the business of storing and shipping TLS certificates has always been inconvenient. The Knative certificate abstraction provides information about the TLS certificate that is desired, without providing it directly.

For example, TLS certificates are scoped to particular domain names or IP addresses. When creating a certificate, a list of `DNSNames` is used to indicate what domains the certificate should be valid for. A conforming controller can then create or obtain certificates that fulfill that need.

I don't go into TLS certificate material in this book, largely because it depends so completely on how your Knative installation is configured and what helper systems are installed. Most of the developer experience in this department is being picked up by each vendor's packaging of Knative.

INGRESS

Routing traffic is always one of those turtles-all-the-way-down affairs. Something, somewhere, is meeting traffic at the boundary of your system. In Knative, that's the Ingress.[1]

Ingress controllers act as a single entrance to the entire Knative installation. These convert Knative's abstract specification into particular configurations for their own routing infrastructure. For example, the default `networking-istio` controller will convert a Knative Ingress into an Istio gateway.

2.2.4 *Autoscaler, Activator, and Queue-Proxy*

Because these components work together quite closely, I've grouped all three under the same heading (figure 2.2).

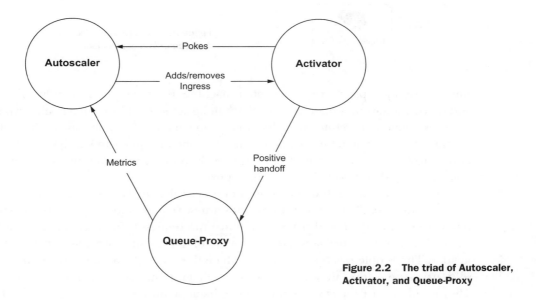

Figure 2.2   The triad of Autoscaler, Activator, and Queue-Proxy

The Autoscaler is the easiest to give an elevator pitch for: observe demand for a Service, calculate the number of instances needed to serve that demand, then update the Service's scale to reflect the calculation (figure 2.3). You've probably recognized that this is a supervisory control loop. Its desired world is "minimal mismatch between demand and instances." Its output is a scale number that becomes the desired world of a Service control loop.

It's worth noting that the Knative Pod Autoscaler operates solely through *horizontal scaling*: it launches more copies of your software when demand rises. *Vertical scaling* means launching it with additional computing resources. In general, vertical scaling is

---

[1] This is distinct from a Kubernetes Ingress.

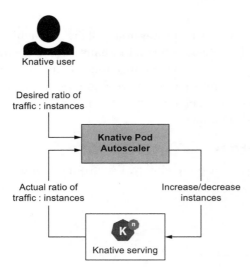

**Figure 2.3   The Knative Pod
Autoscaler is a control loop.**

simpler—you just pay more for a beefier machine. But the costs are highly nonlinear, and there is always an upper limit to what can be achieved. Horizontal scaling typically requires deliberate architectural decisions to make it possible, but once achieved will be more able to face higher demands than any one machine can handle. The Knative Pod Autoscaler assumes you've done the work to ensure that instances coming and going at a rapid clip won't be overly disruptive.

When there is no traffic, the desired number calculated by the Autoscaler is eventually set to zero. This is great, right until a new request shows up without anything ready to serve it. We could plausibly bounce the request with an HTTP `503 Service Unavailable` status; perhaps even, in a fit of generosity, provide a `Retry-After` header. The problem is that (1) humans hate this, and (2) vast amounts of upstream software assumes that network requests are magical and perfect and can never fail. They'll either barf on *their* users or, more likely, ignore your `Retry-After` and just hammer the endpoint into paste. Not to mention (3), which is that all of this will be screencapped and mocked on Reddit.

So what to do when there are no instances running—the dreaded cold start? In this case, the Activator is a traffic target of last resort. Ingress will be configured to send traffic for routes with no active instances to the Activator.

Hence, in figure 2.4, we can see that

1 The Ingress receives a new request. It sends the request to its configured target, which is the Activator.
2 The Activator places the new request into a buffer.
3 The Activator "pokes" the Autoscaler. The poke does two things: First, it carries information about requests waiting in the buffer. Second, the arrival of a poke

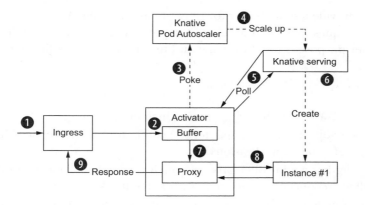

Figure 2.4 The Activator's role in managing cold starts

signal prompts the Autoscaler to make an immediate scaling decision instead of waiting until the next scheduled decision time.

4 After considering that there is a request waiting to be served but that there are zero instances available to serve it, the Autoscaler decides that there ought to be one instance running. It sets a new scale target for Serving.

5 While waiting for the Autoscaler and Serving to do their work, the Activator polls Serving to see if any instances are live.

6 Serving's actions cause Kubernetes to launch an instance.

7 The Activator learns from its polling that an instance is now available and moves the request from its buffer to a simple proxy service.

8 The proxy component sends the request to the instance, which responds normally.

9 The proxy component sends the response back to the Ingress, which then sends it back to the requester.

Does this mean all traffic flows through the Activator? No. The Activator remains on the data path during the transition from "no instances" to "enough instances." Once the Autoscaler is satisfied that there is enough capacity to meet current demand, it updates the Ingress, changing the traffic target from the Activator to the actual running instances. At this point, that Activator no longer has any role in the proceedings.

The exact timing of this update depends mostly on how much traffic has piled up and how long it takes to launch instances to serve it. Imagine that 10,000 requests arrive and the Activator then sprayed these at the first instance foolish enough to stick its head above the trenches. Instead, the Activator throttles its proxy until capacity catches up with demand. Once requests are flowing smoothly, the Autoscaler's own logic removes the Activator from the data path.

The final component of this triad is the Queue-Proxy. This is a small proxy process that sits between your actual software and arriving traffic. Every instance of your Service will have its own Queue-Proxy running as a sidecar. Knative does this for a few reasons. One is to provide a small buffer for requests, allowing the Activator to have a clear signal that a request has been accepted for processing (this is called "positive handoff"). Another purpose is to add tracing and metrics to requests flowing in and out of the Service.

Summary

- `kn` is a CLI tool for interacting with Knative, including Serving.
- `kn service` lets you view, create, update, and configure Knative Services, including splitting traffic between Revisions.
- Knative Serving has a controller process, which is actually a collection of components called "reconcilers." Reconcilers act as feedback controllers.
- There are reconcilers for Serving's core record types (Service, Route, Configuration, and Revision), as well as housekeeping reconcilers.
- Knative Serving has a webhook process, which intercepts new and updated records you submit. It can then validate your submissions and inject additional information.
- The Knative Pod Autoscaler is a feedback control loop. It compares the ratio of traffic to instances and raises or lowers the desired number of instances that the Serving controller controls.
- The Activator is assigned routes for which no instances are available. This assignment is made by the Autoscaler.
- The Activator is responsible for "poking" the Autoscaler when new requests arrive to trigger a scale-up.
- While instances are becoming available, the Activator remains on the data path as a throttling, buffering proxy for traffic.
- When the Autoscaler believes there is enough capacity to serve demand, it removes the Activator from the data path by updating Ingress routes.
- Knative Serving's networking is highly pluggable. Core implementations are provided for two functions: Certificates and Ingress.
- Certificate controllers accept a definition of desired certificates and must provision new certificates or map existing certificates into your software.
- Ingress controllers accept Routes and convert these into lower-level routing or traffic management configurations.
- Ingress controller implementations include Istio-Gateway, Gloo, Ambassador, and Kourier.

References

- knctl—https://github.com/cppforlife/knctl

Configurations
and Revisions

This chapter covers

- A brief history of deployments
- The anatomy of Configurations
- The anatomy of Revisions

My focus in this chapter is to provide a guided tour of Serving's dynamic duo, Configuration and Revision. This separation into two concepts isn't for the mere joy of complexity. To explain the motivation, I'll first give a fictionalized account of the history of software deployment, starting somewhere in the late Triassic period up to the current, slightly more advanced era of Thought Leadership.

After the history lesson, I'll start with Configurations. These are the main way you describe your software and your intentions to Knative Serving. The coverage of Configurations is necessarily brief because Configurations mostly exist to stamp out Revisions.

My discussion of Revisions will be substantially longer, as there is a lot of ground to cover. We will be looking at containers, container images, commands and environments, volumes, consumption limits, ports and probes, concurrency, and timeouts. The style is narrative, but you can skip things you don't care about right now and refer to these later when you need to.

Before we begin, I want you to review a key concept: Revisions are created when a Configuration is created or changed. Revisions don't have an independent existence. In the table of contents for this chapter, you might have formed the sweet illusion that I can deal entirely with Configurations in one place and entirely with Revisions in a different place. That isn't so. The knobs and dials I describe as being part of a Revision get there through a Configuration. This means that while writing about Revisions with my left hand, my right hand is running commands that refer to Configurations. If you get lost or confused, just reorient yourself to this landmark: *Revisions are created only when Configurations are changed or created.*

3.1 Those who cannot remember the past are condemned to redeploy it

Maybe you remember what you had for breakfast. Maybe you don't. But if by lunch your stomach feels ill and you go to a doctor, what you ate for breakfast comes into question. Saying, "well I am not hungry now, so I guess I ate something, but I'm not sure what it was" is unlikely to spark much diagnostic insight. (You will still receive a bill, however.)

Left to its own devices, Kubernetes will make the world appear changeless and timeless—a permanent *steady state*. When the desired and actual worlds become misaligned, it takes action to reconcile the difference. Afterward, it doesn't care that the disturbance ever occurred. It doesn't remember. The ripple of the disturbance has faded, leaving the placid pond of production.[1] So when an outside observer wishes to reconstruct history, they may be out of luck.

Like the doctor, we might, for various reasons, want to know what led us to the current situation, whether for diagnosis or treatment. When you operate without history, you're pretty much swinging across the YOLO ravine on a frayed rope. Eventually, it will snap, sending you hurtling down into the metaphorical crocodiles at the bottom of the ravine (which I have trained to mock you).

This has led to a small cottage industry of mechanisms for capturing history from, or injecting history into, Kubernetes. For example

- Various fields, annotations, and metadata such as `kubernetes.io/change-cause` provide limited historical or causal information directly on a particular Kubernetes record.
- The inbuilt Deployment mechanism provided by vanilla Kubernetes maintains `deployment.kubernetes.io/revision` annotations on `ReplicaSets` that it controls, which provides a partial history of the Deployment.
- The Kubernetes auditing system can be configured to emit an extremely detailed log of changes, allowing later reconstruction of history as seen by the Kubernetes API server.

---

[1] It can be argued that I am wrong, that there are many ways to get a sense of history: logs, Kubernetes events, and so forth. But these can be ephemeral, and besides, alliteration is always alluring to awful authors.

- Tools and practices for GitOps, which rely on capturing submitted changes in a Git repository before applying these to a Kubernetes cluster.
- Specialized history/visualization tools like Salesforce's Sloop.
- And, of course, a teeming multitude of observability and/or monitoring tools offered by a similarly teeming multitude of vendors.

Broadly, these mechanisms fill two related but distinct purposes:

- *What is the history of the cluster? How did it get to its current condition?* None of the previous solutions fully cover these questions. Either these focus on changes to the desired world (Sloop, GitOps), or these produce data that can hint at changes to the actual world (metrics and logs), or some incomplete mix (Kubernetes Audit). But not both.
- *Can I go back in time, please?* The current version of the software is "Wrong," a previous version was "Not As Wrong," so we need to switch back to the previous version. The need for time travel is projected across the entire hierarchy of control, from within a cluster way back into developer-land, because rolling back to a previous version can take many forms: `git revert`, Spinnaker canary analysis, GitOps, and many others.

Knative Serving wants a more general version of the time travel capability. It's not enough to select *a* version to run. Instead, Knative Serving wants to run one or multiple versions concurrently. If I have versions 1, 2, and 3 of my software, I want to be able to run some mix of 1, 2, and 3 (1 only, 1 and 2, 1 and 3 …). And, I want to be able to change the mix whenever I want.

Multiple versions? At once? Am I crazy? Perhaps, but to decide for yourself, I will need to tell you a story.

3.2　*The bedtime story version of the history of deployment as a concept*

Another way to look at the two desires for causality is this:

- Something has gone wrong. Why?
- We changed something and stuff broke. Let's undo the change.

The latter is really what I want to focus on because it's an ancient problem. For as long as there have been production systems, there too have been mandates that it cannot be allowed to stop running during business hours. An obvious logic then unfolded in the early years:

- Axiom 0—If it breaks, you're fired.
- Axiom 1—The system sometimes breaks when it is changed.
- Axiom 2—The changes that cause breakage were due to human error in the change, or in how the change was applied, or in how the change interacted with other changes.
- Theorem 1—*Therefore*, don't change anything.

QED. High fives and slide rules for everyone! But wait, here comes the boss's boss's boss…

- Axiom 3—We need to be able to integrate with Grot-O-Matic 7.36 because our customer will be delivering us records in the form of blurry Klingon hieroglyphs via FTP-over-pigeon-droppings every 24 hours. Oh, and if you don't make this change, you're fired.
- Theorem 2—Ahem. Well. I guess we need to change something or we're fired. But if it breaks, we're fired.
- Theorem 3—*Therefore*, be careful, *extremely* careful, about changes and slather everything that moves with documentation to prove that "It Wasn't Me, Boss."

Fewer high fives this time.

And so, for example, many firms had Change Approval Boards and required would-be mutators to account for their sins in a uniform way. Then the Change Window would open every quarter, and if you were lucky, your change would make it through before the window slammed shut again. And god help you if your change got in, but you realized it was wrong.

Then, later, we developed tools to make this much less painful. For example, version control systems. Version control has been *around* in various forms for ages, but when Git and GitHub came along, these just became standard, the way many folks work. At the same time, folks began to evolve the concepts of continuous integration and continuous deployment. Here there arose three new possibilities: the Blue/Green deployment, the Canary deployment, and the progressive deployment.

3.2.1 The Blue/Green deployment

You have a version of your software already running and serving traffic. Let's call this "Blue" (figure 3.1).

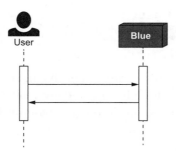

Figure 3.1   Blue

You now want to deploy a new version of your software. Let's call it "Green."

A first approach might be to stop Blue, then deploy Green. The time between "Stop Blue" and "Start Green" is scheduled downtime (figure 3.2). That was roughly the state of the world for Theorem 2.

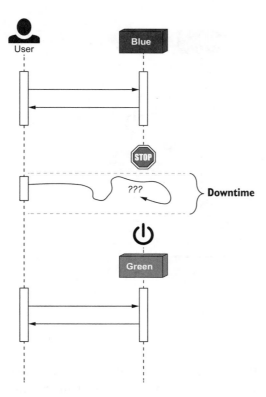

Figure 3.2   Scheduled downtime blues

Scheduled downtimes are still downtimes. It would be nice if we *didn't* have to stop Blue first. And, thanks to the magic of load balancers and proxies and gateways and routers, we don't have to. What we do instead (figure 3.3) is

1 Start Green
2 Switch traffic from Blue to Green
3 Stop Blue

From here, some tools will tick-tock between Green and Blue as the running version. They take turns. This approach is popular because all the software needs to do is to look at a name or label of some kind to see what's in production ("I see we're running Green right now") and pick the other value ("So I will call the next version Blue during this process"). The system managing Blue/Green deployment won't need to maintain state about what's what.

Other systems prefer to keep the meanings stable. The running system is always Blue, the next version is always Green. That works fine, so long as something will keep some records.

Upgrades without taking a scheduled downtime is the basic motivation for Blue/Green deployments. But there are other benefits. One is that we can now ensure

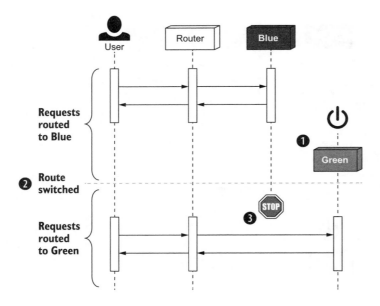

Figure 3.3   A Blue/Green deployment

Green is good before we switch to Blue. Or, alternatively, if Green is bad, we can more easily roll the system back to Blue because our muscle for switching traffic is well-developed. To ensure rollbacks are fast, we can keep Blue running for a little while until Green has proved itself worthy of our trust.

A bad session

The big fly in the ointment for Blue/Green deployment and its successors is that things get *much* harder if you pin user sessions to particular instances of your software (also called *session stickiness*). If user #278 always goes to instance #4, then the person who writes that software can just sorta-kinda *assume* that stuffing information into a variable will be sufficient.

This is mostly *not* how software is written anymore. User session state is typically delegated to some external data store, like a database or caching system. Sometimes, session state is squeezed into HTTP cookies with encrypted payloads. Either way, it means that any request can go to any instance and get identical service.

But software relying on session stickiness still exists. In those cases, you need to add additional steps to drain sessions, or to relocate sessions to another instance, or any number of other clever things. If you are able to avoid tying sessions to instances, I cannot strongly enough insist that you do so.

3.2.2　*The Canary deployment*

Blue/Green deployments are the minimum you should accept from any system, tool, crazy shell script written by the longest-serving engineer, and so on, that is being passed off as "continuous deployment." Done properly, Blue/Green deployment is a safe way to deploy software.

But like many conservative, ultra-safe systems, it can be wasteful. Here's an example (assuming that my production system is always called Blue and my next version is always called Green).

During the normal production steady state, I need enough capacity to run Blue. But during the Blue/Green deployment, I need enough capacity for Blue *and* Green. In fact, I may need additional capacity on top of that to deal with things like database migrations, files being downloaded to new instances of Green, additional consumption due to new Green features, and so on, as well as the overhead imposed on my control plane by the business of rolling out and cutting over to Green. And, of course, for safety, I want to keep Blue around until I am satisfied that Green won't need to be rolled back.

There are now two considerations that are at odds. The first is efficiency; the second is safety. A Canary deployment helps with both of these problems.

In a Canary deployment, we actually roll out a reduced-size sample of Green to run alongside Blue (figure 3.4). For example, it might be that in our normal situation, we would deploy 100 copies of our software. Instead of having 100 Blue and 100 Green during the Blue/Green process, we might start with 100 Blue and 1 Green. This single copy is the "canary."[2]

Instead of cutting *all* traffic over to Green, we instead send a fraction of requests to it and see what happens. Then we might raise the number of Green copies to 10. If we're satisfied with how these run, we then proceed to fully deploy Green. We then cut over and immediately remove Blue. After all, our canaries established that Green was safe, so rollback speed is a less critical consideration.

3.2.3　*Progressive deployment*

Mind you, what we're doing is still fairly wasteful, insofar as we reach a peak level of capacity consumption that is roughly twice the steady state level. So now, we arrive at the third evolution of our approach: progressive deployment.

---

[2]　Canary here is an analogical reference to the birds Victorian-era coal miners brought with them to deep pits and also, one supposes, to their version of tech conventions. Carbon monoxide, somewhat like vaporware announced during a keynote speech, is colorless, odorless, lethal, and it can build slowly. The canary, being small, would die earlier than miners and so they would get an early warning of the danger.

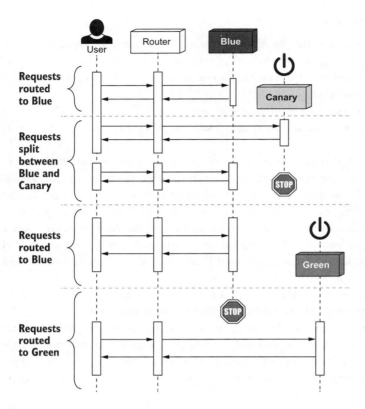

Figure 3.4   A Canary deployment

In progressive deployment, we keep the consumption level much closer to steady state (figure 3.5). Say we have 100 instances of Blue. We first perform a Blue/Green deployment of a *single* instance instead of our entire system. Afterward, we have 99 Blue and 1 Green. We run this 1 Green as a canary for a while. If we're happy, we perform another Blue/Green deployment, this time for 9 instances. Afterward, there are 90 Blue and 10 Green. Then, finally, we might complete the rollout of Green, retiring Blue as we go.

There are a lot of permutations here. For example, to limit the peak surge, we might roll out one instance at a time (or some fixed percentage at a time) rather than perform a Blue/Green deployment for the entire pool. Progressive deployment is essentially the logical endpoint that arises once you split traffic. It limits risk through canaries, and it limits utilization through upgrading a fraction at a time.

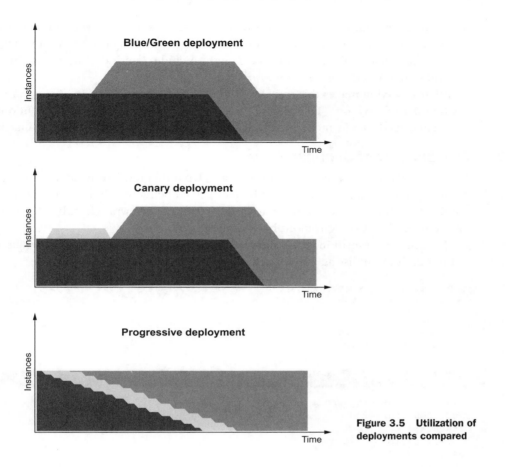

Figure 3.5   Utilization of deployments compared

3.2.4   Back to the future

So what does Knative Serving do? Blue/Green? Canary? Progressive? The answer is: all of these. Sort of.

In my previous discussion, I talked about two major themes: cluster history and safe, efficient deployments. Knative Serving sets out to answer these with two core types: the Configuration and the Revision. The connection is that each Revision is a snapshot of a Configuration, and a Configuration is the template for the *most recent* Revision. An analogy often used is to Git: you can think of each Revision as a particular commit. Then, a Configuration is the HEAD of a branch of Revisions.

How does this design connect back to my discussion? Let's review:

- *History*—Revisions represent snapshots of Configurations over time, giving a partial history of your system.
- *Time travel and deployments*—Multiple Revisions can receive traffic for a single endpoint. This allows the Blue/Green, Canary, and progressive deployment patterns.

But there's something new here. Previously, the business of deployment was a process with a binary outcome. You had version *N* running, something occurs, after which you are running version *N + 1*. That process might include a period of both running, but the end state was *only one version is running*.

Knative Serving makes this easy, but it isn't *limited* to that. You can, if you want, run any number of Revisions. That means that while the binary outcome is conventional, it isn't guaranteed. Deployment is now a fuzzy concept rather than a finite state machine.

3.3   *The anatomy of Configurations*

A *Configuration* is a definition of your software. Up until now, I've avoided showing one in the flesh. I wanted to show you kn first and avoid being too Kubernetes-centric. But now it's time for us to accept our fates as enterprise YAML wranglers. It will be easiest for me to explain Configurations by using the YAML form.

To ease the transition, the following listing shows the kn command we used in chapter 2. Below it, listing 3.2 shows the equivalent Configuration YAML file.

Listing 3.1   The before

```
$ kn service create hello-example \
  --image gcr.io/knative-samples/helloworld-go \
  --env TARGET="First"
```

Listing 3.2   The after

```
apiVersion: serving.knative.dev/v1
kind: Configuration
metadata:
  name: helloworld-example
spec:
  template:
    spec:
      containers:
      - image: gcr.io/knative-samples/helloworld-go
        env:
        - name: TARGET
          value: "First"
```

Everything from the kn CLI is present in the YAML version. We have a name, a container, and an environment variable. We also have a fair amount more besides, including a great deal of whitespace.

This document isn't meant to be used by kn. Those of you who have already drunk the Kule-aid recognize it as a Kubernetes record, which would typically be submitted to Kubernetes using kubectl apply.[3] Consequently, it sports some elements that are there to fit into Kubernetes conventions. For example, the apiVersion and kind

---

[3]   Under the hood, kn is actually doing the same thing that kubectl does. It takes a YAML document and ships it off to the Kubernetes API server.

elements are mostly there to identify the record type so that relevant controllers can be alerted to creations and updates. The metadata section is, under the hood, actually a Kubernetes type that can store many kinds of information. We provided a name here. Lastly, there's this curious little hop-skip-hop:

Listing 3.3 Yo dawg, I heard you like specs

```
spec:
  template:
    spec:
```

Listing 3.3 isn't an accident. There are three "things" here:

- *The outermost* spec *belongs to the* Configuration *itself.* The name spec is another Kubernetes convention meaning "desired world for this thing."
- *The* template *is actually a* RevisionTemplateSpec. I'll discuss this in just a second.
- *The innermost* spec *is a* RevisionSpec. That is, it's the spec of a Revision.

Hopefully, this tips you off to the fact that the template is the "thing" that is converted into Revisions. But it goes further than that: changing the template is what *causes* the creation of Revisions.

This is important, so I will repeat it: changing the template *causes* Revisions to be created. And, in fact, this is true from the moment that I first submit a Configuration. I can see this using kubectl directly, as this next listing demonstrates.

Listing 3.4 Using raw kubectl

```
$ kubectl apply -f example.yaml
configuration.serving.knative.dev/helloworld-example created

$ kubectl get configurations
NAME               LATESTCREATED             LATESTREADY               READY
helloworld-example helloworld-example-8sw7z  helloworld-example-8sw7z  True

$ kubectl get revisions
NAME                      CONFIG NAME         K8S SERVICE NAME          READY
helloworld-example-8sw7z  helloworld-example  helloworld-example-8sw7z  True

# "GENERATION", "REASON" columns excluded from this listing
```

I can see that by submitting the Configuration, I prompted Serving to create a Revision as well. That Revision is not meaningfully different to one created by kn, as I can see in the following listing with kn revision list.

Listing 3.5 kn revision list

```
$ kn revision list
NAME                      SERVICE  AGE    CONDITIONS  READY
helloworld-example-8sw7z           2m24s  3 OK / 4    True

# "GENERATION", "REASON" columns excluded from this listing
```

Your eye might be drawn to CONDITIONS and its value, 3 OK / 4. Despite appearances, this does not mean your Revision is one-quarter evil. It refers to something we've seen before: Revisions scale to zero when there's no traffic. The next listing shows how you can see this with kn revision describe.

Listing 3.6   kn revision describe to the rescue

```
$ kn revision describe helloworld-example-8sw7z
Name:          helloworld-example-8sw7z

# ... snipped ...

Conditions:
  OK TYPE                   AGE REASON
  ++ Ready                  2d
  ++ ContainerHealthy       2d
  ++ ResourcesAvailable     2d
   I Active                 2d NoTraffic
```

Remember that ++ means OK. Counting the conditions from top to bottom, three out of four are ++. Hence 3 OK / 4.

As well as creating Revisions via the creation of Services or Configurations, I can also create *new* Revisions by *editing* a Configuration or a Service. In chapter 2, I used kn service update to amend things, as you can see in the following listing.

Listing 3.7   Updating using kn

```
$ kn service update hello-example --env TARGET=Second
```

Which amends a Service, which amends the Configuration, which causes a new Revision to pop into existence. The equivalent would be to edit my YAML to look like the next listing.

Listing 3.8   The second YAML

```
apiVersion: serving.knative.dev/v1
kind: Configuration
metadata:
  name: helloworld-example
spec:
  template:
    spec:
      containers:
      - image: gcr.io/knative-samples/helloworld-go
        env:
        - name: TARGET
          value: "Second"
```

And then submit this YAML with kubectl again, along the lines of the next listing.

```
Listing 3.9   Amending with kubectl apply
```

```
$ kubectl apply -f example.yaml
configuration.serving.knative.dev/helloworld-example configured

$ kubectl get configurations
NAME                LATESTCREATED            LATESTREADY            READY
helloworld-example  helloworld-example-j4gv5 helloworld-example-j4gv5 True
# "REASON" column excluded from listing

$ kubectl get revisions
NAME                      CONFIG NAME         GENERATION  READY
helloworld-example-8sw7z  helloworld-example  1           True
helloworld-example-j4gv5  helloworld-example  2           True
# "K8S SERVICE NAME" and "REASON" excluded from listing
```

Now I can see *two* Revisions, but there is still only *one* Configuration with the name
helloworld-example. As a helpful hint, Revisions have a generation count that is set
at its creation time. Generations are monotonic numbers. Each Revision will be a
higher number than earlier Revisions, but there's no firm guarantee that all numbers
will be sequential. For example, you might have deleted Revisions yourself.

3.3.1 Configuration status

Is that all that's interesting about Configurations? Not quite. So far we've shown the
spec (a desired world in chapter 1 terms). But there is also a status that is set by the
configuration Reconciler (an actual world in chapter 1 terms). I can use kubectl and
the handy JSON utility jq to display my Configuration status as in the following listing.[4]

```
Listing 3.10   Looking at a status with kubectl and jq
```

```
$ kubectl get configuration helloworld-example -o json | jq '.status'
{
  "conditions": [
    {
      "lastTransitionTime": "2019-12-03T01:25:34Z",
      "status": "True",
      "type": "Ready"
    }
  ],
  "latestCreatedRevisionName": "helloworld-example-j4gv5",
  "latestReadyRevisionName": "helloworld-example-j4gv5",
  "observedGeneration": 2
}
```

---

[4] This example of using jq to stitch up kubectl output is something of a litmus test. On one side, you have the
"Unix pipes are the high watermark of software design" crowd, for whom hoarding one-liners like some kind
of CLI Smaug is right and worthy. Then, there are the "Human-Computer interface research did not end in
1970, which is now 50 bloody years ago" weirdoes like me, who harbour radical notions about just being
allowed to do some damn work without having to learn "Yet Another Minilanguage." This divide is a poetic
illustration of why Knative is at all necessary. The developer experience for Kubernetes is not batteries
included. It's "learn chemistry and try not to poison yourself with lead."

In listing 3.10, you can see two basic sets of information. The first is `conditions`, which I will talk about more later (during my discussion of Revisions). The second set of information is the trio of `latestCreatedRevisionName`, `latestReadyRevision-Name`, and `observedGeneration`.

Let's start with `observedGeneration`. Earlier you saw that each Revision is given a generation number. It comes from `observedGeneration`. When you apply an update to the Configuration, the `observedGeneration` gets incremented. When a new Revision is stamped out, it takes that number as its own.

`latestCreatedRevisionName` and `latestReadyRevisionName` are the same here, but need not be. Simply creating the Revision record doesn't guarantee that some actual software is up and running. These two fields make the distinction. In practice, it allows you to spot the process of a Revision being acted on by lower-level controllers.

These fields are useful for debugging. If you submit an updated Configuration but don't otherwise see expected behavior, compare these. For example, suppose I update my Configuration from `foo-1` to `foo-2`, but I don't see any change in behavior when sending HTTP requests. If I check and see that `latestCreatedRevisionName` is `foo-2` and that `latestReadyRevision` is `foo-1`, then I know something is wrong with `foo-2`, which merits further investigation.

3.3.2   *Taking it all in with kubectl describe*

The observant among you have noticed that `kn` has talked about Services, but I have been talking about Configurations. This is basically because `kn` does not treat Configurations as a standalone concept; it instead sweeps these into Services as the unit of interaction. Given Knative's goals of simplifying and smoothing out the developer experience, that's quite reasonable.

It *does* make it a bit trickier to get a nice readout on a Configuration by itself though. For that purpose, I need to drop down from `kn` to `kubectl`. The helpful `kubectl describe` subcommand allows me to take a closer look at the Configuration as Kubernetes sees it, which the following listing illustrates.

> **Listing 3.11   Inspecting a Configuration with `kubectl describe`**

```
$ kubectl describe configuration helloworld-example

Name:          helloworld-example
Namespace:     default
Labels:        <none>
Annotations:   serving.knative.dev/creator:
                 jacques@example.com
               serving.knative.dev/lastModifier: jacques@example.com
API Version:   serving.knative.dev/v1
Kind:          Configuration
Metadata:
  Creation Timestamp:  2019-12-03T01:17:28Z
  Generation:          2
  Resource Version:    8778016
```

Annotations are key-value metadata attached to the records. Here you can see that Knative Serving identified me as the user who created and last modified the Configuration.

The generation is visible here under Metadata.

```
    Self Link:
      ➥ /apis/serving.knative.dev/v1/namespaces/default/configurations/
      ➥ helloworld-example
    UID:                    ac192f54-156a-11ea-ae60-42010a800fc4
Spec:
  Template:
    Metadata:
      Creation Timestamp:  <nil>
    Spec:
      Container Concurrency:  0
      Containers:
        Env:
          Name:    TARGET
          Value:   Second
        Image:     gcr.io/knative-samples/helloworld-go
        Name:      user-container
        Readiness Probe:
          Success Threshold:  1
          Tcp Socket:
            Port:  0
        Resources:
      Timeout Seconds:  300
Status:
  Conditions:
    Last Transition Time:          2019-12-03T01:25:34Z
    Status:                        True
    Type:                          Ready
  Latest Created Revision Name:    helloworld-example-j4gv5
  Latest Ready Revision Name:      helloworld-example-j4gv5
  Observed Generation:             2
Events:
  Type    Reason              Age     From                          Message
  ----    ------              ----    ----                          -------
  Normal  Created             14m     configuration-controller
    ➥ Created Revision "helloworld-example-8sw7z"
  Normal  ConfigurationReady  14m     configuration-controller
    ➥ Configuration becomes ready
  Normal  LatestReadyUpdate   14m     configuration-controller
    ➥ LatestReadyRevisionName updated to "helloworld-example-8sw7z"
  Normal  Created             6m28s   configuration-controller
    ➥ Created Revision "helloworld-example-j4gv5"
  Normal  LatestReadyUpdate   6m24s   configuration-controller
    ➥ LatestReadyRevisionName updated to "helloworld-example-j4gv5"
```

Our good friend spec.template.spec shows up here again.

Our other good friend status is also visible too.

Events is a log of occurred changes, as reported to Kubernetes.

There is quite a lot of information in listing 3.11, loosely approximating the shape of the underlying record. The code annotations include some highlights. The last one deserves a bit of commentary. The Events list here is a mechanism that Kubernetes provides to applications and extensions. It stores events in a nice, somewhat structured way.

What is the sound of one container flapping?

The Kubernetes Events system has two caveats you should be mindful of. One is that it's an opt-in mechanism. Software running *on* Kubernetes, or which *extends* Kubernetes, is under no obligation to emit events *to* Kubernetes. For a lot of software, this `Events` section is just blank. Knative Serving is a good citizen in this regard and sends meaningful events for Kubernetes to record and display.

But that leads to the second problem. Even if you are dealing with well-behaved software that plays nicely with Kubernetes Events, there's no guarantee that all events will be captured, stored, or retained for long periods, or even protected from deletion. The client API that software calls to pass on an event doesn't return errors, so well-behaved software can be yelling into the void. Once the event reaches the API server, it's about as safe as any other Kubernetes record. It can be deleted by another controller, on purpose or accidentally. And, because events typically share resources with all other records, Kubernetes performs rolling truncations of events. The command today that reports a bunch of events can be ominously silent tomorrow.

The upshot is that the *presence* of an event is meaningful: it means that the described occurrence did actually occur. But the *absence* of an event should not be relied on when forming theories or diagnoses of behavior. It might be absent because the occurrence hasn't happened, or it might be absent because Kubernetes, for whatever reason, never received or stored the event, or because Kubernetes received it but has since deleted it. Absence of evidence isn't evidence of absence.

3.4   *The anatomy of Revisions*

I was deliberately brief in my discussion of Configurations because their primary mission is to stamp out Revisions. Keep in mind the parent/child, template/rendered relationship between a Configuration and its Revisions. In what follows, I will spend a lot of time pointing out the various kinds of settings and fields that can be placed onto a Revision. But *you won't set these directly.* You will instead be applying updates to a Configuration or to a Service, which ultimately leads to a new Revision being stamped out.

In practical terms, this means some of the YAML you see will be from Revisions. But a lot of it will be from Configurations.

Is it a Pod or not?

Those of you with some Kubernetes background will begin to ask: why does a Revision look so much like a Kubernetes Pod?

One reason is that Knative Serving's mission is to improve the developer experience of Kubernetes. That doesn't mean that the whole of Kubernetes is exposed, and it doesn't mean the whole of Kubernetes is hidden. It's case-by-case.

When a feature is provided that's identical to the underlying system, it doesn't necessarily hurt to provide it with an identical name. For example, the `serviceAccountName` field serves the same basic purpose in Knative and Kubernetes, so why not just call it the same thing?

> As of this writing, Knative achieves this by internally storing some configuration in a Kubernetes PodSpec. But it doesn't expose the *whole* of a PodSpec, only a selected allowlist of fields. To this allowlisted set of fields, it adds two of its own: `Container-Concurrency` and `TimeoutSeconds`, which I'll discuss in this chapter.
>
> Note that I said "as of this writing." So far, Knative has only allowlisted a handful of PodSpec fields, and it only uses PodSpecs internally as an implementation convenience. But this is an implementation detail. It's not guaranteed to remain stable.
>
> PodSpecs include lots of knobs and dials that, it might be cogently argued, don't belong there for any reason other than implementation considerations. It's possible in the future that Knative will expose other fields in a different way, or at a different level in its control hierarchy, or introduce new concepts altogether. It's best, therefore, to *ignore* the implementation detail. Consider Revisions to be their own thing.

3.4.1 Revision basics

As you saw in chapter 2, `kn` gives us the basic information about a Revision. The following listing recaps what we can see.

Listing 3.12 What `kn` tells you

```
$ kn revision describe helloworld-example-8sw7z

Name:        helloworld-example-8sw7z
Namespace:   default
Age:         1d
Image:       gcr.io/knative-samples/helloworld-go (at 5ea96b)
Env:         TARGET=First
Service:

Conditions:
  OK TYPE                  AGE REASON
  ++ Ready                 1d
  ++ ContainerHealthy      1d
  ++ ResourcesAvailable    1d
   I Active                1d NoTraffic
```

The key items in listing 3.12 are the `Name` and the `Namespace`. By default, the `Name` is automatically generated when the Revision is created. It doesn't need to be. I can use `kn` to create a revision with a name of my own choosing, as the following listing shows.

Listing 3.13 A Revision by any other name would smell as sweet

```
$ kn service update hello-example --revision-name this-is-a-name
# ... updates

$ kn revision list
NAME                            SERVICE        GENERATION AGE   CONDITIONS READY
hello-example-this-is-a-name    hello-example  6          10s   4 OK / 4   True
hello-example-jnspq-7           hello-example  5          24h   3 OK / 4   True
# "REASON" excluded from listing
```

The Service name here has been baked into the Revision name by Knative Serving as an anti-collision measure. Of course, I could achieve the same in YAML. First, I need to edit my Configuration YAML to look like this listing.

Listing 3.14   Naming the next Revision in the YAML Configuration

```
apiVersion: serving.knative.dev/v1
kind: Configuration
metadata:
  name: helloworld-example
spec:
  template:
    metadata:
      name: this-too-is-a-name       ◁──   Adds the name to
    spec:                                   the Configuration's
      containers:                           metadata.
      - image: gcr.io/knative-samples/helloworld-go
        env:
        - name: TARGET
          value: "It has a name!"
```

You can see that I've added the name in a new `metadata` section. This section can also accept any other standard Kubernetes metadata. What does that include? Quite a lot, including metadata added automatically by Knative. To see more, we need to peek with our `kubectl` + `jq` waltz again. Let's start with the metadata in the following listing.

Listing 3.15   Revision

```
$ kubectl get revision helloworld-example-8sw7z -o json | jq '.metadata'

{
  "annotations": {                                        annotations, taken
    "serving.knative.dev/creator": "jacques@example.com"  ◁──  together with ...
  },
  "creationTimestamp": "2019-12-03T01:17:28Z",          ... labels, capture a fair
  "generateName": "helloworld-example-",                amount of useful information
  "generation": 1,                                      (outlined later).
  "labels": {
    "serving.knative.dev/configuration": "helloworld-example",
    "serving.knative.dev/configurationGeneration": "1",
    "serving.knative.dev/service": ""
  },
  "name": "helloworld-example-8sw7z",        ◁──   name and namespace tell you
  "namespace": "default",                          the name of your Revision and
  "ownerReferences": [                             where it lives in Kubernetes-
    {                                              land. These are the same
      "apiVersion": "serving.knative.dev/v1",      values that kn shows as
      "blockOwnerDeletion": true,                  Name and Namespace.
      "controller": true,
      "kind": "Configuration",
      "name": "helloworld-example",
      "uid": "ac192f54-156a-11ea-ae60-42010a800fc4"
    }
```

```
    ],
    "resourceVersion": "8776259",
    "selfLink": "/apis/serving.knative.dev/v1/namespaces/default
        ➥ /revisions/helloworld-example-8sw7z",
    "uid": "ac1a8358-156a-11ea-ae60-42010a800fc4"
}
```

What about `ownerReferences`? It's interesting at one level, but strictly speaking, it's an implementation detail. Try not to fixate on it too closely. The same information is more easily found in the `annotations` and `labels`, some of which I describe in table 3.1.

Table 3.1 Important labels and annotations on Revisions

Name	Type	Description
`serving.knative.dev/configuration`	label	Which Configuration is responsible for this Revision?
`serving.knative.dev/configurationGeneration`	label	When the Revision was created, what was the current value of `generation` in the Configuration metadata?
`serving.knative.dev/route`	label	The name of the Route that currently sends traffic to this Revision. If this value is unset, no traffic is sent.
`serving.knative.dev/service`	label	The name of the Service that, through a Configuration, is responsible for this Revision. When this is blank, there's no Service above the Configuration.
`serving.knative.dev/creator`	annotation	The username responsible for the Revision being created. `kn` and `kubectl` both submit this information as part of their requests to the Kubernetes API server. Typically, it's an email address.
`serving.knative.dev/lastPinned`	annotation	This is used for garbage collection.
`client.knative.dev/user-image`	annotation	This is the value of the `--image` parameter used with `kn service`.

The names of labels and annotations follow a pattern: `<subject area>.knative.dev/<subject>`. This allows each of the subprojects to namespace their own annotations without trampling each other.

3.4.2 *Container basics*

A lot of the "meat" of what you'll provide to a Revision lives in the `containers` section. The following listing is a first glimpse.

Listing 3.16 The `containers` array

```
apiVersion: service.knative.dev/v1
kind: Revision
# ...
```

```
spec:
  containers:
  - name: first-and-only-container
    image: example.com/first-and-only-container-image
```

The `name` in listing 3.16 reveals a secret: you can, if you really want to, ask for more than one container to be run for each instance of a Revision. This wasn't always so.

In its original design, Knative only permitted one container image to be set and would reject attempts to set more than one. This assumption then flowed through other parts of the design. For example, if there is only one image that's turned into a running process, then there is only one possible process where traffic needs to be sent.

So why support multiple containers? Mostly because of *sidecars*: containers run alongside your own processes to add extra functionality. This pattern is widely used for tools intended to be run across some or all of a cluster, such as service meshes like Istio, antivirus tools, monitoring system agents, and so on.

Because this capability was added later in Knative's history, it's slightly inelegant. It's also quite new. At the time of writing, I can't refer you to official documentation. For simplicity, I'll ignore multi-container support.

In my example, I give the container a name. Technically, this isn't necessary. But names are a good idea, even simple ones. Lots of monitoring and debugging tools now slurp data out of the Kubernetes API. In the future, others may be more Knative-centric or Knative-aware. Either way, giving the container a name makes it easier to understand, identify, and correlate with other systems.

3.4.3   Container images

The *container image* is the software that ultimately runs on something, somewhere.[5]

> **What is a container image?**
>
> Container images (originally called Docker images, now better referred to as OCI images) are primarily about the shipment of bits that wind up looking like a disk to your software. But container images can also carry a bunch of additional settings and instructions: environment variables, startup commands, user names, and so on.
>
> Container images are interpreted and executed by container runtimes. The Docker daemon is the best known, along with its offspring `runc` and `containerd`. There are now others such as CRI-O, gVisor, Kata, Firecracker, and Project Pacific. These are independent implementations that can create identical runtime behavior, often with other desirable features.

---

[5]   It irks me that while the motivational analogy for Docker containers was shipping containers, the word "container" refers to the *running process* rather than the *bag of bits*. Instead, we say "container *image*." Reflecting the analogy back into logistics would mean calling container ships "containers" and calling containers "container rectangular prisms."

In specifying a container, you must provide an `image` value. This will be a reference that allows a container runtime, such as `containerd`, to fetch the image from an image registry. I showed this earlier in my examples of Configurations and Revisions.

There are, however, two other relevant keys to know about: `imagePullPolicy` and `imagePullSecrets`. Both of these are intended for consumption by a container runtime.

The `imagePullPolicy` setting is an instruction about *when* to pull an image to a Kubernetes node. It is one of those annoying details that surfaces at the wrong level of abstraction, but which is nevertheless important to know about. You can give it three values: `Always`, `Never`, and `IfNotPresent`.

The `Always` policy ignores any local cache that a container runtime maintains and instead forces a complete re-pull anytime the Revision is launched on a Kubernetes node. The `Never` policy prevents any attempt to pull, so that success relies on that relevant image being pre-populated into a local cache. `IfNotPresent` basically says "use a cached copy if you have one; otherwise, pull it."

As a rule, you don't need to set `imagePullPolicy`. If you do set it for Configurations, `IfNotPresent` is a safe and efficient choice. If you are setting it for a raw Kubernetes record, like a PodSpec, then you are in a world of hurt. I'll return to this topic when we reach chapter 9.

The `imagePullSecrets` setting is another Kubernetism poking up through the dirt. You might be used to slinging `docker pull` commands about willy-nilly to get public images. This is fine and well, but not all container images are public. And, further, not all container registries are prepared to talk to unidentified strangers. That means that some kind of authentication is required.

Kubernetes has a `Secret` record type which, among other things, can be used for image registry credentials. Like all Kubernetes records, a `Secret` must have a name that can be used to identify it and refer to it. It is this name to which the `imagePull-Secrets` will refer.

Suppose I have an image that lives in a private repo at registry.example.com. I might have put credentials for registry.example.com into a `Secret` called registry-credentials-for-example-dot-com. Then, I wind up with something like that shown in the following listing.

> ### Listing 3.17 Can you keep a secret?

```
apiVersion: service.knative.dev/v1
kind: Configuration
# ...
spec:
  template:
    spec:
# ...
      imagePullSecrets:
      - name: registry-credentials-for-example-dot-com
```

After applying the YAML in listing 3.17, the container runtime uses the credentials provided by the `Secret` any time that it pulls a container image from registry.example.com. And as with the `containers` section, `imagePullSecrets` is an array. In a raw Kubernetes PodSpec, this makes sense because it allows multiple containers to be defined. And because each container can potentially come from a different registry, it's necessary to allow multiple sets of credentials.

The nameless dread of container image names

Image names are, incidentally, also a mess. At the time of writing, all of these are legal image names:

- ubuntu
- ubuntu:latest
- ubuntu:bionic
- library/ubuntu
- docker.io/library/ubuntu
- docker.io/library/ubuntu:latest
- docker.io/library/ubuntu@sha256:bcf9d02754f659706...e782e2eb5d5bbd716 8388b89

More to the point, these are all *identical*. Each name refers to the same pile of bits, because if you don't specify `docker.io`, it is assumed on your behalf.

"Very convenient," you might be thinking. Well, maybe. Suppose I instead ask for example.com/ubuntu/1804@sha256:bcf9d02754f659706...e782e2eb5d5bbd7168388b89. And further suppose that it is bit-for-bit identical to the others. Is this the same image? The answer is no. Not from the point of view of the way images are named and addressed.

"But that makes sense," you say. "They're different URLs, so they should be treated as different." But what happens when you want to pull from a private repository behind your firewall? Suddenly, everything is hard because you (1) can't reach docker.io and (2) can't simply rename the images because that would make these "different."

The problem is that there is no distinction made between identity and location. Knative cannot fully resolve this mess.

Knative Serving's `webhook` component resolves partial container image names into full names with a digest included. For example, if you told Knative that your container is ubuntu, it dials out to Docker Hub to work out the full name including the digest (e.g., docker.io/library/ubuntu@sha256:bcf9d02754f659706...e782e2eb5d5bbd7168388b89).

This resolution happens just before the Revision gets created because the `webhook` component gets to act on an incoming Configuration or Service record before the rest of Serving sees these.

You can see the resolved digest in two different ways. Let's first look at it with `kubectl` and `jq` in the following listing.

Listing 3.18   What `kubectl` sees

```
$ kubectl get revision helloworld-example-8sw7z -o json |
  ➡ jq '.status.imageDigest'

"gcr.io/knative-samples/helloworld-go
  ➡ @sha256:bcf9d02754f659706...e782e2eb5d5bbd7168388b89"
```

The `gcr.io/knative-samples/helloworld-go` is recognizable from earlier. The rest of it, the `@sha256:…` stuff, is what Knative resolved and recorded. It's actually guidance to the container runtime that it should ask for an *exact* version of the container image, rather than whatever container image happens to be identified by `gcr.io/knative-samples/helloworld-go` at the next pull.

The `sha256:` bit is telling it to verify the exact identity by using the SHA-256 hashing algorithm. If the registry doesn't have an entry that hashes to that digest value, it throws a 404 error. But `kn` does something slightly different in the next listing.

Listing 3.19   Seeing the digest with `kn`

```
$ kn revision describe helloworld-example-69cbl

Name:        helloworld-example-69cbl
Namespace:   default
Age:         4h
Image:       gcr.io/knative-samples/helloworld-go (at 5ea96b)
# ... other stuff I'm ignoring right now
```

You can see (at `5ea96b`) in the `Image` field. It's the first 6 hexadecimal digits of the full SHA-256 digest value.

What about collisions? Is it possible that two images will have the same first 6 hex digits? At one level, yes, absolutely. In terms of uniquely identifying a given image from the universe of all images, 6 hex digits is not enough. It can express only millions of permutations, instead of quintillions for the full digest. But you're not comparing the universe of *all* images, just the universe of images for that base URL. The odds of collision there pretty much become noise unless you're doing something Very Interesting (please email me to tell me what it is). Six hex digits is easier to compare with the Mark I eyeball and doesn't cause terminal wrapping. You accept it for Git, after all.

3.4.4   The command

So far, I have thrown container images at Knative and magic has happened: these got converted into running containers with little fuss. But that hasn't wholly been due to Knative's efforts. Let me demonstrate with some `kn` action in the next listing.

Listing 3.20   The Knative doesn't know where to begin

```
$ kn service update hello-example --image ubuntu

Updating Service 'hello-example' in namespace 'default':
```

```
RevisionFailed: Revision "hello-example-flkrv-9" failed with message:
                ➥ Container failed with: .
```

Listing 3.20 reveals that kn doesn't show us the most helpful message. Let's look more closely at the Revision with the next listing.

Listing 3.21   What's going down?

```
$ kn revision describe hello-example-flkrv-9

Name:         hello-example-flkrv-9
Namespace:    default
Age:          2m
Image:        ubuntu (pinned to 134c7f)
Env:          TARGET=Second
Service:      hello-example

Conditions:
  OK TYPE                 AGE REASON
  !! Ready                20s ExitCode0
  !! ContainerHealthy     20s ExitCode0
  ?? ResourcesAvailable    2m Deploying
   I Active               11s TimedOut
```

The output in listing 3.21 is slightly more helpful. I can at least see that Ready and ContainerHealthy are !!. That's the Knative symbolism for "bad."

!! Ready means that the container won't come up because Kubernetes just doesn't know how to run it. Or, rather, Kubernetes can't guess at what I want to actually run. Here I used ubuntu, which out of the box has hundreds of executables. Which one did I want to bring to life? It has no idea.

Meanwhile, ResourcesUnavailable is ?? (unknown) because, if the container can't come up, it doesn't hit resource limits. What *actually* happened, though? There are two parts to the answer:

- The container image I nominated doesn't have a defined ENTRYPOINT.[6] That means that when the container runtime picks it up, it can't find out which command to run by inspecting the container image itself.
- *Neither did I set a* command *field on my Configuration.* If I had, it would have been passed into the container runtime as a parameter.

Because it's set by someone closer to production, a command setting will override an ENTRYPOINT. Hence, you get this basic set of combinations:

- ENTRYPOINT with command ⇒ command
- ENTRYPOINT without command ⇒ ENTRYPOINT

---

[6] In addition to ENTRYPOINT, images can also have a CMD. These sorta kinda do the same thing, and for the purposes of our discussion it won't matter, so I'm going to keep pretending that only ENTRYPOINT is relevant.

- command without ENTRYPOINT ⇒ command
- Neither command nor ENTRYPOINT ⇒ it goes kerflooie

Your first instinct might be to try for a sneaky command: bash -c echo Hello, World! as a cost-cutting measure. It was certainly my first thought. But it won't do what you want either. Knative observes that the process exits, which violates its expectations.

Most of the time, you shouldn't use command; you should rely on the ENTRYPOINT set by the container image you nominate. This is for a number of reasons. The most important is: it's easier. Whoever builds the container image (whether that's you or someone else) probably intends for it to be used as is. Especially if it's going to be used by Knative.

If you *do* use command, there's one more thing to know: args. As you might imagine, this is an array of arguments that are passed to whichever command you define.

But to reiterate: you probably shouldn't use command. The assumption that you won't is baked into kn, which does not expose a way to set command.

3.4.5 *The environment, directly*

You've already seen the easy way to add or change environment variables: use kn with --env. I used it in chapter 2 to advance "Hello world" to state-of-the-art. A lot of systems use or at least support setting environment variables as a configuration mechanism. Often, this is an alternative to command-line arguments or configuration files. Whether I want to add new environment variables or update existing variables (and thereby create a new Revision), I use --env, as the following listing demonstrates.

Listing 3.22 Adding another environment variable

```
$ kn service update hello-example --env AGAINPLS="OK"

# ... Output from updating the service ...

$ kn revision describe hello-example-gddlw-4
Name:       hello-example-gddlw-4
Namespace:  default
Age:        16s
Image:      gcr.io/knative-samples/helloworld-go (pinned to 5ea96b)
Env:        AGAINPLS=OK, TARGET=Second
Service:    hello-example

# ... Conditions ...
```

If this seems too easy, you can use YAML again by setting env. As the name suggests, env sets environment variables. In Configuration YAML, the env parameter is set on the lonely occupant of containers, which this listing shows.

Listing 3.23 Some YAML again

```
apiVersion: service.knative.dev/v1
kind: Configuration
```

```
# ...
spec:
  template:
    spec:
      containers:
      - name: first-and-only-container
        image: example.com/first-and-only-container-image
        env:
        - name: NAME_OF_VARIABLE
          value: value_of_variable
        - name: NAME_OF_ANOTHER_VARIABLE
          value: yes, this is valuable too.
```

As listing 3.23 illustrates, you can set as many `name` and `value` pairs as you like because the `env` section is an array. It's not required to use SHOUTY_SNAKE_CASE for `names`, but it's idiomatic.

Remember that Knative Serving spits out a new Revision every time you touch the `template`. That includes environment variables, which can be used to change system behavior. Knative's dogma is that a Revision should be a faithful snapshot. If configuration can be changed out-of-band, then it will not be possible to later know how a system was configured at a particular time. Yes; it's the problem of history that I spent so much time talking about earlier in this chapter.

Knative's approach is not without drawbacks. First, updating configuration now costs you a redeployment. If your software starts fast, that might well be fine. If, for whatever reason, your software takes a long time to deploy or become ready, then tweaking configuration values can become prohibitively expensive. There is a school of thought (championed by Netflix among others) that configuration ought to be distributed independently from the code that obeys it. This doctrine intends for the deployment of configuration changes to be decoupled from the deployment of software. This enables configuration changes to be made much more quickly.

On the downside, history is now sprinkled into different places again, meaning that reconstruction is back to correlation of independent timelines. If you build powerful automation and consistent tooling, this is less of a problem, but that *if* can be a mighty big *if*. Knative's decision emphasizes simplicity and safety by pushing all changes through the same mechanism.

Apart from environment variables that you set yourself, Knative Serving injects four additional variables. These are

- PORT—The HTTP port your process should listen on. You can configure this value with the `ports` setting (I'll get to it before long). If you don't, Knative typically picks one for you. Now, it might be something predictable, like 8080, but that is *not* guaranteed. For your own sanity, only listen in on the port you find in PORT.
- K_REVISION—The name of the Revision. This can be useful for logging, metrics, and other observability tasks. Also fun for party tricks.
- K_CONFIGURATION—The name of the Configuration from which the Revision was created.

- K_SERVICE—The name of the Service owning the Configuration. If you are creating the Configuration directly, there will be no Service. In that case, the K_SERVICE environment variable will be unset.

3.4.6 *The environment, indirectly*

Of course, when I said environment variables get snapshotted, I wasn't telling the whole story (in the degenerate argot of today's youth, this is called "lying"). It is true that directly setting variables with name and value under env will be snapshot into a Revision. Once this snapshot is taken, the value is frozen for all time, or until the next cosmic whoopsie in your cluster, whichever comes first (never bet against heat death).

But there are actually two alternative ways of injecting environment variables: --env-from/envFrom and valueFrom. What these have in common is that you don't provide the values of variables directly; envFrom goes further and even does away with providing a name. In both cases, the values come from either a ConfigMap or a Secret.

Which means, to start with, you need ConfigMaps and Secrets from which to draw values. These are Kubernetes records and kn doesn't support either. So to begin, I need to create a ConfigMap and a Secret (listing 3.24), and ship these off with kubectl (listing 3.25).

Listing 3.24 The ConfigMap and Secret

```
---
apiVersion: v1
kind: ConfigMap
metadata:
  name: example-configmap
data:
  foo: "bar"
---
apiVersion: v1
kind: Secret
metadata:
  name: example-secret
type: Opaque
data:
  password: <...redacted but it's definitely certainly not 'password123'...>
```

Listing 3.25 Applying the YAMLs

```
$ kubectl apply -f example-configmap.yaml example-secret.yaml
configmap/example-configmap created
secret/example-secret created
```

The first and easiest way to use these is with --env-from. This essentially says, "I want you to look up this record, then create variables from what you find under data." In listing 3.24, the ConfigMap has foo: bar and the Secret has password: <redacted>.

Listing 3.26 Setting variables with `kn` and `--env-from`

```
$ kn service update hello-example \
    --env-from config-map:example-configmap \
    --env-from secret:example-secret

# ... Output from update ...
```

When I use `--env-from` (listing 3.26), then inside the container, there are two additional environment variables: `foo=bar` and `password=<redacted>`. Now I can validate that the injection has occurred, but I can't see *what* was injected, as the next listing reveals.

Listing 3.27 Partial information only

```
$ kn revision describe hello-example-gkfmx-7
Name:         hello-example-gkfmx-7
Namespace:    default
Age:          12s
Image:        gcr.io/knative-samples/helloworld-go (pinned to 5ea96b)
Env:          AGAINPLS=OK, TARGET=Second
EnvFrom:      cm:example-configmap, secret:example-secret
Service:      hello-example
```

I can use `kubectl describe` for a more verbose look at the same information as the following listing shows. Note that in the listing, there is a distinction being drawn as evidenced by the annotations.

Listing 3.28 Did it work or not?

```
kubectl describe pod/hello-example-gkfmx-7-deployment-6cb9fbbd58-8mm7b
Name:         hello-example-gkfmx-7-deployment-6cb9fbbd58-8mm7b
Namespace:    default
# ... snip

Containers:
  user-container:

# ... snip

    Environment Variables from:          ◁─┐  Environment Variables from:
      example-configmap  ConfigMap  Optional: false   validates that the ConfigMap
      example-secret     Secret     Optional: false   and the Secret are used.

    Environment:                         ◁─┐  Environment: shows stuff
      AGAINPLS:            OK                that's injected explicitly
      TARGET:             First             and directly through env.
      PORT:               8080
      K_REVISION:         hello-example-gkfmx-7
      K_CONFIGURATION:    hello-example
      K_SERVICE:          hello-example

# ... snip
```

If you are so inclined and don't want to use kn's `--env-from`, then it's possible to do this in YAML with `envFrom`, as in the following listing.

Listing 3.29   Using `envFrom` to stamp out environment variables

```
apiVersion: serving.knative.dev/v1
kind: Configuration
metadata:
  name: values-from-example
spec:
  template:
    spec:
      containers:
      - image: example.com/an/image
        envFrom:
        - configMapRef:
            name: example-configmap
        - secretRef:
            name: example-secret
```

This mechanism is relatively convenient because it takes everything in the `ConfigMaps` and `Secrets` you provide and stamps out the environment variables. If you have software that expects a bunch of environment variables to be set, then it's easier to do it through `ConfigMaps` than to laboriously concatenate all of the settings into a long kn command.

But the `--env`/`envFrom` mechanism is not *always* convenient. Sometimes you have a big bag of values in a `ConfigMap` or `Secret` that were not originally intended to be environment variables. In this situation, you want to be able to pick and choose which values will be imported from the available selection.

This brings us to the mysterious contender, `valueFrom`. It looks a lot like `envFrom`, but with some subtle and important differences. For one thing, it's not exposed through kn, so it's all YAML from here. It also has a slightly different structure because of the need to be able to select specific values. The selections are achieved by `config-MapKeyRef` and `secretKeyRef`. Unfortunately, these are a little bit on the chatty side, as the next listing proves.

Listing 3.30   Using `valueFrom` to pull in values

```
apiVersion: serving.knative.dev/v1
kind: Configuration
metadata:
  name: values-from-example
spec:
  template:
    spec:
      containers:
      - image: example.com/an/image
        env:
        - name: FIRST_VARIABLE
```

```
          valueFrom:
            configMapKeyRef:
              name: example-configmap
              key: firstvalue
        - name: PASSWORD
          valueFrom:
            secretKeyRef:
              name: example-secret
              key: password
```

Listing 3.31   Applying the YAMLs

```
$ kubectl apply -f example.yaml
configuration.serving.knative.dev/values-from-example created
```

After applying the new version (listing 3.31), how can I see if this worked? As with
`--env-from`, I can't see it through `kn`. At least, not directly. The following listing
demonstrates the veil of mystery.

Listing 3.32   kn does not show the resolved value

```
$ kn revision describe values-from-example-626da
Name:        values-from-example-626da
Namespace:   default
Age:         48m
Image:       example.com/an/image (at 1a2bc3)
Env:         FIRST_VARIABLE=[ref]
             PASSWORD=[ref]
Service:

Conditions:
  OK TYPE                   AGE REASON
  ++ Ready                  48m
  ++ ContainerHealthy       48m
  ++ ResourcesAvailable     48m
   I Active                 38m NoTraffic
```

You can see in listing 3.32 that there are references, but not what value these resolve
to. This is one advantage of the `env.valueFrom` approach over the `envFrom` approach.
In this case, `kn` at least points to the fact that a variable exists.

Now to the lying bit—I didn't lie. What I said was completely accurate: a Revision is
a snapshot of a Configuration. This snapshot does not contain the *value* of an environment variable, but rather the exact configuration, which might happen to include the
value of environment variables. When I use `valueFrom`, I am snapshotting the *reference*
to a variable, not the value that could have been found on the other side of the reference at the moment of the snapshot.

This opens the door back to the independent updating of configurations without
the updating of Configuration. Put another way: if you want to, if it makes sense, you
can change environment variables by modifying the `ConfigMap` or `Secret` that a Revision's `valueFrom` points to.

There's a caveat here. The change won't be effective until the Revision is relaunched. These references to values are resolved to actual values at container creation time. These are *not* updated dynamically. If you update the `ConfigMap` or `Secret` that you referred to, that update won't be reflected in the running Revision.

To pick up the change, the Revision needs to be scaled to zero and then relaunched. This is not in your direct control, and so in practice, you should not rely on this mechanism for fast configuration changes. In particular, you should not rely on it to rotate credentials quickly. Your choices are

- To edit the Configuration to force the creation of a new Revision that takes over from the previous Configuration, accepting the cost thereof
- To use an alternative mechanism for configuration key/values (such as Netflix Eureka), which is more proactive in managing TTLs or pushing new values to consumers, and to use out-of-band secrets management systems like Vault or CredHub.

Which should you choose? That's partly a matter of taste. My advice is that you should prefer to edit the Configuration whenever possible for data you would put into a `ConfigMap`. For a `Secret`, you should strongly consider using a credential manager because keeping secret material in environment variables leads to a fascinating kind of security hell.

If you absolutely must have some kind of secret or sensitive material in your environment, then for pity's sake, use a `Secret` and `valueFrom` *and* also do a new Revision whenever you rotate it. Yes, I know, it's a schlep. But you want to make key material as inconvenient to reach as possible.

3.4.7 Configuration via files

Passing configuration via the command line is easy: use `args`. Via the environment is also easy: use `env` or `envFrom`. But these options have two problems.

First, some software requires parameter files, or you might prefer parameter files over other possibilities. For these cases the command line and environment variables won't do.

Second, command lines and environment variables aren't a safe place for secrets to hang out. Too many tools and systems have some way of laying eyes on a command line or an environment variable. Exfiltration opportunities abound. Can you SSH into the running container? Run `ps` on the container or on the Node underlying it? Do you have monitoring system agents that extract environment variables? Or that can be configured to do so? Are you checking secrets into Git? The list goes on and on (and can be sung as a hymn to the tune of "We're So Boned, Time To Update My LinkedIn Profile").

One way out of this is to take your `Secrets` and `ConfigMaps` and expose these as files in a filesystem. This first of all enables grumpy old software the luxury of not changing. Secondly, it behaves like a filesystem, adding another permissions hoop attackers will need to hop through. Finally, these get mounted as `tmpfs` volumes. Your sensitive keys and values never touch a disk and become inaccessible once the container goes away.

Let's start with the `kn`-centric view of things by mounting a `Secret` into our container. The following listing demonstrates this.

Listing 3.33   Volumes of secrets

```
$ kn service update hello-example --mount /sikkrits=secret:example-secret

Updating Service 'hello-example' in namespace 'default':
# ...
```

The key in listing 3.33 is the `--mount` parameter, which maps from `example-secret` into `/sikkrits`. The `secret:` prefix tells `kn` what kind of record it will ask Knative to map; the alternative option is `configmap:` for `ConfigMaps`.

Having added a secrets mount, my first instinct is to see if it worked using `kn revision describe`. The next listing shows how that's done.

Listing 3.34   The secret `Secret`

```
$ kn revision describe hello-example-yffhm-12

Name:       hello-example-yffhm-12
Namespace:  default
Age:        3m
Image:      gcr.io/knative-samples/helloworld-go (pinned to 5ea96b)
Env:        TARGET=Second
Service:    hello-example
# ... Conditions table
```

Listing 3.34 gives no sign of the `Secret` being mounted. It won't show `ConfigMaps` either. If I want to see what happened, I need to pop the bonnet ("crack the hood" for my American friends) and cop a squizz ("take a look") at the raw YAML with `kubectl` and `jq`, per the following listing.

Listing 3.35   Volumes and mounts

```
$ kubectl get -o yaml revision hello-example-yffhm-12

apiVersion: serving.knative.dev/v1
kind: Revision
metadata:
# ... lots of YAML
spec:
  containers:
    name: example-container
    # ... more YAML
    volumeMounts:
    - mountPath: /sikkrits
```

```
      name: exsec-9034cf59
      readOnly: true

  volumes:
  - name: sikkrits-9034cf59
    secret:
      secretName: example-secret
# ... still more YAML
```

You can see in listing 3.35 that the configuration is in two places: `volumeMounts` (under the lonely member of `containers`) and `volumes` (which hangs directly off `spec`). These different levels reflect YAML's meaningful whitespace. These also reflect another Kubernetism bubbling up into Knative. I will take a second to explain.

Raw Kubernetes allows more than one container in a PodSpec. Containers might want to share one or more filesystems. That means there needs to be (1) a way to list all the volumes that might exist and (2) a way to decide which containers can see which volumes. Dumping everything into a single pile might be convenient at first, but down the road, it leads to bugs and security hassles.

Incidentally, the business of volumes shows up in `kn` in a confusing way. As well as `--mount`, you'll find there's a `--volume` option. The help text for both is close to identical. So which should you use? You should stick to `--mount`. It does more or less what one might expect in terms of creating a directory, putting `ConfigMaps` and `Secrets` onto a volume, and then mounting it for you.

3.4.8 Probes

Broadly speaking, software is dead or alive. When it's alive, it's ready or it's not ready. This is, at least, one of the ways Kubernetes (and therefore Knative) sees your software: as having the properties of *liveness* and *readiness*. In raw Kubernetes, you are given the ability to set `livenessProbes` and `readinessProbes` on your containers. Knative exposes this functionality, but with caveats.

First, what are probes? A *probe* is a simple mechanism that Kubernetes can use to determine the liveness or readiness of the software. Typical liveness probes include stuff like "is it listening on port 3030?" or "if I run this shell command inside the container, does it exit with code 0?" Typical readiness probes are mostly centered on making HTTP requests to known endpoints and expecting a `200 OK` response.

Superficially, these might look the same. For example, both liveness and readiness probes might check for an HTTP response or sniff a TCP port. But there *is* a distinction.

Software that's otherwise alive might not be ready for traffic. For example, during a long startup, the software is *alive*, but it's not *ready*. This leads to different treatment for each kind of probe. When liveness checks fail, Kubernetes eventually kills the container and relaunches it someplace else. When readiness checks fail, Kubernetes prevents network traffic from reaching the container. The following listing shows the configuration for liveness and readiness probes.

Listing 3.36   Knative probes

```
apiVersion: service.knative.dev/v1
kind: Configuration
# ...
spec:
  template:
    spec:
      containers:
      - name: first-and-only-container
        image: example.com/first-and-only-container-image
        livenessProbe:
          httpGet:
            path: /deadoralive
        readinessProbe:
          tcpSocket:
```

The first thing to note is that you can pick between `httpGet` and `tcpSocket` for your probes. Table 3.2 shows the key fields for these two types.

Table 3.2   Fields for probes

Type	Field	Description	Required?
`httpGet` and `tcpSocket`	`host`	A hostname or IP address	No
`httpGet`	`path`	An HTTP path	Yes
`httpGet`	`scheme`	Can only be one of "http" or "https"; defaults to "http"	No
`httpGet`	`httpHeaders`	If you really need these, see the Kubernetes docs	No

You can also set configurations that can be applied to either of the probe types. For example, you can make a `livenessProbe` wait for 5 seconds by using `initialDelaySeconds: 5`. Or, you can require three successful probings in a row with `successThreshold: 3`.

If you came from Kubernetes, these features of probes are familiar to you. You also may be wondering, what happened to `port`? The answer is that Knative takes control of this value to satisfy its "Runtime Contract." It modifies any probes so that their `port` value is the same as the `port` value of the container itself, which will be the same as the `PORT` environment variable that's injected.

A slight quirk of this behavior is that `tcpSocket:` can just hang out by itself without needing anything underneath it. I think that looks a little weird, but it's allowed in this case.

If you don't provide one or both probes, Knative Serving creates `tcpSocket` probes with `initialDelaySeconds` set to zero. By setting these to zero, Knative is telling Kubernetes to immediately begin checking for liveness and readiness in order to minimize the time it takes for an instance to begin serving traffic.

If I may be frank: probes are not likely to be the most pressing thing to think about. Unless you have a proven need to adjust the defaults, you might as well save yourself some YAML. kn sees things this way, and consequently, it doesn't provide a means for setting or updating probes.

3.4.9 Setting consumption limits

Knative lets you set minimum and maximum levels for CPU share and bytes of RAM. This is another case of directly exposing the underlying Kubernetes feature, which is called resources.

In practice, you are most likely going to find yourself using this to set minimum levels, which is known to Kubernetes as requests. The following listing shows how to update limits with kn.

Listing 3.37 Requesting CPU and RAM

```
$ kn service update hello-example \
  --requests-cpu 500m \
  --requests-memory 256Mi
```

The 500m format refers to "milliCPUs," or thousandths of a CPU. In this case, it's for 500 milliCPUs, which is half a CPU. However, what "half a CPU" means depends on where you're running Knative. You'll need to consult your vendor or provider documentation.

The memory format for 256Mi is referring to mebibytes (not megabytes), which is the value we'd typically think of as 256 megabytes (not mebibytes). It confuses me too, but *mostly* you can substitute Mi for MB in your head and get it right. The same goes for Gi (gibibyte) and GB (gigabyte) and, lucky you, Ti (tebibyte) and TB (terabyte) as well.

The upper ceiling is known as limits and follows the same format as requests. The following kn listing illustrates setting limits.

Listing 3.38 Limiting CPU and RAM

```
$ kn service update hello-example \
  --limits-cpu 800m \
  --limits-memory 512Mi
```

And, of course, there's a YAML equivalent too. As well, the next listing reveals this.

Listing 3.39 Requesting and limiting in YAML

```
apiVersion: service.knative.dev/v1
kind: Configuration
# ...
spec:
  template:
    spec:
      containers:
```

```
- name: first-and-only-container
  image: example.com/first-and-only-container-image
  resources:
    requests:
      cpu: 500m
      memory: 256Mi
    limits:
      cpu: 800m
      memory: 512Mi
```

Many folks leave off limits entirely, because most of the time what they want is "burstable" behavior. That means that the container process is guaranteed to get its `requests` allocations and will burst to consume any spare capacity that the operating system is willing to allocate to it. This is a useful property for helping containers launch as quickly as possible, because it is typical for launching processes to do a whole bunch of preliminary bookkeeping and preparation that isn't yet about directly serving traffic.

This advice isn't perfect though. Where possible and manageable, I think it's better to set a high set of limits; for example, setting a limit of 3500 Mi on 4-core worker nodes. That's high enough that you get *most* of the benefits of burstiness, but not so high that a single container process can inadvertently starve all of its neighbors. However, doing so involves a lot more work than sticking to bursty behavior. In particular, you will need to know the CPU and RAM capacity of worker nodes *in advance* and update your Service definitions when the nodes are upgraded. That might not be very practical or desirable.

Serverlessless

And now for a rant: Serverless isn't. I wish it was. Episode eleventy jillion.

What happens if you don't set `limit` and `request`? Nothing special, really. Left to its own devices, Kubernetes places a completely undefined workload any old where and then leaves it to fend for itself against other workloads landing on the same machine. Unless you set `limit` and `request` records, Knative accepts whatever Kubernetes dishes up as default values.

Default values are configurable by the platform engineers who set up and operate the Kubernetes cluster using `LimitRange` records. On GKE, for example, this is configured so that `requests.cpu` is `100m`, setting a floor CPU allocation of 10%.

I would prefer not to go down a rabbit hole here, because I happen to know it is a quite deep and elaborate rabbit hole. Somewhat efficient packing of workloads is, after all, part of the superhero origin story for Kubernetes, so it should come as no surprise that there are many knobs and levers to be twisted or pulled by relevant persons. But this necessity has led to a complicated set of rules and ideas that no developer should be required to care about. As an exercise, look up the Kubernetes documentation for Quality of Service levels, then try to reassure yourself that you can reliably predict what Kubernetes will do in times of trial and tribulation.

To be sure, autoscalers solve some of this problem, but, as I will repetitively repeat in the upcoming chapter on autoscaling, autoscalers aren't magical. And neither is the Kubernetes scheduler. Both must work in a world where raw compute resources like CPU and RAM are not completely fungible. There are boundaries to what can be done, set by the capacity of the nodes that Kubernetes is managing. A container has to sit *somewhere*, and its activities consume *something*. The mechanisms of `request` and `limit` are there so that you can provide hints to the Kubernetes scheduler about what that will look like. The reality that there are discrete machines leaks up through the nice abstraction of Revisions.

It turns out that Kubernetes, the closed-loop-feedback champion, has a giant gaping open loop at its heart: container placement. Once placed, the container is placed for good. The Kubernetes scheduler doesn't perform rebalancing of workloads. Rebalancing that does occur is a side-effect of other causes, such as container crashes or autoscaling.

Is there any hope for the future? Maybe. One line of attack is VM-based runtimes like Firecracker or Spherelets. Because these are VMs, each can be more easily and robustly relocated between physical nodes without appearing to be restarted, meaning that transparent rebalancing can occur without needing to modify the Kubernetes scheduler. Another more science-fiction-y line of attack is to unbundle the resources offered by compute nodes and have directly network-connected chunks of RAM, CPUs, and so forth.

3.4.10 Container concurrency

Speaking in broad terms, the purpose of the Autoscaler is to ensure that you have *enough* instances of a Revision running to serve demand. One meaning of enough is to ask, "How many requests are being handled concurrently per instance?"

Which is where `containerConcurrency` comes in. It's your way of telling Knative how many concurrent requests your code can handle. If you set it to 1, then the Autoscaler will try to have approximately one copy serving each request. If you set it to 10, it will wait until there are 10 concurrent requests in flight before spinning up the next instance of a Revision. That is at least *approximately* what happens, because the Autoscaler has quite a few knobs and dials that affect what it does, not to mention a moderate amount of internal subtlety that I'll need to explain carefully.

You can set a concurrency *limit* with kn, as the following listing shows.

Listing 3.40 Using `kn` to set container concurrency limits

```
$ kn service update hello-example --concurrency-limit 1

# ... Output from the update ...

$ kn revision describe hello-example-pyhcm-6

Name:        hello-example-pyhcm-6
Namespace:   default
```

```
Age:            2m
Image:          gcr.io/knative-samples/helloworld-go (pinned to 5ea96b)
Env:            AGAINPLS=OK, TARGET=Second
Concurrency:
  Limit:        1
Service:        hello-example
```

Note the new section under `Concurrency`, which in turn gives a `Limit`. The concurrency limit is a hard threshold for scaling. If average concurrent requests rise above this number, the Autoscaler creates more instances. There is also another setting, `--concurrency-target`, but this works differently. Instead of setting a *maximum* level of concurrency, it sets a *desired* level of concurrency. Right now you can use --concurrency-limit, and Knative sets --concurrency-target to the same level. In chapter 5, I will break this down further. Naturally, you can set this value in the YAML too, as this listing shows.

Listing 3.41   But is it YAML scale?

```
apiVersion: service.knative.dev/v1
kind: Configuration
# ...
spec:
  template:
    spec:
      containerConcurrency: 1
```

The YAML in listing 3.41 does the same as `--concurrency-limit`, setting a maximum on concurrent requests being served per instance. There isn't an equivalent in the YAML for `--concurrency-target`.

If you don't use `--concurrency-limit` or set `containerConcurrency` in YAML, the value defaults to 0. In turn, this sets up a whole bunch of other default settings that I'll ignore for now and discuss in chapter 5. What should you set it to? That's really up to your own judgment. Leaving it unset (i.e., leaving it at 0) is basically OK. Autoscaling up from zero instances and back down to zero instances will occur.

Of course, if you have a closer insight into what level of concurrency makes sense for your software, you should take advantage of that. For example, you might have a system that is strongly threadbound, so that a pool of 4 threads can handle 4 requests simultaneously. In this case, it probably makes sense to set the value to 4, or perhaps 5 to account for other kinds of buffering.

But remember, because we find it easier to build complex systems than to build simple ones, performance tuning will always be a mostly empirical affair. You need to apply load and observe performance, then adjust your settings accordingly.

NOTE Wouldn't this be easier if it were expressed as Requests Per Second (RPS) instead of concurrent requests? Yes, it would, and the Autoscaler can be configured to use RPS targets instead. In chapter 5, I'll explain how to do that. But here's a teaser: concurrent requests and RPS are actually closely related. If you have one, you can typically derive the other. I'll explain why when we get to chapter 5.

3.4.11 Timeout seconds

Knative Serving is based on a synchronous request-reply model, so as a matter of necessity, it needs timeouts. The `timeoutSeconds` setting lets you define how long Knative Serving will wait until your software begins to respond to a request.

The default value is generous: 5 minutes. More specifically, 300. Note that this is not a duration value, it's an integer value. You don't set it to "300s" or "5m". If you want 5 minutes, you set it to "300".

On the upside, the default value is pretty much guaranteed to avoid flakiness due to slow responses. On the downside, if you have a bug that causes stalled responses, you're going to see the Autoscaler busily stamping out copies as unattended requests pile up.

This setting is not directly surfaced through kn and, instead, has to be set using `kubectl apply`. Out of the box, you can set values up to 600 (10 minutes). If you attempt to set a higher value, Knative will complain. Suppose that I want the visually distinct 9999 as my value. First, I'd tinker with the `Configuration` record to look like the following listing.

Listing 3.42 Putting up big numbers

```
apiVersion: service.knative.dev/v1
kind: Configuration
# ...
spec:
  template:
    spec:
      timeoutSeconds: 9999
```

Then in the next listing, when I use `kubectl` to apply the change, the computer says no.

Listing 3.43 Nein nein nein nein!

```
$ kubectl -f example.yaml

error: configurations.serving.knative.dev "hello-example" could not be
  patched: Internal error occurred: admission webhook "webhook.serving
  .knative.dev" denied the request: validation failed: Saw the following
  changes without a name change (-old +new): spec.template.metadata.name
*{*v1.RevisionTemplateSpec}.Spec.TimeoutSeconds:
  -: "300"
  +: "9999"
expected 0 <= 9999 <= 600: spec.template.spec.timeoutSeconds
```

This error message is relatively helpful, in that it identifies what the offending change was (300 to 9999), what the inoffensive expectations were (to be between 0 and 600), and which component took offense (the webhook).

The downside to this sanity check is that maybe you have a good reason for letting something run for more than 5 or 10 minutes. Batch or batch-like scenarios, in particular, typically want to run for as long as it takes.

Knative Serving's timeout limit can be raised by tinkering with the installation configuration. But it's unlikely that you, as a developer, will have the authority to set such values, because these can impact everything that runs on Knative. In these cases, you will need to undertake the mature engineering step of engaging in a jello fight over whether the value should be raised (or, if it comes to that, lowered).

Summary

- Deployment processes have improved over the years from scheduled downtimes to Blue/Green deployment, to Canary deployment, and finally to progressive deployment.
- Blue/Green deployment works by launching the next version of software (Blue) alongside the existing version (Green), then switching over traffic when the new version is ready.
- Canary deployment works by first rolling out one or a few copies of the next version of the software and seeing if these are stable. If these are, further deployment (usually Blue/Green) occurs.
- Progressive deployment combines elements of both Blue/Green and Canary deployments, focusing on progressively moving traffic from existing software to new software.
- Knative Serving supports all these patterns of deployment.
- Additionally, Serving is able to run multiple versions of software at the same time. This is made possible using Revisions.
- Configurations are a definition of the software you want to run on Knative Serving.
- Revisions are created when Configurations are created or changed.
- Specifically, changes to the `spec.template.spec` settings in a Configuration trigger the creation of new Revisions.
- Configuration `status` provides information about what Revision is currently running.
- Revisions have a `container`, which must include an `image`. You should also provide a `name` for easier debugging.
- You can set `imagePullSecrets` if you are using private image repositories.
- You can set `imagePullPolicy`, but you probably won't need to.
- Knative will try to run the image you give it, first by looking for an ENTRYPOINT on the image itself, then by looking for a `command` on the Revision. If these are both missing, the Revision will not work.
- While you can configure `command` and `args`, you probably shouldn't. Instead, build and use images that have ENTRYPOINTs.

- You can set environment variables directly using the `env` setting. You can also set environment variables indirectly using `envFrom`. These values can be pulled from Kubernetes `ConfigMaps` and `Secrets`.
- Variables that you set using `env` are directly copied into the Revision. Variables you set via `envFrom` are not, meaning that these might change between Revision launches.
- You can mount configuration files easily with `kn`. Less easily by using `kubectl` with `volumeMounts` and `volumes`.
- You can define liveness and readiness probes for your software.
- If you don't define probes, Knative assumes that it can probe for an HTTP server at a known port. If doesn't get a `200 OK`, Knative assumes something is broken.
- You can set upper and lower bounds on CPU and RAM allocations for your Revision instances. You can use `kn` or `kubectl` with `requests` and `limits`.
- You can tell the Autoscaler how many simultaneous requests your software can handle by setting the container concurrency.
- If you don't set container concurrency, Knative will set reasonable defaults for its Autoscaler behavior.
- You can tell Knative how long it should wait for your software to respond to requests. The default is 5 minutes, but you can set values up to 10 minutes.

References

- k8saudit—https://kubernetes.io/docs/tasks/debug-application-cluster/audit/
- sloop—https://github.com/salesforce/sloop
- Alexis Richardson, "What is GitOps, Really?" (August 21, 2018), https://www.weave.works/blog/what-is-gitops-really
- Evan Anderson and Dan Gerdesmeir, "Knative Serving API Specification: Container," v. 1.0.1, (2019), http://mng.bz/ZPVR
- k8s-probe-docs—http://mng.bz/RXNZ
- The Knative Authors, *Knative Runtime Contract*, "Meta Requests," https://github.com/knative/serving/blob/master/docs/runtime-contract.md (Accessed Thursday, Jan 23, 2020)
- Yizhou Shan, et. al., "LegoOS: A Disseminated, Distributed OS for Hardware Resource Disaggregation," *Proceedings of the 13th USENIX Symposium on Operating Systems Design and Implementation*, http://mng.bz/XdV6
- hey—https://github.com/rakyll/hey
- max-timeout—http://mng.bz/2egg (Accessed Wednesday, Jan 22, 2020)

Routes

This chapter covers

- Using `kn` to inspect Routes
- Using `kn` to update Routes by updating Services
- The anatomy of Routes

It seems like only pages ago that I was extolling the virtues of history and of Knative's ability to juggle it a bit with Revisions. And I wasn't wrong. But by itself, this is just an exercise in decorative bookkeeping. I need my Revisions to *do* something.

In Knative Serving, this brings us to *Routes*. These are the way you can describe to Knative how to map from an incoming HTTP request to a specific Revision. In this chapter, my focus is going to be on the business of what you can ask Knative to do. I'll pay much less attention to *how* Knative does the network magic.

So what *is* a Route? Briefly, a Route is where you answer three questions:

- At what public address or URL will traffic arrive *from*?
- What targets can I send traffic *to*?
- What *percentage* of traffic goes to which targets?

The first two points (from and to) are pretty typical of generations of proxies, routers, traffic doodads, and thingamajiggers. The third, traffic splitting or weighting, isn't universal, but it's common. Everything you can do with a Route can be done some other way. You might, for example, already have some elaborate tooling built around using a Kubernetes Ingress controller. Or, you might just run Nginx by hand with a bit of spit and elbow polish.

So at one level, you don't need Routes. But you don't need Routes in the same way that, if you already have a collection of bicycles you built yourself, you don't need a Honda Civic. Both will get you from place to place, but one of these will be easier to maintain.

This leads me to a second point about Routes. Whether you've used Perl and Apache VirtualHosts, or Rails, or Spring Boot, you put your rules about the "traffic from"/"traffic to" mapping *somewhere*. The question is who owns the somewhere? Is it defined by the application developers? Or is it owned and managed in a centralized system? In practice, there will be some mix of these, but even for a single app, you need to answer this question.

Knative provides Routes because if you are signed up for the Configurations and Revisions world, you want something that's closely adapted to that world. While I can use a central routing tool or API gateway, these don't know out of the box what a Configuration or Revision is. If you roll your own routing, then you will rely on implicit relationships. Whereas with Routes, the connection between the Route and its targets is explicit.

4.1 Using kn to work with Routes

If I used kn to create a Knative Service, then a Route was created automatically. This was (hopefully!) obvious in the previous chapter, where I gleefully poked and prodded Revisions without giving much thought to routing. I was typically finding a poke-able address by looking at service list or service describe.

Am I stuck with these? No. The route list and route describe commands give me information specific to Routes as shown in the following listing.

Listing 4.1 Using kn route list

```
$ kn route list

NAME                URL                                             READY
hello-example       http://working-example.default.example.com     True
broken-example      http://broken-example.default.example.com      False
```

From route list (listing 4.1), I can see the basic information of name, URL, and readiness. If I want to look more closely, I'd use route describe.

The output in the following listing should look familiar; it follows the basic structure that you would see from kn service describe. The key differences to note are explained in the code annotations.

Listing 4.2   Using `kn route describe`

```
$ kn route describe hello-example

Name:        hello-example
Namespace:   default
Age:         2d
URL:         http://hello-example.default.example.com
Service:     hello-example

Traffic Targets:
  100% @latest (hello-example-zcttz-8)

Conditions:
  OK TYPE                AGE REASON
  ++ Ready               3h
  ++ AllTrafficAssigned  4h
  ++ IngressReady        3h
```

A new Traffic Targets section of kn route describe doesn't need to show information about Revisions in the way that kn service describe does, so it's more compact.

The Conditions have different names from what you'd see in kn service describe or kn revision describe.

The easiest way to create a Route is to let a Service do it for you, and this is what shapes the approach kn takes. When you use kn service create, kn creates a Service, and the Service (in turn) causes the creation of a Route. Similarly, when you use kn service update, the Route is updated to point to the new Revision that got stamped out. And, unsurprisingly, using kn service delete ultimately causes the Route to be deleted.

Well, that was a short chapter! Thanks for tuning in. Next time on .... *Wait!* Is that *all*?

4.2   *The anatomy of Routes*

No. There is more to Routes that, by design, kn does not let you *directly* control. You can *look* with route list and route describe, but there's no such thing as a route update or route create.

> **NOTE** I'll be following a "break-and-fix" approach to examples in this chapter, rather than a "happy-path-then-sad-path" approach.

Mostly, that's fine. But I'd like you to understand what it is you're looking at, meaning that I will again need to go into the YAML forest. Let's first see what I've cooked up in my trusty example.yaml file, shown in the next listing.

Listing 4.3   The Route as YAML

```
apiVersion: serving.knative.dev/v1
kind: Route
metadata:
  name: route-example
spec:
  traffic:
  - configurationName: hello-example
    latestRevision: true
    percent: 100
```

Hopefully `metadata.name` is familiar, as well as the `apiVersion` and `kind` keys. The core of Route's work lives in `spec.traffic`. And, in fact, `traffic` is the *only* key in a Route's spec.

The `traffic` key is an array of traffic *targets*. And it is traffic targets that are the meat of a Route. More on those in a second, but first I will send my YAML off to Kubernetes (listing 4.4) and ask `kn` to read it back to me (listing 4.5).

Listing 4.4 Creating the Route with `kubectl`

```
$ kubectl apply -f example.yaml

route.serving.knative.dev/route-example created
```

Listing 4.5 Reading back my Route

```
$ kn route describe route-example

Name:         route-example
Namespace:    default
Age:          1m
URL:          http://route-example.default.example.com

Traffic Targets:
  100%  @latest (hello-example-zcttz-8)

Conditions:
  OK TYPE                  AGE REASON
  ++ Ready                 1m
  ++ AllTrafficAssigned    1m
  ++ IngressReady          1m
```

In listing 4.5, Route conditions are summarized with the tidy `++/!!/??` style that kn provided for other `describe` commands. There are three main conditions to watch for:

- `AllTrafficAssigned`—This means that Knative found all of the targets that were given in `traffic`. If this is `false`, you might have mistyped the target name.
- `IngressReady`—This says that the Ingress, the software responsible for the first bit of traffic management in Knative, is ready to manage the Route. If it is `false`, then you need to go and investigate whether your Ingress system is up and running.
- `CertificateProvisioned`—This means that an automated system that sets up a TLS certificate was able to do so (e.g., by using LetsEncrypt).[1]

---

[1] In my examples, you're not going to see this, because setting up certificates in Knative Serving largely rests with the platform operators. It's operators who will be either manually attaching certificates to the underlying infrastructure or will alternatively set up automated certificate systems that set the `CertificateProvisioned` condition. And so I am skipping jauntily past this essential bedrock of modern security, pausing only to warn you against doing the same. While going without TLS makes for convenient development, it's frankly irresponsible by production time. And slower, too, because HTTP/2 sets a hard dependency on TLS as its transport layer. The Knative project website has guidelines on adding TLS certificates either manually (https://knative.dev/docs/serving/using-a-tls-cert/) or automatically (https://knative.dev/docs/serving/using-auto-tls/).

The Ready condition *is* relevant, but by itself, it doesn't tell you much. That's because it rolls up the other two conditions. If any of the other conditions are bad (!!), then so is Ready.

WARNING   Knative Services and Kubernetes Services are not the same. In fact, these are deeply unalike. Refer to the sidebar for more.

Service vs. Service

A Kubernetes Service is approximately half of a Route. It defines a name where traffic can be sent and where that traffic will wind up being sent. This is needed because copies of software can come and go, appearing with new unique names each time. A downstream client shouldn't have to keep track of the exact location of its upstream server. If you define a Kubernetes Service, you can send traffic there and let Kubernetes find the running software for you.

But a Kubernetes Service is at its best in dealing with traffic inside a cluster. Traffic that comes from outside the cluster can, in theory, be sent through a Kubernetes Service, but it isn't pretty. You wind up needing a specialized kind of Service (a Load-Balancer) that lashes you to the particular infrastructure you're running on. Meaning that if you ask the Kubernetes Service to be the outside world face of your software, you will need to get AWS or Azure or vSphere or what-have-you to set up a load balancer that will shuffle traffic between the underlying platform's network and your Kubernetes cluster's internal network.

The more idiomatic way in Kubernetes is to have the Service as an internal thing and to provide a Kubernetes Ingress that knows how to listen for outside world traffic and send it to the Kubernetes Service. If you look carefully, you might have realized that Routes roll up both of these problems. It deals with the business of wiring Ingresses and Kubernetes Services on your behalf. Easy peasy.

But a Knative Service, as we've seen before, is not purely about networking stuff. Instead, it rolls up Configurations and Routes; it's a high-level statement of all the things you want Knative to do for a particular piece of software.

I know the name collision here is less than ideal. It's passable for folks who are new to both Knative and Kubernetes, for whom we can say "just ignore the Kubernetes stuff as much as possible." For seasoned Kubernetes pros, it's a bit annoying. As it happens, "seasoned pros" is a decent description for some of the folks who designed Knative. The name "Service" was not chosen by accident and, I promise you, there were naming discussions that took bikeshedding to new and exciting levels. "Service" came out as the least worst.

4.3   *The anatomy of TrafficTargets*

I said earlier that traffic is the meat of Routes. Then, while that thought sizzled, I dropped it. Now it's time to look more closely at targets because these are used for both spec and status.

4.3.1 configurationName and revisionName

In listing 4.3, I started with a configurationName. By the time Knative Serving finished, my Route pointed at a revisionName. And then I neglected to ask any hard questions.

Such as: can you set revisionName on the spec? Yes, you can, and in the same way as a configurationName. Let's update our YAML (listing 4.6), renaming the Route to avoid fuss, then apply it (listing 4.7).

Listing 4.6   Configuring a `revisionName`

```
apiVersion: serving.knative.dev/v1
kind: Route
metadata:
  name: route-revname-example
spec:
  traffic:
  - revisionName: hello-example
    latestRevision: true
    percent: 100
```

Listing 4.7   Angriness about `latestRevision`

```
$ kubectl apply -f example.yaml

Error from server (InternalError): error when creating "example.yaml":
➥Internal error occurred: admission webhook "webhook.serving.knative.dev"
➥denied the request: validation failed: may not set
➥revisionName "hello-example" when latestRevision is true:
➥spec.traffic[0].latestRevision
```

The first thing I learn in listing 4.7 is that I can't set a revisionName while latestRevision is true. To avoid learning what the heck that means, I just mark it as false and continue on my merry way through the following listing.

Listing 4.8   This time for sure

```
$ kubectl apply -f example.yaml

route.serving.knative.dev/route-revname-example created

# hooray!

$ curl -I http://route-revname-example.default.example.com
HTTP/1.1 404 Not Found
date: Thu, 06 Feb 2020 21:33:28 GMT
server: istio-envoy
transfer-encoding: chunked

# booo!
```

Listing 4.8 looked promising at first and then, it wasn't promising at all. What happened? The following listing reveals the answer, which is that three different things are wrong. The code annotations explain why.

Listing 4.9 Unhappiness abounds

```
$ kn route describe route-revname-example

Name:        route-revname-example
Namespace:   default
Age:         4d
URL:         http://route-revname-example.example.com

Traffic Targets:

Conditions:
  OK TYPE                   AGE  REASON
  !! Ready                  4d   RevisionMissing
  !! AllTrafficAssigned     4d   RevisionMissing
  ?? IngressReady           4d
```

Unsurprisingly, the combination of the other two conditions means that the top-level Ready condition is !!.

AllTrafficAssigned is !! (bad) because of RevisonMissing. It makes sense: if the Revision is missing, then it's impossible to assign traffic.

IngressReady is ??, meaning unknown. Again, this makes sense. Without a place to send traffic, Knative can't even begin to work out the Ingress situation.

Before I leave, I'm going to first point out that if you'd relied on kubectl apply to signal that things had gone wrong, you would be out of luck. It helps to remember that kubectl is responsible for submitting the *spec*, but it is not necessarily in charge of reporting the *status* of that particular submission. If you want to know how the story ends, you need to come back and ask. This is one spot where kn has a nicer experience as an interactive CLI tool if you're working through Services—it will wait for a Route to look good before it declares success.

Let's assume for a second that I know what I'm doing and use the name of a Revision that actually exists (shown in the next listing). And then, we'll see if it works (listing 4.11).

Listing 4.10 Configuring a `revisionName`, take 2

```
apiVersion: serving.knative.dev/v1
kind: Route
metadata:
  name: route-revname-that-works-example
spec:
  traffic:
  - revisionName: hello-example-zcttz-8
    latestRevision: false
    percent: 100
```

Listing 4.11 Hooray!

```
$ kubectl apply -f example.yaml

route.serving.knative.dev/route-revname-that-works-example created

$ curl http://route-revname-that-works-example.default.example.com

Hello world: First
```

What happens if you set *both* configurationName and revisionName? The answer, as the following listing shows, is that you make Knative mad. You can only set one of these at a time.

Listing 4.12 Just one name, please

```
expected exactly one, got both:
    spec.traffic[0].configurationName, spec.traffic[0].revisionName
```

4.3.2 latestRevision

The latestRevision key is provided as a courtesy for those who also provide a configurationName. By setting this to true, you ask Knative Serving to update the Route to point at the newest Revision at any given time. If this wasn't the case, you'd wind up having to (1) update the Configuration, (2) find the latest Revision, and then (3) update the Route yourself.

This connection to Configurations is why I had trouble earlier when I just switched from configurationName to revisionName. A Revision, by itself, does not know if it is the latest. The concept of "latest-ness" belongs to a Configuration.

When you set latestRevision to false, or omit it entirely (which gets counted as false), you will need to provide a revisionName. This is referred to as a "pinned" Route. This means that when the Configuration changes, the Route will *not* change automatically to point to a new Revision. It will keep pointing where it's already pointing. Taken together, table 4.1 shows what you get.

Table 4.1 How latestRevision and names interact

	revisionName is set	configurationName is set
latestRevision is true	Nope. You asked for both pinned and floating behavior. Pick one!	OK. The Route updates to point at the latest Revision of a Configuration.
latestRevision is false or missing	OK. The Route is pinned to the Revision. Changes to the Configuration will be ignored.	Nope. You said you wanted to pin the Route to a particular Revision, but you didn't provide a name.

When you use kn service create or submit a Service record using kubectl, latestRevision defaults to true. This is a sensible default because it requires the least effort from a developer.

But if you are using a tool to more deliberately control traffic allocations, then what you *don't* want is for Configurations to shuffle the world beneath you. In that situation, latestRevision: false tells Knative that you will keep your own routing books.

4.3.3   *tag*

Way, waaaay back in chapter 2, I performed the cool party trick shown in the following listing.

```
Listing 4.13   Splitting traffic 50/50
```

```
$ kn service update hello-example \
  --traffic hello-example-bqbbr-2=50 \
  --traffic hello-example-nfwgx-3=50

Updating Service 'hello-example' in namespace 'default':

  0.057s The Route is still working to reflect the latest
        ➥ desired specification.
  0.072s Ingress has not yet been reconciled.
  1.476s Ready to serve.

Service 'hello-example' updated with latest revision 'hello-example-nfwgx-3'
        ➥ (unchanged) and URL: http://hello-example.example.com

$ curl http://hello-example.example.com
Hello Second!

$ curl http://hello-example.example.com
Hello world: Second
```

The gist was that using `--traffic` enabled me to set routing percentages on particular Revisions. Sometimes, though, I don't want percentages—I want certainties. Suppose I have two Revisions, `rev-1` and `rev-2`. If I want to be *sure* to hit `rev-1`, I can set its percentage to 100%.

This might not be what I want, however. While it guarantees that *my* requests all go to `rev-1`, it also guarantees that everyone's requests will as well. If my purpose was to debug a flaky function, this is going to cause some problems. What's needed is to separate two different problems:

- How do I divvy up traffic between Revisions using a shared name?
- How can I refer to Revisions directly?

Setting a `tag` is what gives us the ability to directly target a particular Revision. Let's assume I've created a Service with two Revisions. I want to tag these `satu` ("one") and `dua` ("two"), respectively.[2] It looks like the next listing.

```
Listing 4.14   Setting a tag
```

```
$ kn service create satu-dua-example \
    --image gcr.io/knative-samples/helloworld-go \
    --env TARGET=Satu
```

---

[2] Proof, if any was required, that three years of studying Bahasa Indonesia in middle school achieved approximately *nol*, because *Saya tidak bisa bahasa Indonesia.*

```
# ... creation of Service and a Revision, "satu-dua-example-brvhy-1"

$ kn service update satu-dua-example \
    --env TARGET=Dua

# ... another Revision, "satu-dua-example-snznt-2"

$ kn service update satu-dua-example \
    --tag satu-dua-example-brvhy-1=satu \
    --tag satu-dua-example-snznt-2=dua

Updating Service 'satu-dua-example' in namespace 'default':

  0.052s The Route is still working to reflect the latest
         ➥ desired specification.
  0.246s Ingress has not yet been reconciled.
  1.568s Ready to serve.

Service 'satu-dua-example' with latest revision 'satu-dua-example-snznt-2'
  ➥ (unchanged) is available at URL:
  ➥ http://satu-dua-example.default.example.com
```

Note that adding a tag *doesn't* cause a new Revision to be stamped out. That's because tag is part of a Route, not part of a Configuration. And besides, if tagging Revisions created new Revisions, you'd never catch up.

What does the world look like now? I check the following listing for revelations.

Listing 4.15   Three targets

```
$ kn route describe satu-dua-example
Name:       satu-dua-example
Namespace:  default
Age:        16d
URL:        http://satu-dua-example.default
              ➥ .example.com
Service:    satu-dua-example

Traffic Targets:
  100% @latest (satu-dua-example-snznt-2)

    0%  satu-dua-example-brvhy-1 #satu
        URL:  http://satu-satu-dua-example.default
                ➥ .example.com

    0%  satu-dua-example-snznt-2 #dua
        URL:  http://dua-satu-dua-example.default
                ➥ .example.com

Conditions:
# ... snip
```

The main URL is still available. Anything sent to this URL flows according to the configuration of the Traffic Targets.

100% of traffic is flowing to @latest because I didn't update any --traffic settings while updating --tag. The @latest tag is a floating pointer to the latest Revision. This is the same Revision that will be pointed to when latestRevision is true.

satu-dua-example-brvhy-1 has the tag satu attached to it. Likewise, satu-dua-example-snznt-2 has dua attached.

Now the fun bit: in addition to the normal URL, I now have special URLs that only route to particular tags.

I'll test the theory with the following listing.

```
$ curl http://satu-satu-dua-example.default.example.com
Hello Satu!

$ curl http://dua-satu-dua-example.default.example.com
Hello Dua!
```

Note that these URLs follow a predictable pattern. The main URL, where traffic flows according to the Traffic Target rules, includes the service name only (http://<service-name>.default.example.com). But each tagged Revision now has a URL of the form http://<tag>-<servicename>.default.example.com. In these, the main URL is prepended with the tag. Hence, **satu**-satu-dua-example points to #satu, which points to satu-dua-example-brvhy-1.

Now that I have tags, I can use those to split up traffic, as the next listing demonstrates. This is exactly the same as splitting traffic using a Revision name.

```
$ kn service update satu-dua-example \
  --traffic satu=50 \
  --traffic dua=50

# ... updates

$ kn route describe satu-dua-example

Name:       satu-dua-example
Namespace:  default
Age:        3h
URL:        http://satu-dua-example.default.example.com
Service:    satu-dua-example

Traffic Targets:
   50%  satu-dua-example-brvhy-1 #satu
        URL:  http://satu-satu-dua-example.default.example.com
   50%  satu-dua-example-snznt-2 #dua
        URL:  http://dua-satu-dua-example.default.example.com
```

In listing 4.17, I can see that traffic will be split 50/50 between satu and dua. What I no longer see is @latest as one of the targets. By setting the traffic totals explicitly, I told Knative Serving that I know what I'm doing. Under the hood, this shows up as latestRevision: false.

What happens if I create another Revision? Something you might not have expected: the Revision *exists* but can't receive traffic. The following listing shows how it will look in kn.

Listing 4.18 No love for `Tiga`

```
$ kn service update satu-dua-example --env TARGET=Tiga
# ... creates new Revision

$ kn service describe satu-dua-example
Name:        satu-dua-example
Namespace:   default
Age:         3h
URL:         http://satu-dua-example.default.example.com

Revisions:                                            Instead of seeing 0%,
    +   satu-dua-example-rbbxk-5                  ⟵┘  I see a + symbol.
            ➥ (current @latest) [3] (36s)
        Image:  gcr.io/knative-samples/helloworld-go (pinned to 5ea96b)
    50%   satu-dua-example-snznt-2 #dua [2] (3h)
        Image:  gcr.io/knative-samples/helloworld-go (pinned to 5ea96b)
    50%   satu-dua-example-brvhy-1 #satu [1] (3h)
        Image:  gcr.io/knative-samples/helloworld-go (pinned to 5ea96b)

# ... conditions
```

The arrow points to the new thing in listing 4.18. Right now, this Revision isn't excluded because of how routing arithmetic works when given zeroes—it's excluded from the routing arithmetic altogether. You can figure this out from the next listing, because if you look at the Route instead of the Service, the third Revision isn't there at all.

Listing 4.19 No `Tiga`

```
$ kn route describe satu-dua-example
Name:        satu-dua-example
Namespace:   default
Age:         3h
URL:         http://satu-dua-example.example.com
Service:     satu-dua-example

Traffic Targets:
    50%   satu-dua-example-brvhy-1 #satu
        URL:  http://satu-satu-dua-example.default.example.com
    50%   satu-dua-example-snznt-2 #dua
        URL:  http://dua-satu-dua-example.default.example.com
```

Maybe you're still confused. I think a diagram is in order (figure 4.1).

At face value, this whole dance may seem a bit silly. Why create a Revision if you're not going to feed it any traffic? Shouldn't the latest and greatest always be in the spotlight? Often, yes. In development environments, definitely. That's why the default Knative Serving behavior sets `latestRevision: true` and then updates a floating `@latest` tag automatically.

But when you manually assign traffic percentages, this automatic behavior is disabled and you are given full control. This is a reasonable thing to do because, otherwise,

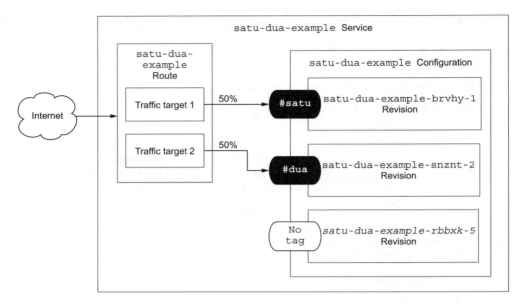

Figure 4.1   The relationship of Services, Routes, Configurations, Revisions, and Tags

you'll be constantly stuck in weird slapfights with Serving's controllers. Setting traffic manually is a useful escape hatch.

Mind you, escaping is sometimes a mistake. Happily, you can undo it pretty easily because `@latest` is always available as a tag. Take a peek at the following listing.

Listing 4.20   Switching the autopilot back on

```
$ kn service update satu-dua-example \
  --traffic satu=33 \
  --traffic dua=33 \
  --traffic @latest=34

# ... updates

$ kn service describe satu-dua-example
Name:        satu-dua-example
Namespace:   default
Age:         3h
URL:         http://satu-dua-example.example.com

Revisions:
    34%  @latest (satu-dua-example-rbbxk-5) [3] (20m)
         Image:  gcr.io/knative-samples/helloworld-go (pinned to 5ea96b)
    33%  satu-dua-example-snznt-2 #dua [2] (3h)
         Image:  gcr.io/knative-samples/helloworld-go (pinned to 5ea96b)
    33%  satu-dua-example-brvhy-1 #satu [1] (3h)
         Image:  gcr.io/knative-samples/helloworld-go (pinned to 5ea96b)
```

```
# ... conditions

$ kn route describe satu-dua-example
Name:       satu-dua-example
Namespace:  default
Age:        3h
URL:        http://satu-dua-example.example.com
Service:    satu-dua-example

Traffic Targets:
    33%   satu-dua-example-brvhy-1 #satu
          URL:  http://satu-satu-dua-example.example.com
    33%   satu-dua-example-snznt-2 #dua
          URL:  http://dua-satu-dua-example.example.com
    34%   @latest (satu-dua-example-rbbxk-5)

# ... conditions
```

In listing 4.20, I can now see that my third Revision is visible in *both* the Service and the Route. And, in figure 4.2, I can see what it looks like.

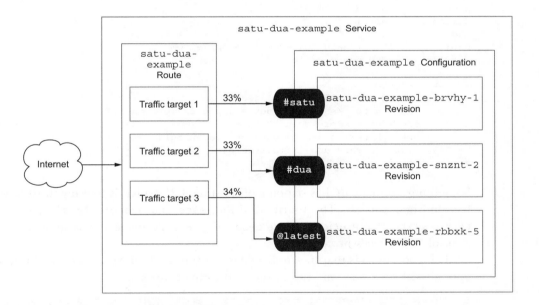

Figure 4.2   After `@latest` is set as a target

But let's keep rolling. I've re-enabled `@latest` and, under the hood, the `latest-Revision: true` setting has been placed on `satu-dua-example-rbbxk-5`. If I add a fourth Revision, what will happen to the third Revision? Will it still get traffic? Will the others shuffle down, or something? Saunter to the next listing for an answer.

```
$ kn service update satu-dua-example --env TARGET=Empat
# ... creates new Revision

$ kn service describe satu-dua-example
Name:       satu-dua-example
Namespace:  default
Age:        3h
URL:        http://satu-dua-example.example.com

Revisions:
    34%  @latest (satu-dua-example-lqlqj-7) [4] (38s)
         Image:  gcr.io/knative-samples/helloworld-go (pinned to 5ea96b)
    33%  satu-dua-example-snznt-2 #dua [2] (3h)
         Image:  gcr.io/knative-samples/helloworld-go (pinned to 5ea96b)
    33%  satu-dua-example-brvhy-1 #satu [1] (3h)
         Image:  gcr.io/knative-samples/helloworld-go (pinned to 5ea96b)

# ... conditions

$ kn route describe satu-dua-example
Name:       satu-dua-example
Namespace:  default
Age:        3h
URL:        http://satu-dua-example.example.com
Service:    satu-dua-example

Traffic Targets:
    33%  satu-dua-example-brvhy-1 #satu
         URL:  http://satu-satu-dua-example.example.com
    33%  satu-dua-example-snznt-2 #dua
         URL:  http://dua-satu-dua-example.example.com
    34%  @latest (satu-dua-example-lqlqj-7)
# ... conditions
```

Something unfortunate has happened in listing 4.21, which is that my third Revision has vanished entirely. The fourth Revision, satu-dua-example-lqlqj-7, has taken over as @latest. But neither route describe nor service describe shows any other signs of its predecessor.

The good news is that the *Revision* has not vanished forever. I can see this quickly enough with kn revision list, as the next listing reveals.

```
$ kn revision list

NAME                       TRAFFIC  TAGS   GENERATION   CONDITIONS   READY
satu-dua-example-lqlqj-7   34%             4            3 OK / 4     True
satu-dua-example-rbbxk-5                   3            3 OK / 4     True
satu-dua-example-snznt-2   33%      dua    2            3 OK / 4     True
satu-dua-example-brvhy-1   33%      satu   1            3 OK / 4     True
# "SERVICE", "AGE" and "REASON" excluded from listing
```

Listing 4.22 shows the whole gang, complete with traffic percentages and tags. Figure 4.3 shows the whole gang in diagrammatic form.

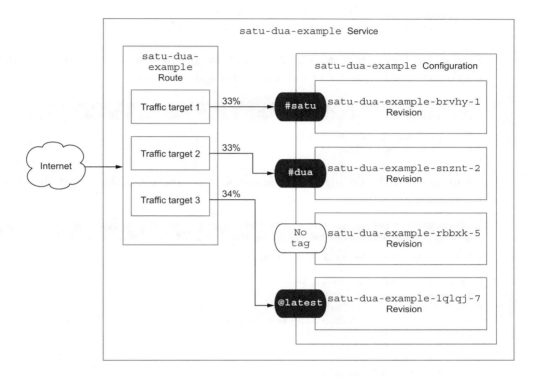

Figure 4.3   After adding a fourth Revision, the third Revision no longer receives traffic.

Did I lie earlier when I said you could re-engage autopilot using `@latest`? The answer is, as usual, "sort of." You *could* re-engage the way that `@latest` acts as a floating target based on the creation of Revisions, but this doesn't unpin anything else that you've manually configured. Only the fraction that was assigned to `@latest` will float. Everything else is fixed in place until you change it.

And if you stop to think about it, this means that the fully automatic setting is actually a special case of the partly automatic setting. If 100% of traffic flows to `@latest`, which is the default rule, then everything looks fully automated. For development, that's an excellent experience, but in production, you may want to exert a more precise control.

The trade-off is that the illusion of magic and automation is shattered once we begin to pin things down. And because we've shattered the illusion, let's just keep going and grind it into dust by moving tags across Revisions.

My first instinct is to just use `--tag` again, but with a different target. This turns out not to work, which the following listing illustrates.

Listing 4.23   Tags can't be overwritten in-place

```
$ kn service update satu-dua-example --tag satu-dua-example-lqlqj-7=satu

refusing to overwrite existing tag in service,
   ➥ add flag '--untag satu' in command to untag it
```

But luckily, I get a hint from kn about what to do. I need to --untag the target to free up the tag itself. I can see how that goes in the next listing.

Listing 4.24   Untagging `satu`

```
$ kn service update satu-dua-example --untag satu
# ... Route gets updated
```

And now that I've untagged it, what happens to satu's 33% share of traffic? The following listing shows us.

Listing 4.25   The Route after untagging `satu`

```
$ kn route describe satu-dua-example

Name:       satu-dua-example
Namespace:  default
Age:        4h
URL:        http://satu-dua-example.example.com
Service:    satu-dua-example

Traffic Targets:
   33%  satu-dua-example-brvhy-1
   33%  satu-dua-example-snznt-2 #dua
        URL:  http://dua-satu-dua-example.example.com
   34%  @latest (satu-dua-example-lqlqj-7)

# ... conditions
```

Knative Serving opts for safety. This means that as it removes the satu tag as the Traffic Target, it substitutes the Revision that was pointed at by the tag. Meaning that the 33% previously assigned to satu is now assigned to satu-dua-example-brvhy-1 instead (figure 4.4)

For users coming through the front door, via the main URL, there will not be a perceptible change. The traffic is still being split three ways among the same three Revisions.

For users who were directly hitting the <tag>-<servicename> URLs, there *is* a perceptible change. That URL stops working and begins to return 404s.

But now, at least, the tag is free to be reassigned. I perform that reassignment in listing 4.26.

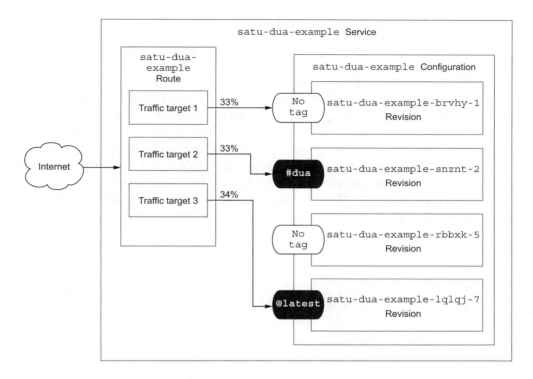

Figure 4.4   The first Revision still receives 33% of the traffic after the `#satu` tag is removed.

Listing 4.26   Assigning `satu` to a different Revision

```
$ kn service update satu-dua-example --tag satu-dua-example-lqlqj-7=satu

# ... updates the Route
```

But when I inspect the Route, I am again caught out by an unexpected behavior. The next listing sheds some light.

Listing 4.27   Hmmm

```
$ kn route describe satu-dua-example
Name:       satu-dua-example
Namespace:  default
Age:        4h
URL:        http://satu-dua-example.default.example.com
Service:    satu-dua-example

Traffic Targets:
    33%  satu-dua-example-brvhy-1
    33%  satu-dua-example-snznt-2 #dua
         URL:  http://dua-satu-dua-example.default.example.com
```

```
34%  @latest (satu-dua-example-lqlqj-7)
 0%  satu-dua-example-lqlqj-7 #satu
     URL:  http://satu-satu-dua-example.default.example.com
```

What I expected to see in listing 4.27 was that the 33% of traffic currently going to the untagged Revision `satu-dua-example-brvhy-1` would snap over to the newly tagged `satu-dua-example-lqlqj-7` once it took over the `satu` tag. But this didn't happen.

On reflection, it should be clear why. When I untagged the first time, Knative's knowledge of `satu` was destroyed, and it subbed in the Revision to ensure that the Route would continue to function largely as before. When I reintroduce `satu`, Knative has forgotten its previous existence. It gets the same treatment that any other tag would get: a direct URL is created, the tag is added to the Route, but 0% traffic is assigned. Afterward, it looks like figure 4.5.

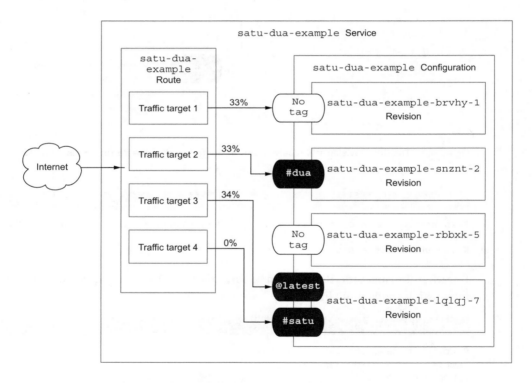

Figure 4.5   Adding the #satu tag doesn't shift traffic allocations.

If you're not confused, it's only because you got bored. The purpose of `--tag` and `--traffic` is to allow you to precisely control how deployment occurs. For right now, if you are just kicking tires, the default `@latest` behavior is fine. It will behave like a

Blue/Green deployment, traffic won't get dropped, all will be well. I'll sketch how to use the more advanced capabilities in chapter 9.

Summary

- Routes are how you describe to Knative where you want traffic to come from and go to.
- Routes are included as part of Services.
- You can use `kn routes` subcommands to `list` and `describe` Routes.
- Routes can have various conditions; the main ones include `AllTrafficAssigned`, `IngressReady`, and `CertificateProvisioned`.
- The heart of a Route is its list of traffic targets. These are visible in `kn` as Traffic Targets and visible in YAML under `spec.traffic` and `status.traffic`.
- Traffic Targets can have a `configurationName`, `revisionName`, or a tag.
- Traffic Targets can be "automated" by using `latestRevision: true` or by using the special `@latest` tag.
- Tags are names that you can attach to particular Revisions and then use as names for targeting. You can add and remove tags at will.
- The rules for how tags and `@latest` behave are not completely obvious. You can skip using tags until you need precise control of your deployment process.

Autoscaling

This chapter covers

- Problems that autoscalers set out to solve
- How Knative Serving's autoscaling works under various scenarios
- A walkthrough of the core autoscaling algorithm
- Configuration options and how these affect autoscaling

Autoscaling awakens the engineering imagination in a way that few topics do. Most of the systems we build seem lifeless or mindless. But to build a system that appears to *breathe* is somehow uniquely fascinating. Depressingly, though, *autoscaling* turns out to be easy to spell, yet hard to achieve. The system that breathes peacefully today is yelling obscenities tomorrow.

My goal in this chapter is to explain the basic structure and functioning of the components responsible for the management of scaling in Knative Serving: the Autoscaler, the Activator, and the Queue-Proxy. Most of the time, you will not need to think of these because these embody the accumulated observations and insights of the Knative authors. But, these are dynamic systems and exhibit dynamic complexity, which means that you will occasionally be surprised. A grasp of the components will help you to moderate your surprise.

I refer to the Autoscaler, Activator, and Queue-Proxy as the "Autoscaling Triad." This name is meant to convey that these are jointly responsible for the behavior of autoscaling; it's not so much about whether each of these is autoscaled in themselves (answer: they are, sort of, but it doesn't matter for us). Their respective roles and responsibilities have evolved throughout the life of the Knative project to their current allocations.

5.1   *The autoscaling problem*

As a problem, autoscaling is easy to describe. I have demand. I want to serve that demand. I obtain some amount of capacity to serve the demand. I would like the business of calculating and obtaining capacity to be automated.

Sometimes, I would like the calculations and capacity provisioning steps to be done ahead of anticipated demand (usually called *predictive autoscaling*), and sometimes I want the decisions to be made on short notice according to current conditions (*reactive autoscaling*). Knative's Pod Autoscaler (KPA) is classified as a reactive autoscaler.

If you stare for a bit, predictive and reactive autoscalers turn out to have the same basic structure: a control loop. What distinguishes these is different windows of observation and frequency of decisions.

This control loop, whether slow-moving or fast-moving, is intended to reduce mismatch between demand and capacity (figure 5.1). But even that definition hides volumes of complexity. For example, how is demand measured? How is capacity measured? The Horizontal Pod Autoscaler (HPA) that's included in Kubernetes defaults to using CPU consumption as its measurement for both demand and capacity. This certainly makes its calculations easy, but CPU is often a poor proxy for demand as an end user might perceive it. If I order a pizza, I am not interested in the temperature of the pizza oven. I am interested in timely delivery.

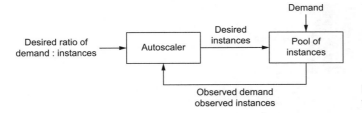

Figure 5.1   The Autoscaler viewed as a control loop.

But this is not the hardest thing that the KPA has to solve. The tricky problem is scaling down to zero and scaling up from zero. The transition from 1 copy to 10 copies to 100 copies of your software is mostly a quantitative difference. It is a difference in *count*. But the transition between zero and one is qualitative. It is a difference in *kind*.

Paradoxically, this qualitative difference arises because we want to conceal that there is a qualitative difference. End users are meant to be blissfully ignorant that software has scaled down to zero or up to a thousand. They just want to see a timely response.

To achieve this, the software must be able to buffer traffic when there are no instances. It must be able to observe demand—traffic—in order to make sensible scaling decisions. Once it has made such decisions, it must ensure that buffered traffic doesn't overwhelm instances. The problem for Knative is to deal with the autoscaling problem sensibly, subject to these basic constraints:

- End users should not see an error just because there are no running copies of software.
- Software should not be overwhelmed by demand.
- The platform shouldn't waste resources unnecessarily.

The triad behaves differently along two axes: number of requests arriving and number of instances available to serve requests. I can loosely divide each into three categories:

- Requests
  - Zero requests
  - One request
  - Many requests
- Instances
  - Zero instances
  - One instance
  - Many instances

Together this gives roughly nine different operating regimes (figure 5.2) in which the Autoscaler is variously scaling up, down, or simply staying put. You can refer to figure 5.2 each time you need to quickly predict (*roughly*) what the KPA will do. One instance, many requests? That's a panic. Zero requests, zero instances? Time for snoozing.

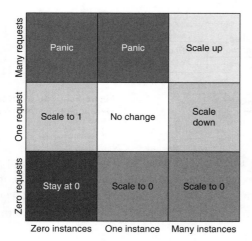

Figure 5.2   The Grid of Fortune

In this chapter, I'll organize my discussion by instances first and requests second on the theory that instances coming and going magically is what you came to read about. Requests coming and going is more or less like the tides, background radiation, or pizza delivery: very important, but largely beyond your control.

5.2   *Autoscaling when there are zero instances*

When there are no instances, the Activator (which you first met in chapter 2) is the undisputed star of the show. Or, perhaps more accurately, it's the unsung hero. This is because when a Revision is scaled down to zero, the Activator becomes the target for any traffic that will arrive.

Perhaps this is a surprise, given all the pretty diagrams in the previous chapter. Traffic appeared to flow magically from traffic targets in the Route directly to individual Revisions, perhaps using tags as targets. Further inspection reveals that I drew direct arrows. Arrows! Where was the Activator when there were arrows at large?

We can begin to understand what's going on by zooming in a bit on the magical arrows in figure 5.3. To make room in the diagram, let's assume there's only one Revision. I'm also going to ditch all of the fluff about Service, Configuration, and Route. Let's just focus on traffic and Revisions (figure 5.4).

In the last chapter, the explanation I gave was that the Route sends 100% of traffic to the `@latest` tag, which happens to be hanging off the sole Revision, `autoscaler-example-qstha-1`. What is new in figure 5.4 is the dotted box saying "No instances." And now for the big reveal (figure 5.5).

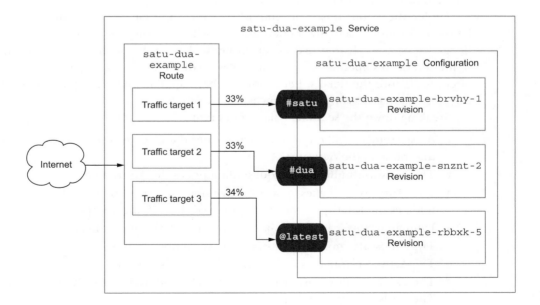

Figure 5.3   Lies!!

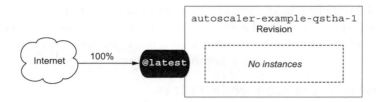

Figure 5.4   Just the Revision

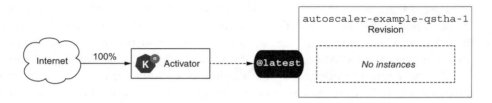

Figure 5.5   Enter the Activator

Figure 5.5 shows the world when you have configured Routes and Revisions, but have no running instances. The Activator becomes the actual target of traffic management. The fancy dashed line indicates that, in actual fact, no traffic is actually flowing right now. No traffic, no instances. Just the Activator, listening.

Under the hood, this is accomplished with some fairly fancy footwork. Several kinds of footwork, actually, depending on whether you are using Istio as a fully-fledged service mesh that takes over all networking functionality. But to an outside requester, or to someone using kn, it makes no difference. You can, and I believe you ought to, ignore the details. Let's look at what happens when a request arrives for a Revision that has no running instances (figure 5.6).

Breaking down the sequence diagram in figure 5.6, we get this:

1 A user sends a GET request. It first reaches the gateway, which is currently sending traffic to the Activator.
2 The Activator buffers the request, then pokes the Autoscaler.
3 The Autoscaler makes a scaling decision to scale up to 1. The Autoscaler updates the Knative Service to the desired state of one instance.
4 Ultimately, this leads to the launch of a new Revision instance.
5 The Autoscaler notes that instances have climbed to one.
6 The Activator notices that a Revision instance is now live.
7 The Activator now forwards the request it buffered to the Revision instance. The Revision sends its response.
8 The response then flows from the Activator, through the gateway, to the user.

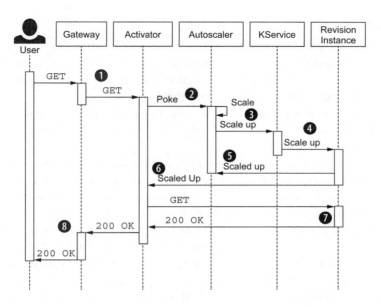

Figure 5.6   The First Request waltz

After this process is concluded, a single instance is now running (figure 5.7). Note, however, that in figure 5.7, traffic is still flowing through the Activator. This is a safety measure called *burst capacity*. The Activator performs a kind of mirror calculation to the Autoscaler. It's not deciding how many instances should be running based on the number of requests. Instead, it decides whether to remain on the data path based on how many requests it thinks available instances can actually service.

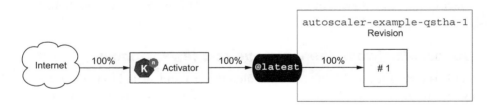

Figure 5.7   A single instance

This is most noticeable when scaling from zero. When there are no instances running, the available capacity is necessarily zero. But it's true up until several instances are running.

5.2.1   *The Autoscaler panics*

You might be wondering what happens if many requests show up at once. In the previous example, I discussed going from zero to one instance, triggered by going from zero to one requests. It was all very polite and calm. But if many requests show up in a short time, the Autoscaler does something different: it panics.

That's the real name: *panic mode*. I think it's a good name, giving some sense of the degree to which behavior shifts. In panic mode, the Autoscaler does two main things differently from its normal mode.

First, it becomes more sensitive to current request counts. The Autoscaler typically makes its decisions based on a trailing average of the past 60 seconds. In panic mode, this drops to 6 seconds. This makes the Autoscaler more sensitive to bursty traffic. You might wonder why panic mode is needed at all in that case. Couldn't we just use a short window and always remain sensitive? Don't I *want* the Autoscaler to act quickly?

You might now, but you won't. Relying on a short window makes the Autoscaler vulnerable to noise in the signal. There is a certain amount of randomness in the arrival of requests; periods of tightly-packed activity or deafening silence that appear in the space of a few seconds can be smoothed out over one minute. An Autoscaler that's always highly sensitive would end up "seeking." That is, it would keep fiddling with its desired count of instances. Imagine you managed a car factory and ran around hiring and firing workers based on sales figures reported in the last hour. You would pretty soon be fired yourself.

So that explains why panic mode is a special mode. But won't it still exhibit seeking behavior?

Which leads to the second thing that's different about panic mode: it does not scale down. The Autoscaler still performs its calculations and, given the increased sensitivity, the calculated value from a 6-second window is going to jump around like fleas in a bouncy castle. But in the interests of safety, the Autoscaler simply ignores any decision to scale down until the panic is over. This prevents seeking behavior because the system can only move one way—up.

5.3   *Autoscaling when there are one or a few instances*

This is a distinct regime from the scaled-to-zero and scaled-to-many cases. Typically, you wind up here if you are in a steady state, where traffic is relatively constant over a minute with slow changes in demand.

This is common when you're dealing with humans because demand generated by humans follows fairly regular cycles in their usage. Over the course of a day, a week or a year, you can find repeating patterns.

Statisticians refer to this property as *seasonality*. Adjusting for seasonality is a big deal in order to distinguish "something unusual is going on" from "yeah this happens every Monday." If we were building a predictive autoscaler, then this is useful (Netflix's proprietary Scryer does this).

Seasonality is a problem for predictive autoscalers, but not so much for reactive autoscalers like Knative's. Whether an increase is due to seasonality or due to some irregular surge in demand doesn't matter to Knative. It will try to match capacity to demand either way.

Depending on its exact configuration, the Activator will remove itself from the data path at this level of activity. Instead, the responsibility for buffering requests now falls on the Queue-Proxy.

The Queue-Proxy is a sidecar container. When you submit a Service or Configuration, Knative adds the Queue-Proxy to the Pod specification that it ultimately sends to Kubernetes on your behalf. The Queue-Proxy runs in a separate container from your code, but it is given control of HTTP networking (figure 5.8). Every instance of a Revision will have its own Queue-Proxy running.

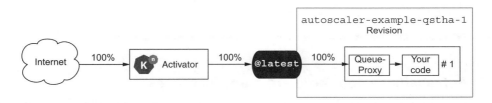

Figure 5.8   The Activator and the Queue-Proxy

This is for two reasons. The first is that the Queue-Proxy is a small, shallow buffer in front of your app to smooth out the flow of requests and responses. The second, related purpose is to gather request statistics for the Autoscaler.

But wait, doesn't this mean there are *two* buffers now—Activator and Queue-Proxy? It does, yes. But for good reasons.

First, once a request is sent to a Revision instance, it cannot be sent to a different instance. If the Queue-Proxy buffer was deep, you would see increased response-time variance and error rates. Requests served by warm, healthy instances are served quickly, so the buffer doesn't fill up much. Requests served by slow, sickly instances can pile up fast. Overall, a larger fraction of total time spent by requests will be from requests that got stuck on unhealthy instances than would otherwise be the case. Shallowness at the Queue-Proxy buffer means that instances struggling to keep up quickly drop out of the pool of instances where traffic is sent.

Second, there aren't always two buffers. When enough instances are live and healthy, the Activator removes itself from the data path. This means that the Queue-Proxy is the only buffer, though still shallow. The Queue-Proxy is still needed, in this case, to collect statistics and to perform limited smoothing.

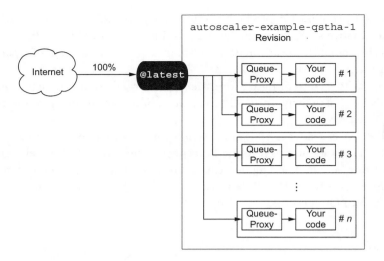

Figure 5.9   Queue-Proxy works by itself when there are several instances.

5.4   *Autoscaling when there are many instances*

By the time your traffic is running at a high level, Knative will have launched many instances for you to serve the demand. As noted previously, this means that traffic flows directly to the Queue-Proxy sidecar sitting next to your code, without Activator involvement (figure 5.9).

The many instances situation has an interesting property, which is that you need proportionally smaller increases in capacity as demand rises. An economy of scale, called the *square-root staffing rule*, is in play. The name comes from call centers.

Call centers face a problem much like an autoscaler. Demand has seasonality but is somewhat random from moment to moment. Customers hate waiting, but call center companies hate paying for idle agents ("hate" being a word that comes up often in the context of call centers). How many call center employees should be assigned to each shift?

You might think that ten times as many calls means ten times as many agents are needed. But that's actually not so. The arrival of demand and the time it takes for a call to be completed are variable. As staff increases, the odds that at least one agent is available to answer a call right now increases too. After these facts endure some tense interrogation by queueing theorists, it transpires that increasing staff proportional to the square root of demand is a decent rule for approximately dealing with demand.

The Autoscaler doesn't directly apply this rule, but because it tries to target a particular level of load per instance, it behaves more or less as if it does. At low traffic levels, you will see instances increasing in proportional leaps. At high traffic levels, the changes will be relatively gentler. Going from one instance to two instances is a 100% increase. Going from 100 to 101 instances is a 1% increase.

5.5 A little theory

I've so far described how the Autoscaling Triad of Autoscaler, Activator, and Queue-Proxy work together in a somewhat narrative fashion. Hopefully, this gave you a taste of the ebb and flow these three components have when they work in combination. But now, I want to look more closely at the Autoscaler in itself, partly so that I can point out various knobs and levers you can adjust.

Sike! You don't get to do that yet. Let's first take a second to discuss some basic theory; specifically, that the Autoscaler is a control loop and a queueing system. Along the way, I will endeavor to personally enrage every control engineer and queueing theorist who happens to read my drastically oversimplified descriptions of these absolutely vast topics.

5.5.1 Control

First, control. One form of a control system is a "PID controller." While the Autoscaler is not designed as a PID controller, PID control is still a useful framework for thinking about how the Autoscaler works. (A good introductory book is *Feedback Control for Computer Systems* by Philipp K. Janert. After that, *Feedback and Control for Everyone* by Pedro Albertos and Iven Mareels is a deeper introduction.)

The *P* in PID stands for "Proportional." Proportional control means that the controller's decisions are related to the *size* of the difference between desired worlds and actual worlds. If there is a large difference, the controller makes large moves to correct it. The Autoscaler makes decisions about desired instances that are based on its calculation of the gap between demand and capacity. In that sense, it is a proportional controller.

The *I* in PID stands for "Integral." Integral controllers don't just look at the most immediate state of the world, they smooth it out over some amount of time. This means integral controllers are less likely to lurch around. A common way to use integral control is taking a weighted average of differences between desired and actual. The Autoscaler calculates desired instances from statistics gathered in two sliding windows (normal and panic), meaning that its reactions have an integral aspect.

The *D* in PID stands for "Differential." Differential control adjusts its response based on *how fast* the difference between desired and actual is changing. At first glance, that might look like what proportional control does, but it's not. "I'm going too fast" is proportional control. "I'm accelerating too hard" is differential control. The Autoscaler doesn't calculate the rate of change, so it does *not* have a differential aspect.

5.5.2 Queueing

Now let's touch on queueing systems. I mean this in the sense of queueing *theory*, not in the sense of particular software systems like RabbitMQ. A queueing system has a few different terms and variables.[1]

---

[1] Naturally, there are multiple terms for all of these, so it can be difficult to compare discussions between sources. Even more naturally, there are a bunch of mathematical notations in which λ, ρ, and μ battle for supremacy against L, W, R, and U.

- *Arrival rate*—Represents how demand shows up over time. HTTP requests are arrivals in this sense.
- *Server*—Represents the thing that does work. Your software is a server in that sense so, happily, words mean the same thing in two different fields.
- *Queue length*—Constitutes the number of arrivals waiting in a queue to be processed.
- *Service time*—Represents the time it takes for a server to process the work necessary for one arrival. Service time does not count time spent queueing. For your software, that's typically the time between an HTTP request arriving at your software and the response coming from your software.
- *Service rate*—Represents the amount of work done per time unit. It's the inverse of service time. In our field, this is usually called "throughput."
- *Wait time*—Represents the average amount of time spent queueing for a server.
- *Residence time*—Sums up wait time and service time. You probably call this *latency*, depending on how you measure the start and end of a request/response.
- *Utilization*—Indicates the fraction of time the server is busy doing something.
- *Concurrency*—Constitutes the total number of arrivals either waiting in a queue or being processed.

Easy introductions are hard to come by; this topic is often considered a branch of probability mathematics. I found *Performance Modeling and Design of Computer Systems* by Mor Harchol-Balter to be slow going, but it has the advantage of being specifically focused on computing systems.

One of the most interesting simple rules that comes out of queueing theory is *Little's Law*. Using the previous terms, it looks like this (assuming that the Arrival Rate is less than or equal to the Service Rate):

$$\textit{Average Concurrency} = \textit{Average Arrival Rate} \times \textit{Average Service Time}$$

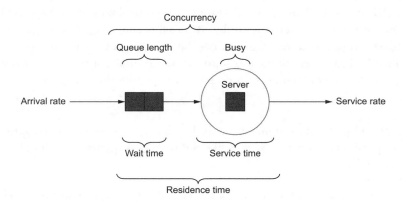

Figure 5.10   Some queueing theory terms

The "average" is important because from moment to moment, the rule might not be true. But it holds true over the long term, on average, no matter what. You might not be immediately impressed by this, but it's actually amazing, because the pattern of arrivals can take so many different forms. Reliable, square waves? Little's Law applies. Sinusoidal waves? Little's Law. All over the place? Little's Law. Beta, poisson, logit-normal, uniform? Little's Law applies for all of these.

The practical upshot here is twofold. First, you have a fairly useful tool for sanity checking your understanding of a system. You can use it for back-of-the-envelope estimates of steady-state systems. You can use it to see if the numbers you look at in production add up over the long run or whether deeper investigation is required.

Second, you can rearrange the terms. Given any two of the figures, you can work out what the third must be. This is relevant to the Autoscaler because it gives you two different ways of configuring it. One is based on concurrent requests, the other on requests per second. In the previous terms, these are concurrency and arrival rate. These are related through *service time* (how quickly your software can process a given request). But otherwise, in the long run, these are interchangeable. Pick the one you prefer. Because I'm most used to concurrency, that's what I'll focus on.

Another useful little finding from queueing theorists is that service time and utilization are also related. You already knew that, of course. I knew it. We all knew it. But could we *predict* it, even approximately? Ah … in the simplest case—a single server that can process one request at a time—you get this relationship:

$$Utilization = \frac{Arrival\ Rate}{Service\ Rate}$$

Seems obvious so far. But now I can do this:

$$Residence\ time \propto Service\ time \times \frac{Utilization}{1-Utilization}$$

The punchline is that slowdown is *exponential with increased utilization* (figure 5.11). The difference between operating at 80% utilization and 90% utilization isn't 10%. It's more like twice as long. And between 98% and 99% isn't 1% longer. It's more like 50 times longer. Like the square-root staffing rule, this is an example of where a linear intuition of how things behave is painfully wrong (table 5.1).

Table 5.1 Exponential hell

Utilization	Slowdown Factor
70%	2.33 x
80.00%	4 x
90.00%	9 x
95.00%	19 x
98.00%	49 x

Table 5.1   Exponential hell *(continued)*

Utilization	Slowdown Factor
99.00%	99 x
99.50%	199 x
99.90%	999 x

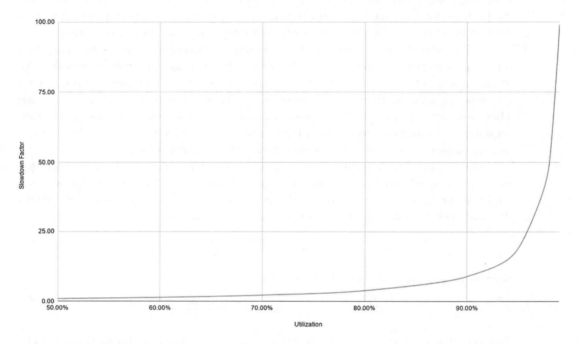

Figure 5.11   Utilization slowdowns can get bad in a hurry.

5.6   *The actual calculation*

OK, enough stalling: I will explain how the Autoscaler algorithm works. I'm going to use four flowcharts to walk you through it. I'd be flattering myself if I said this was because I wanted to break the algorithm up into logical units. The main reason is that each flowchart has to fit on a single page. But for partial self-flattery credits, I've at least *tried* to break it up into logical units.

The Autoscaler typically runs on a schedule, waiting 2 seconds between decisions. This gives a little time for data to accumulate and means that data is collected in "buckets" of 1-second duration. The exception to the 2-second rule is *poking*. The Activator, being a rude sort of thing, can directly signal the Autoscaler to make an immediate decision, without needing to wait for the current 2-second interval to elapse.

First, the algorithm does some basic sanity work (figure 5.12).

1 The Autoscaler retrieves a count of "ready" instances. Readiness is defined using the readiness healthcheck (see chapter 3).

2 If the count of ready instances is 0, the count is directly changed to 1. More on that momentarily.

3 The Autoscaler checks to see whether it has any accumulated metrics available. If there are, it proceeds to the next stage (figure 5.13).

4 If there are no metrics, the Autoscaler signals that it could not make a decision, which includes setting the desired scale to 0.

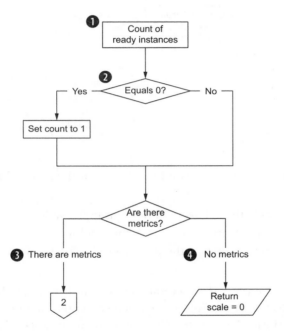

Figure 5.12   Algorithm flowchart, part 1

Why force the number of ready instances to 1? The answer has two parts. The first is that it prevents awkward divide-by-zero errors. The second, more important reason is that the 1 here stands for the Activator.

The clue leading to the Aha! moment here is that the Activator reports metrics to the Autoscaler, enabling the Autoscaler to treat the Activator as being another Revision instance. This makes sense when there are zero running instances: the Autoscaler still needs information about the state of demand, even when capacity is non-existent. The Activator has that information.

Figure 5.13 is where I've buried the most detail. The boxes are symmetrical (and hence, I only number one side of the diagram) because the Autoscaler calculates

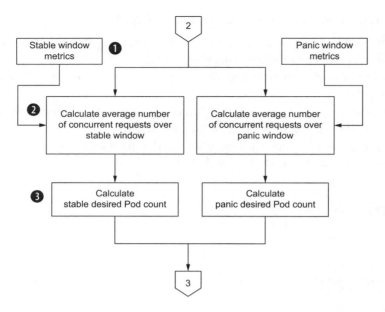

Figure 5.13   Algorithm flowchart, part 2

numbers for *both* the stable and panic cases. The logic is identical; all that differs is the data.

1 The Autoscaler uses metrics gathered over a window as input data.
2 The Autoscaler averages concurrent requests over the window.
3 Using the average concurrent requests, the Autoscaler calculates desired pod counts.

The metrics in use here are retrieved in one of several ways. When there are only a few instances running, Knative collects metrics from every instance. As the number grows, this becomes impractically slow. Instead, the Autoscaler begins to sample a statistical subset of instances.[2] On one hand, this means that the Autoscaler's decisions are less accurate. But on the other hand, if you recall the square root staffing rule, it matters less.

Scraping is run on the same 2-second schedule as scaling decisions. Thus the data gathered is "bucketed" into 60 buckets for each minute. Each bucket contains an estimated average number of requests, divided up per Revision.

---

[2] A difference arises here between how this sampling works in the service mesh case and non-mesh case. When there is no service mesh, Knative is able to obtain the direct IP address of each instance it manages. Sampling is then fairly simple; it selects a random subset and then scrapes the data from the instances found on those IPs. But, by design, a service mesh interposes itself between each instance in the cluster. That means Knative can't pick which instance will be scraped when it sends a scraping request. Instead, Knative keeps track of which instances have responded to a given scrape request. It then keeps retrying scraping until it has seen "enough" unique instances to satisfy its statistical requirements. The practical upshot is that scraping is slower in the service mesh case.

The last sentence deserves a place in hell next to all other word problems, such as "if Fred speeds at 20 kms/h for 6 hours and exceeds the limit by 10 kms/h for 2 hours, how many celery sticks does he owe in interest?" And, thus, we are swept back to a diagram, this one breaking the flow of flowcharts.

Suppose I am popular and now have nine—nine!—running instances of my Revision. Roughly speaking, it would look like figure 5.14.

Traffic flows through the usual plumbing until it lands at each instance's Queue-Proxy. But how much; to which? You might think you could just count how requests were *sent* to each Queue-Proxy. But different requests take different amounts of time to process. And, because of the exponential slowdown, overloaded instances are slower than unloaded instances. Just counting the arrivals does not show the number of queued requests.

Instead, the scraping process directly pulls the count of currently enqueued and currently processing requests from Queue-Proxy instances. If I show both of these values (queued and processing), it looks something like figure 5.15.

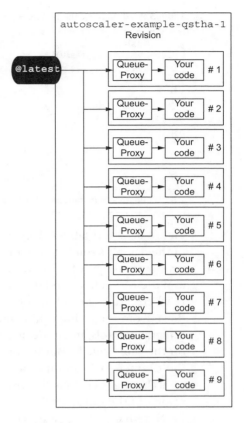

Figure 5.14 Nine instances are running for one Revision.

The key to note is that some requests are in the Queue-Proxy, some are currently in your software, but all are counted towards the total used to calculate an average. After some crunching, it transpires that there are approximately 5.67 concurrent requests per instance (table 5.2).

Table 5.2 Crunching the numbers

Instance	Queued	Processing	Total
1	2	5	7
2	1	1	2
3	2	4	6
4	4	5	9

Table 5.2   Crunching the numbers *(continued)*

Instance	Queued	Processing	Total
5	2	3	5
6	2	4	6
7	3	5	8
8	0	2	2
9	2	4	6
9 instances	*18 queued requests*	*33 processing requests*	*51 requests*

51 requests ÷ 9 instances ≈ 5.67 requests per instance

Figure 5.15 and table 5.2 show a snapshot of the data. It's roughly true in that the figures over the past 2 seconds are reported as if these are an instantaneous value. Here is where true control theorists, rapelling down from the ceiling while dual-wielding integral symbols, might decide to disagree on the finer details. But for our purposes, the distinction is unimportant. These are what the numbers look like from the point of view of the Autoscaler.

Now that we have gathered metrics over a window, we can average the averages over the windows. This gives the average number of concurrent requests, per instance, per time bucket.

I hope this makes your is-this-on-the-exam? sense tingle, because we've stumbled onto something that fits into Little's Law. The average concurrent requests over your instances is going to be a function of arrivals (aka, how many requests are being made per time unit) and processing time. If you double the arrivals, you have to double the requests sitting *somewhere*. You can either wear the exponential slowdown or you can increase capacity.

Which brings me to my next point: the Autoscaler calculates the desired number

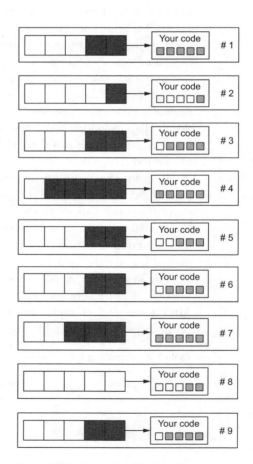

Figure 5.15   Queued and processing requests across instances

of instances by trying to maintain a utilization ratio. Given a *maximum* level of concurrent requests (say, 100) and a desired utilization (say, 70%), the Autoscaler's goal is to provide enough instances so that the average number of concurrent requests is 70 per instance.

That 70% ratio is basically sound. You might want a higher utilization. As tempting as this is, I'd hold off. When you picked Knative, you probably had it in mind to deal with variable demand, but if your goal is to be close to optimal, you better hope that your demand isn't very variable. Alas, these wishes are largely in conflict.

Now I can convert the previous description into some formulae. First, there's a formula applied each time metrics are collected:

$$Average\ Concurrent\ Requests\ Per\ Sample = \frac{Sum\ of\ Concurrent\ Requests\ Per\ Instance}{Number\ of\ Instances\ Sampled}$$

"Number Sampled" is one of the Count of Ready Instances, or a sampled subset, or the number 1. These figures are collected each cycle and stored in 1-second buckets. Then, when making decisions, the Autoscaler averages the buckets:

$$Average\ Concurrent\ Requests\ Over\ Window = \frac{Sum\ of\ Average\ Concurrent\ Requests\ Per\ Instance}{Number\ of\ Buckets}$$

This formula is applied over the stable window (default 60 seconds, 60 buckets) and over the panic window (default 6 seconds, 6 buckets). The next step is to calculate the target value of concurrent requests:

$$Target\ Concurrent\ Requests\ Per\ Instance = Maximum\ Concurrent\ Requests \times Target\ Utilization$$

Now, at last, we can calculate the number of desired instances:

$$Desired\ Instances = \frac{Average\ Concurrent\ Requests\ Over\ Window}{Target\ Concurrent\ Requests\ Per\ Instance}$$

Let's try crunching some numbers. In table 5.2, I showed how the Average Concurrent Requests Per Sample was calculated over 9 instances. Suppose I do that every 2 seconds for 20 seconds, giving 10 buckets (table 5.3).

Table 5.3 Bucketed request statistics

Bucket #	Sum of Req / Instance	Avg Req / Instance
1	51	≈ 5.6
2	53	≈ 5.8
3	40	≈ 4.4
4	47	≈ 5.2
5	49	≈ 5.4

Table 5.3   Bucketed request statistics *(continued)*

Bucket #	Sum of Req / Instance	Avg Req / Instance
6	55	≈ 6.1
7	56	≈ 6.2
8	61	≈ 6.7
9	59	≈ 6.5
10	58	≈ 6.4
Sum	529	58.3
Average	≈ 58	≈ 5.83

To get Average Concurrent Requests Per Instance Over Window, I sum the averages in table 5.3 and divide by the number of buckets to get the Average Concurrent Requests Per Instance Over Window: 58.7 ÷ 10 = 5.87. Now suppose I set my Maximum Concurrent Requests at 10 and my Target Utilization at 0.8. Then I will have a Target Concurrent Requests Per Instance of 10 × 0.8 = 8.

Now I can calculate Desired Instances: it's the recorded figure divided by the target figure. In my case, it's 58.7 ÷ 8 ≈ 7.35. Unless the Autoscaler is in panic mode, it will now try to scale down the number of instances from 9 to 7.

This is the heart of the algorithm that picks a number of instances. You might reasonably have felt that we're done here. But not just yet, because we calculated two values: one for stable mode, one for panic mode.

5.6.1   *To panic, or not to panic, that is the question*

Having dealt with the raw calculation in figure 5.13, we can return to a discussion of panics. I can at last dispel the gloomy, misty mystery surrounding the ominous-sounding "Panic Threshold." It's actually simple, but to explain it, I will introduce another quick formula:

$$\textit{Absolute Instance Error} = \textit{Desired Instances} - \textit{Actual Instances}$$

This is a formula borrowed from control theory, for what it's worth, which is why I've used the term "error" here. It reflects the size of the mismatch (the error) between what is desired and what is actual.

Note that this formula does not measure concurrent requests or utilization. This one focuses on the absolute number of instances. But that number isn't always super meaningful. Saying "the Absolute Instance Error is 1" doesn't make a clear distinction between "2 desired, 1 actual" and "100 desired, 99 actual." So we need a relative error:

$$\textit{Relative Instance Error} = \frac{\textit{Absolute Instance Error}}{\textit{Actual Instances}}$$

In the case of "2 desired, 1 actual", Relative Instance Error is $(2 - 1) \div 1 = 1.0$. The 1.0 here represents an error of 100%. Meanwhile, in the "100 desired, 99 actual" case, I find that $(100 - 1) \div 99 \approx 0.01$. That's an error of approximately 1%. Much less worrying.

The panic threshold is the point at which Relative Instance Error becomes "too high." It's expressed as a percentage in Configuration, the default is 200% or a Relative Instance Error of 2.0.

Because it relies on a *relative* value, the likelihood of the panic threshold being exceeded falls as the number of instances increases. That's more or less the behavior we want anyway: freaking out over a shortage of 10 instances isn't sensible when the current pool has 500.

This means you needn't panic over panics. When scaling from zero instances, or from a few instances, *panics will be common.* That is to be expected and should not be a cause for alarm on your part. In fact, if you crunch the numbers, you'll find that when scaling from zero, only three requests are needed to cause a panic.

Does exceeding the panic threshold put the Autoscaler into panic mode? Here enters figure 5.16. This diagram sketches out the logic devoted to switching between

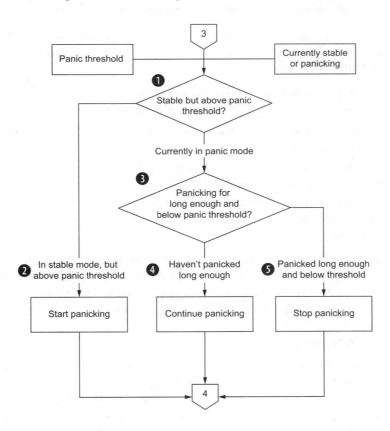

Figure 5.16 Algorithm flowchart, part 3

stable and panic modes. Coming into this stage, the Autoscaler starts with two pieces of information. First, is it currently stable or panicking? Second, has the panic threshold been exceeded?

1   The Autoscaler first considers the case of being in a stable mode but exceeding the panic threshold. In this case …

2   … the Autoscaler flips the mode to panic.

3   If the Autoscaler is already panicking, it needs to decide if it should *stop* panicking. It does this by looking at how long the panic has been going on and whether the panic threshold is currently unmet. More in a second.

4   If the panic is so far too short, or if the panic threshold is still exceeded, the panic continues.

5   If the panic window has elapsed and the panic threshold isn't exceeded, the panic ends and the Autoscaler returns to stable mode.

Starting a panic is the simple case. Fiddlier is the decision between continuing a panic or ending a panic. To end a panic, the Autoscaler needs for the current calculation to be below the panic threshold, *and* it needs for the panic duration to have elapsed.

> **NOTE** The panic *duration* is set to the value of the stable *window*. By default, this means it's 60 seconds long. The duration is *not* the same as the panic window, which defaults to 6 seconds.

Now for the final step, which is deciding what value to return (figure 5.17). This is where the distinction between stable and panic modes becomes a deciding factor.

1   If the current mode is stable, the Autoscaler returns the Stable Desired Instance Count it has already calculated.

2   If the Autoscaler is panicking, and the calculated Panic Desired Instance Count has increased, the Autoscaler returns that calculated value.

3   If the calculated Desired Instance Count is equal to or lower than the current actual number of instances, the Autoscaler returns the current number of instances instead.

Put another way, in stable mode, the Desired Instance Count can rise and fall with traffic. But during a panic, it can *only go up*. The name is again appropriate—a panicking Autoscaler is inclined to hoard resources until it feels safety is restored. In stable mode, the Autoscaler breathes; during a panic, it holds its breath.

5.7   *Configuring autoscaling*

So far, in this chapter, I've gone over the Autoscaler's behavior in some basic scenarios, then followed with a tour of the inner workings. I've given you two passes at understanding it. But there are gaps in these accounts. A survey of the Autoscaler's knobs allows me to fill in gaps without having to add even more digressions to the narrative discussions.

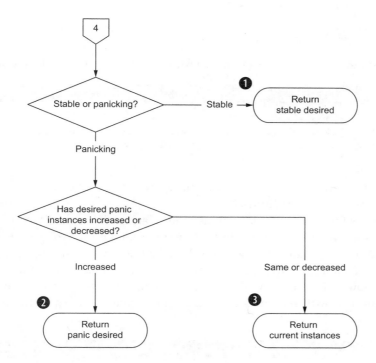

Figure 5.17 Algorithm flowchart, part 4

Most of the configuration settings I'll discuss can either be set globally by an operator or set at a Configuration or Service by a developer. It's best not to set things globally because everything under a given Knative Serving installation will be affected. And besides, the defaults are fairly sensible for most cases.

Put another way: My goal is to improve your understanding, not to encourage unnecessary changes. Naming and explaining a setting isn't an endorsement of tinkering with it.

5.7.1 How settings get applied

The Autoscaler can receive settings via a number of means. One such means is to create a Kubernetes `ConfigMap` record in the `knative-serving` namespace, named `config-autoscaler`. It would look something like the following listing.

Listing 5.1 Config mapping in example.yaml

```
apiVersion: v1
kind: ConfigMap
metadata:
  name: config-autoscaler
  namespace: knative-serving
```

```
data:
  enable-scale-to-zero: 'true'
```

The YAML in listing 5.1 can then be submitted with kubectl, as the next listing shows.

Listing 5.2   Setting the ConfigMap with kubectl

```
$ kubectl apply -f example.yaml
Warning: kubectl apply should be used on resource created by either
        ➥ kubectl create --save-config or kubectl apply
configmap/config-autoscaler configured
```

The warning here occurs because, in fact, the config-autoscaler ConfigMap is already present, but without any active settings on it.

A second means for setting configurations is annotations. These are the little key-value pairs that you can set on anything in Kubernetes, which means you can set these on a Configuration. Annotations are a mixed bag, by the way. On the upside, these provide a kind of dynamically-typed escape hatch from the schema of any Kubernetes record. On the downside, they … well … refer to the upside. One way to create and change annotations is with the kubectl annotate command, shown in the following listing.

Listing 5.3   Setting a /minScale with kubectl annotate

```
$ kubectl annotate revisions \
  hello-example-fvpbc-1 \
  autoscaling.knative.dev/minScale=1

revision.serving.knative.dev/hello-example-fvpbc-1 annotated
```

Actually, I don't need kubectl for this, if I don't want it. I can use kn instead, as in the following listing.

Listing 5.4   Using kn to set /minScale

```
$ kn service update \
  hello-example \
  --annotation autoscaling.knative.dev/minScale=1

Updating Service 'hello-example' in namespace 'default':

  4.294s Traffic is not yet migrated to the latest revision.
  4.500s Ingress has not yet been reconciled.
  5.884s Ready to serve.

Service 'hello-example' updated with latest revision 'hello-example-bvxyn-2'
  ➥ and URL: http://hello-example.default.example.com
```

Note that autoscaling annotations have the form autoscaling.knative.dev/<name>. For convenience, I'll just refer to this with the shorthand /<name>.

5.7.2   *Setting scaling limits*

Autoscaling is always enabled, but you needn't always scale to zero. You can disable that in two ways. The first is to use `enable-scale-to-zero` on the `ConfigMap`. This is a fairly consequential decision, of course, because you'd be disabling it for *everyone*.

The alternative is setting a `/minScale` annotation on a Service or a Revision. In the previous section, I set it on the Revision by using `kubectl` and then `kn`.

The minimum and maximum scale options are sufficiently likely to be used that `kn` allows you to set these at creation time or when updating a Service with `--min-scale` and `--max-scale`. The following listing gives an example.

Listing 5.5   Using `kn` to set scaling limits

```
$ kn service update \
  hello-example \
  --min-scale 1 \
  --max-scale 5

Updating Service 'hello-example' in namespace 'default':

  3.327s Traffic is not yet migrated to the latest revision.
  3.574s Ingress has not yet been reconciled.
  5.046s Ready to serve.

Service 'hello-example' updated with latest revision 'hello-example-cxsqv-3'
    and URL: http://hello-example.default.example.com
```

Doing so creates a new Revision. You can use `kn` to see the scaling limits on a Revision as part of `revision describe`, as this listing shows.

Listing 5.6   Looking at scaling limits with `kn revision describe`

```
$ kn revision describe hello-example-jpgbl-2

Name:         hello-example-jpgbl-2
Namespace:    default
Annotations:  autoscaling.knative.dev/maxScale=5,
                autoscaling.knative.dev/minScale=1
Age:          23s
Image:        gcr.io/knative-samples/helloworld-go (pinned to 5ea96b)
Env:          TARGET=First
Scale:        1 ... 5
Service:      hello-example

# ... conditions
```

Note the `Scale: 1 … 5` line in listing 5.6, showing the inclusive scaling range. You might also notice that the same information appears in `Annotations` as well.

I think it's worth forming the view that these settings are really about economics rather than engineering. Setting `/minScale` is a statement of how much delay you can afford to tolerate, whereas /maxScale is a statement of how much capacity you can afford to carry.

You should consider using /minScale if you are sure that you can never allow a slow response due to a cold start. Otherwise, don't. Using /maxScale is worth doing as a general policy, even if you set the value to an "impossible" level, such as 100 or 500 or 1,000—a level high enough to give you heartburn without seeming like something you will plausibly reach.

As they come around the bend ...

"But what about limitless scaling?" you ask, grimly clutching dim memories of Google blog posts. It's true that given enough money and given enough cluster capacity, you might be well served in a sudden surge by allowing scaling to an unlimited level.

As an answer, I draw your eye to the odds board of those notoriously merciless bookies, Murphy & Sons, posted down at the Production Is Broken Racing Ground. For "sudden wave of interest and success," Murphy & Sons have posted long odds of 200:1. This doesn't happen often in practice and, when it does, you'll probably hear about it.

For "bad person hates your guts," our flint-eyed bookmakers have posted shorter odds of 50:1. And this situation favors using /maxScale, because it constrains the blast radius of a DDOS attack.

Finally, Murphy & Sons know the form and have posted short odds for the most likely case: "bug caused by mistake obvious only in hindsight" of just 3:1. If asked, they'll explain that they've seen far more DDOSes caused by an infinite loop, suddenly enormous error log, suddenly large response size, escalating mutual deadlocks, and so on, than from any other action of Lady Fortune. "No need to worry about zebras," they politely explain, "when a startled horse can trample you to death just as well."

Here too, /maxScale can help. You reach a limit but you don't exceed it. This gives you a sporting chance to at least rollback a version or two until things clear up, and it stops a single piece of software from choking something—your network, your cluster, your wallet perhaps—to death.

So whaddya reckon, punter? Feel like taking a flutter? Placeyerbets, place yer beeeets!

5.7.3   *Setting scaling rates*

There's a limit to how fast a cluster can respond to autoscaler desires, whether scaling up or down. When calculating the desired instance values, the Autoscaler actually clips these so that they don't exceed a ratio of the current actual instances.

Scaling up is governed by max-scale-up-rate, which defaults to 1,000. It allows the Autoscaler to jump in multiples of up to 1,000 times at each decision point, but *only* from the actual currently running instances. So for example, if there are two instances, this limit allows the Autoscaler to jump by 2,000. This hefty limit doesn't show up in stable mode and, in fact, only rarely in a panic mode. But because each decision to scale up is partly based on multiplication, you'll typically see a double jump during panics.

The scaling down is governed by `max-scale-down-rate`, for which the default is 2. This might seem like weak tea compared to `max-scale-up-rate` and, in some sense, that is true. But halving at each step is still an exponential function. In terms of panics coming to an end, you will see a characteristic curve of exponential delay, with desired instances first falling quickly and then tapering off.

The `max-scale-down-rate` limit is meaningless *during* a panic, mind you, because in the midst of panicking, no downscaling occurs. This limit acts as a constraint in stable mode only.

Another setting affecting scale-down behavior is `scale-to-zero-grace-period`, which defaults to 30 seconds (more literally, it's a string that gets converted into a number: `30s`). When Knative decides to scale to zero, this grace period is how long Knative is prepared to wait for networking systems to unplug the instance from a network before Knative asks Kubernetes to kill it. After the grace period, Knative just considers the instance as killed. This setting is most useful to bump up if you are finding that networking updates are so slow that traffic is being misrouted. But otherwise, it is dark magic and should be left undisturbed.

As these three settings can only be set on the `ConfigMap`, these apply to the entire installation. The demand patterns of a system that receives dribs and drabs, and a system that receives steady load with occasional bursts, demand different treatment from a grace period. In general, without good reason, and without understanding how your traffic looks, you ought to leave these alone.

5.7.4 Setting target values

Two magic numbers have an outsized influence on the Autoscaler: `container-concurrency-target-default` (default value 100, the annotation is `/target`) and `container-concurrency-target-percentage` (default value 70, the annotation is `/targetUtilizationPercentage`). These are the values that determine the ratio of requests to instances that the Autoscaler tries to maintain. The basic logic is that `-default` ultimately gets treated as the *maximum possible* value for concurrent requests for any one instance, while `-percentage` is used to calculate the *actually desired* value for concurrent requests for each instance on average.

The practical upshot is that, out of the box, the Autoscaler targets 100 * 0.7 concurrent requests per instance: 70, in other words. You might at this point be slightly confused as to why 100 is the default value. It might seem a little on the high side. The explanation requires a callback to chapter 3, specifically the discussion of container concurrency in section 3.4.10. In that discussion I said, slightly vaguely, that this value defaults to zero and that zero is the signal to set a bunch of other default values.

And this is what `-target-default` is about. You can set `containerConcurrency` for your Service or Configuration, and it will show up on a Revision. But if you don't do that, then Knative Serving needs to pick *something* as an upper limit. The splashy label on the cereal box might say "Unlimited Requests Per Instance!", but the small print says "* *not applicable in finite universes.*" 100 is a nice round number that many systems will not reach in practice, and 70% is a reasonable utilization figure to avoid the exponential slowdown.

Mind you … it's not super likely that this value will be what you want. It's conservative on the upper bound for concurrency, not on the lower bound. This is where a little bit of load testing is a worthy investment (and also a deep rabbit hole, for which, see *The Art of Computer Systems Analysis* by Raj Jain and *Systems Performance: Enterprise and the Cloud* by Brendan Gregg). Even doing this on your local development system can give you an order-of-magnitude approximation for what figure to pick. Once you have a figure, you can set the container concurrency on your Service or Configuration using `--concurrency-target` for a direct target figure, or `--concurrency-limit` as the upper limit from which the target is then derived.

A special case to keep in mind is setting concurrency to 1. This means that each request gets its own instance to work with. This is useful if, for whatever reason, your software has some kind of zany thread-safety or shared-state issue. Hopefully, this isn't the case.

What about utilization? Should you fiddle with that? Briefly, no. The default is typically fine, assuming that your selection of container concurrency is roughly accurate. Fiddling with *both* concurrency and utilization settings just ensures that you will increase confusion about what's what. Don't do it.

Now, one last thing before I move on. You can configure the Autoscaler to use requests per second (RPS) as the scaling metric (which, as I previously noted, is likely to behave similarly because of Little's Law). This can be done in one of two ways.

First, if you want to set it globally, you can configure `requests-per-second-target-default` in the `ConfigMap`, implicitly switching the autoscaler to use RPS as its scaling metric. You can't use the `container-concurrency-target-default` key as well, though, because these options are mutually exclusive.

Second, if instead you want to switch to RPS-based scaling on a particular Service or Revision, you need to attach two annotations: `/metric` and `/target`. The `/metric` annotation explicitly sets the scaling metric. You can set it to `concurrency`, which gives you the normal behavior, or to `rps` for RPS-based scaling. The `/target` annotation is a number of requests, interpreted differently according to the `/metric` that you set. For `concurrency`, `/target` means the number of concurrent requests, and for `rps`, it means the number of requests per second.

These `/target` values are not 1:1. If you flip from `concurrency` to `rps`, behavior changes. How much does it change? By rearranging Little's Law, the RPS for a given level of concurrency is approximated by

$$Arrival\ Rate = \frac{Concurrency}{Service\ Time}$$

Say my requests take an average of 400 milliseconds. For a default calculated concurrency target of 70 requests, I get $70 \div 0.4 = 175$ RPS.

5.7.5 Setting decision intervals

The Autoscaler surveys the world and renders judgement on a regular 2-second interval. This is configurable in the `ConfigMap` by setting the `tick-interval` key. Lowering this interval means that the Autoscaler makes more frequent, perhaps more timely, decisions at the expense of greater thrashing and operational overhead. Increasing the interval spares resources, but makes the system more sluggish when responding.

Indirectly, the effect of the `tick-interval` is to contribute to the integral control facet of the Autoscaler's behavior. It creates regular pauses in which data about the actual world has time to accumulate into meaningful signals. No guesses for my advice here: leave `tick-interval` alone, unless you have a demonstrated need to tinker.

5.7.6 Setting window size

And speaking of accumulating data, it's possible to adjust the all-important window sizes. First is the stable window, defaulting to 60 seconds. Shortening this window makes the Autoscaler more jittery; it reacts more to what might be random fluctuations in demand. Making it longer smooths reactions, but means that sustained increases or decreases in demand might not be heeded as quickly.

Unlike `tick-interval`, which is a global setting that is hard to tune for everyone, it's possible to set the stable window either globally (using `stable-window` on `Config-Map`) or on your own Service or Configuration. To do this, you set a `/window` annotation. The format here is Golang's shorthand for units of time. For example, `60s` and `1m` will be considered the same, but you need to identify the unit of time (s = second, m = minute, etc.) in order to provide a valid value.

You should absolutely be open to tuning this value using the annotation if it makes sense for your workload. The balance here is between jitteryness and smoothness. On the surface, it might seem as though a jittery autoscaler would be OK—wouldn't I *want* the system to quickly react? The problem is that those reactions are not free; these place pressure on the Kubernetes cluster itself. This is part of why panic mode exists: it divides the skittery-jittery cases at the edge of scaling from zero from the smoother cases when traffic is high and instances already numerous.

The panic window is not defined directly. Instead, it's defined as a percentage of the stable window. You can set this percentage globally with `panic-window-percent-age` or use the `/panicWindowPercentage` annotation on a Service or Configuration. The default is 10%, which is how the panic window comes out to being 6 seconds by default.

I would be wary of tinkering with the panic window percentage *too* much. It needs to be substantially shorter than the stable window; otherwise, it won't be able to catch sudden shifts in demand. That argues for a small percentage. But the final resolved time can't be too short, or you will run into the problem of having insufficient data on which to base decisions. The Autoscaler *will* make decisions, of course, but as you zoom in towards 1 second, it becomes less like a sensible control loop and more like a noise amplifier.

You should basically only tinker with the panic window percentage if you set the stable window to unusually high or low values. If your stable window is an hour, for example, then you might set your panic window at 1% so that the Autoscaler can panic in 36 seconds instead of 6 minutes. At the other end, if you lowered your stable window to 20 seconds, then raise the panic a bit, perhaps to 25%, because 2 seconds of data is getting close to jumping at radio static.

5.7.7 *Setting the panic threshold*

The other major knob to twist for panic behavior is the panic threshold. You can set this globally with `panic-threshold-percentage`, but you probably shouldn't. But there can be a case for adjusting it for individual Services or Configurations, for which you can use the `/panicThresholdPercentage` annotation.

In some ways you don't need this option, as you can recreate some amount of its behavior by adjusting the panic window percentage. But adjusting the threshold has the advantage that it's easier to connect back to the economic problem of deciding what to scale and how much to scale.

For workloads that are valuable, you might choose to lower this threshold so that panics continue to occur even though you have more than a few running instances. You'd accept, in this case, heavier churn in your instances, but that may well be acceptable (but do consider `/minScale` as a more stable option). For other workloads with predictable demands that can be made to wait, you might instead choose to raise the threshold to a high value so that panics are unlikely to occur.

5.7.8 *Setting the target burst capacity*

The target burst capacity (TBC) subsystem is mostly about the ratios at which the Activator stays in the data path or steps out of it. The name comes from the idea that the Activator needs to understand how much capacity the current instances will be able to safely absorb in a "burst" so that it can decide whether it should stay in the data path as a buffer.

This can be set globally with `target-burst-capacity`, or on a Service or Configuration with `/targetBurstCapacity`. The calculation is fiddlier to describe than I would like, but there are a few key values:

- `0` means "only use the Activator when my software scales to zero."
- `-1` means "always use the Activator, regardless of scale."
- Other positive values represent a fixed target of "burst capacity."

The default is 200. The Activator will only begin to back out of the data path if it calculates that there is a "spare" 200 request capacity available. In general, this will be truer of larger pools of instances, so the Activator in this respect more or less works in line with the square root staffing rule.

The trade-off here is that placing the Activator in the data path creates an additional hop. That's more latency, more contention, more variability. For cases with demanding performance requirements, you should consider whether to disable the TBC and rely on `/minScale` and `/targetUtilizationPercentage` instead. On the other hand, if you have workloads that are bursty but that can wait, setting the TBC to a higher value gives you a free buffer proxy to allow your software to get started.

5.7.9 *Other autoscalers*

The Knative Pod Autoscaler isn't the *only* autoscaler you can use with Knative Serving, it's just the one you get by default. Out of the box, you can also use the Horizontal Pod Autoscaler (HPA), which is a subproject of the Kubernetes project. The HPA was originally built around using CPU load as its scaling target but has lately grown to be more featuresome. If you have already built tooling and know-how around the HPA, don't be shy about using it.

But, at the time of writing, that's your major alternative. The HPA's stablemate— the Vertical Pod Autoscaler (VPA)—is not directly supported and doesn't really fit the way Knative thinks anyhow. The Kubernetes Event-Driven Autoscaler, aka KEDA, works on what is arguably a sounder principle, but integration with Knative is currently only at an experimental stage.

5.8 *A cautionary note*

The Autoscaler is not magical. It's not psychic. It can't repeal the laws of physics or call on the aid of mystical forces.

What it *can* do is to reduce *some* categories of risk and some forms of wasteful toil. You get some protection against unpredictable variability, but not infinitely so. You'll still need to do work to understand how your system behaves at different scales and under different inputs. The Autoscaler can't scale its way out of problems like database contention or a recursive regex explosion attack. These still require human intervention.

There is one thing you can do to help the Autoscaler to do a better job, however— software that starts quicker. This means a combination of smaller images and faster-launching processes. If you can shave time from 30 seconds down to 15 seconds, then for bursty workloads, you really should take that option.

Don't turn this into a fetish, mind you. I have a particular pet peeve with the obsession over running everything on Alpine: it uses a weird libc, nobody is paid to patch CVEs in a timely fashion, and the performance gains are negligible once image layers are cached. Just use Ubuntu or Red Hat/Fedora. And don't over obsess over the difference between your-choice-of-language and not-your-choice-of-language, unless you have a *provable need*. What I'm saying is, take the free wins. The *free* wins, not the twenty-days-of-fiddling wins.

Oh, and one more thing: *the Autoscaler is not magical.*

Summary

- Autoscaling is easy to say, but difficult to do. Scaling from zero makes the problem substantially more difficult.
- When there are zero instances, traffic is handled by the Activator.
- When traffic arrives and there are zero instances, the Activator pokes the autoscaler, which scales up instances above zero. Traffic is held by the Activator until instances are ready.
- The Autoscaler can "panic," during which it scales up aggressively but does not scale down.
- As the number of instances rises, the Activator removes itself from the data path.
- The autoscaling problem and autoscalers are better understood with a small amount of control theory and queueing theory.
- The Autoscaler algorithm can be loosely divided into four phases: a basic metrics phase, a phase to calculate desired stable and panic instances, a phase to decide whether to be in stable mode or panic mode, and a final phase that selects the scale value to return.
- The calculation is based on the average number of concurrent requests collected into 2-second buckets, then averaged over stable (60 s) and panic (6 s) windows.
- Desired instances are calculated based on the ratio between average concurrent requests per instance and target concurrent requests per instance.
- Panicking is determined by the panic threshold, which is a ratio of panic desired instances to stable desired instances.
- The Autoscaler's configuration parameters can be configured in multiple ways. Parameters set via ConfigMap are global to the installation and not recommended. Parameters can be applied to specific Services or Configurations with Kubernetes annotations.
- You can use the Kubernetes Horizontal Pod Autoscaler (HPA) as an alternative to the Knative Pod Autoscaler (KPA).
- Autoscalers are not magical.

References

- Philipp K. Janert, *Feedback Control for Computer Systems* (O'Reilly Media, 2013)
- Pedro Albertos and Iven Mareels, *Feedback and Control for Everyone* (Springer, 2010)
- Mor Harchol-Balter, *Performance Modeling and Design of Computer Systems: Queueing Theory in Action* (Cambridge University Press, 2013)
- Daniel Jacobson, Danny Yuan, Neeraj Joshi, "Scryer: Netflix's Predictive Autoscaling Engine," *The Netflix Tech Blog*, November 5, 2013, http://mng.bz/nMgg
- Daniel Jacobson, Danny Yuan, et.al., "Scryer: Netflix's Predictive Autoscaling Engine—Part 2," *The Netflix Tech Blog*, December 4, 2013, http://mng.bz/vz8J

- Raj Jain, *The Art of Computer Systems Analysis: Techniques for Experimental Design, Measurement, Simulation, and Modeling* (John Wiley & Sons, 1991)
- Brendan Gregg, *Systems Performance: Enterprise and the Cloud* (Prentice Hall, 2013)
- hpa—http://mng.bz/4ZJa
- vpa—http://mng.bz/QmZw
- keda—https://keda.sh/

Introduction to Eventing

Here comes the next big section. I approach it with some trepidation.

In some sense, Serving is simple: *do* a thing. Eventing is: *say* a thing, *hear* a thing. In Serving, the intention to do and thing done have a relatively predictable temporal coupling. But in Eventing, I can be saying things long before these are heard. I can listen for things that will never be heard. I can hear things long since said. The shoe store point-of-sale system can emit events for sales before the sales forecasting system exists to process events. The inventory system can listen for stock shrinkage alerts that might not occur. And so on.

The underlying model of Eventing is this: things happen in the world. Some of these happenings are observed. Some of these observations are transmitted from place to place. Receivers of the transmission read the observation, deduce some state of the world, then perhaps take actions. These actions perhaps cause still other observations to arise.

Eventing is for the bit in the middle. It doesn't do the happenings. It doesn't observe the happenings. But it does take observations and transmit those. The format used for this purpose is CloudEvents, the mechanisms are Channels and Filters, Brokers and Triggers, Sources and Sinks, Sequences and Parallels. I will spend the next few chapters explaining these to you.

6.1 The road to CloudEvents

Because CloudEvents are the coin of the realm, let's take a closer look at these first.

> **NOTE** As I did in my introduction to Serving, I'm going to start with a fictional scenario to show why and how CloudEvents can be useful. If that's not to your taste, feel free to skip ahead.

Suppose I have raised twenty umptillion dollars for my new startup, Exampleomatics. Our first product is revolutionary and will reshape the entire world. In short, we have developed an AI-enabled, blockchain-compatible device for intercepting, observing, and controlling connections in a non-wireless connectivity energy distribution system—the world's first and only Electron Proxy. (Later, when cynics suggest that we've reinvented $200 "light switches," I will post the kind of tweets that my PR team will sprint to delete within seconds.)

The Exampleomatic Electron Proxy can be "on" or "off." This information is going to be necessary for our full-VR home-management system, so we need for the Proxy to emit events describing what's happening. The following listing shows my first attempt.

Listing 6.1 Simple

```
case status {
    when status.ON  -> http.POST('https://example.com/v1/proxy/on')
    when status.OFF -> http.POST('https://example.com/v1/proxy/off')
}
```

So far, so good. We've made sure to assume that the internet is never down and that only one endpoint will ever receive this information. There are a few problems, though.

For one thing, I can't tell which of our Electron Proxies is on or off. This scheme just counts the on and off events. At first this doesn't matter, because I can just use the totals to create impressive "up-and-to-the-right" plots for my venture capitalist (VC). All is well in the land of synergistic disruptivity.

But one day, I get a phone call from an early, important customer: the VC's son-in-law. He bought a PhriendlyPhoton electro-lumen (TechCrunch described it as a total revolution, introducing for the first time in history the ability to transform electrical energy into lighting) from our bitter rivals, the PhriendlyPhactoryCompany. When he sets the Electron Proxy to "on," he expects that electricity will flow through it to the PhriendlyPhoton, which will then convert electrons to photons. But it didn't work. He called Phriendly, and they said to call Exampleomatic.

Now I need to identify *which* Electron Proxy is emitting which on/off event. One way to do that is to bake it into the requested URL, which the next listing illuminates.

Listing 6.2   Slightly less simple

```
case status {
    when status.ON  ->
        ⇒ http.POST('https://example.com/v2/proxy/on?id=$id', id)
    when status.OFF ->
        ⇒ http.POST('https://example.com/v2/proxy/off?id=$id', id)
}
```

The change adds an identity to the request so I know which Electron Proxy has turned on or off. I call back the VC's son-in-law, whose business card identifies him as "Special Chief Analyst (Without Portfolio)," and tell him to try turning it on and off again. Relief washes over me when it turns out that the Electron Proxy is working fine. It's Phriendly's problem now.

Or so I thought. Phriendly also has a basic event telemetry system in their devices (which was #3 on BusinessInsider's "5 reasons Phriendly is disrupting the electromagnetic force market and nothing will ever be the same"). *Their* telemetry shows that no received_electrons event is ever sent. So either our events are faulty or theirs are. But how are we supposed to tell?

Our handsome overlord (Yale School of Management '19) doesn't care. "Just fix it," he says. My CTO cautiously meets their CTO. After establishing rapport by trash-talking any technology that's older than 30 minutes, they come up with a plan. We'll put our logs next to their logs and work out what happened that way.

After a day locked in a room, the result comes back: it's the wire. The wire is faulty. Time for some Visionary Leadership! I pull sixteen engineers off three projects and tell them to Fix It Now. Fifteen sit with me in a meeting, while the sixteenth slinks off to a hardware store to buy wire and some tools. Nobody dares to ask how many engineers will be required to replace the lightbulb itself.

A few days later, my CTO asks the rhetorical question: why was this so hard? If we had all the events from our Electron Proxies and events from PhriendlyPhotons going to the same place, we could have used $550,000 of machine learning model-training to determine that the wire was faulty.

But there's a problem: in no universe will I send *our* sensitive, proprietary data to Phriendly! And, in an act of pure selfishness, they refuse to send any of their data to *us*.

There the matter rests for a few days. Then our joint customer, the VC's son-in-law—James Richard Thomas III, two-time Tea & Crumpets secret society coxswain (3rd alternate)—calls us both to a conference at his father-in-law's office. He has been installing more devices from both of us and wants to be able to answer questions such as "Should I send my kid to military school for messing with the effing light switches?"

I begin explaining that "light switch" is reductionistic and that, actually, our Electron, Prox- …

"I don't care," he says, cutting me off. "Work out something that I can do."

My CTO and Phriendly's CTO lock themselves in a room again. They come out with a radical idea: we make it so that *customers* can collect the data. In fact, they can decide *where it goes.* We return to our codebase and before long, this listing come to light.

Listing 6.3 Configurability arrives!

```
baseURL = configuration.baseURL

case status {
    when status.ON  -> http.POST('$baseURL/proxy/on?id=$id', id)
    when status.OFF -> http.POST('$baseURL/proxy/off?id=$id', id)
}
```

Now our users can send their data anywhere. We lose the ability to sell them abercisers, old Chuck Norris films, or denture glue based on the advanced user profiles we assembled with on/off data, the undocumented microphone that listens for clapping sounds (and also everything else), and some judicious TensorFlow. But, we're moving away from the consumer market anyhow. The enterprise electron-management market is much more profitable.

This goes well, but soon there is another complaint from JRT 3.0 (a name my engineers use on Slack to describe the VC's son-in-law and which I have threatened to make into a firing offense for uttering). Our data goes to different endpoints and is in different formats. We're using the industry standard—XDR—but those morons at Phriendly are using ASN.1 DER instead. We're sending it to /v3/proxy, but they are using /phriendly/v3. In order to use this data, JRT 3.0's team of crack Excel-wielders (Assistant Underassociate Analysts) have to write a whole pile of hideous VBA. While it will soon be replaced by hideous Python written by the crack data science team (Associate Underassistant Analysts (Junior Intern)), the overhead of massaging different endpoints and packaging is obnoxious.

My CTO and Phriendly's CTO lock themselves in a room *again* for what will, one way or another, be the last time. They first of all define their problems:

- We have different endpoints.
- We have different data encoding formats.
- We have different metadata.

Meaning, we need something that's indifferent to HTTP endpoint URIs, which can support multiple encoding formats, but that has consistent metadata.

During a lunch break, they discover CloudEvents and decide to build a quick spike. Before long, our codebase looks a bit like that in the following enlightened listing.

Listing 6.4   JSON, like cockroaches, will survive the nuclear apocalypse

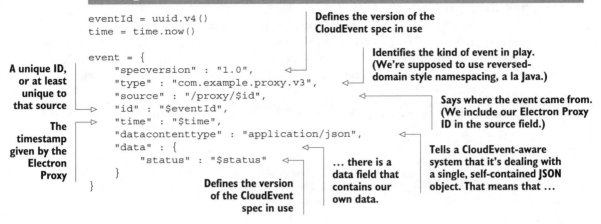

```
eventId = uuid.v4()
time = time.now()

event = {
    "specversion" : "1.0",
    "type" : "com.example.proxy.v3",
    "source" : "/proxy/$id",
    "id" : "$eventId",
    "time" : "$time",
    "datacontenttype" : "application/json",
    "data" : {
        "status" : "$status"
    }
}
```

A unique ID, or at least unique to that source

The timestamp given by the Electron Proxy

Defines the version of the CloudEvent spec in use

Identifies the kind of event in play. (We're supposed to use reversed-domain style namespacing, a la Java.)

Says where the event came from. (We include our Electron Proxy ID in the source field.)

Defines the version of the CloudEvent spec in use

... there is a data field that contains our own data.

Tells a CloudEvent-aware system that it's dealing with a single, self-contained JSON object. That means that ...

My CTO sits down and explains what all those notations in the code listing mean. All good and well, I point out, but how does the data actually *get* to us? And, if it gets to us, how do we combine it with CloudEvents created by Phriendly? The CTO points to an empty space on the whiteboard titled "Knative Eventing" and says: "Actually, I was hoping you would fill this in for me."

6.2   *The anatomy of CloudEvents*

While I enjoyed flexing my bad fiction skills, there's more to be said about Cloud-Events. First, let's talk about *layering*. In networking, there's a well-known model for layering—the OSI model (figure 6.1). It defines seven layers, ranging from "what are the electrons doing?" through "what is the user doing?" Different layers have rhyming solutions to rhyming problems, but the layers *are* logically distinct and the distinction is quite useful.

These days it's common to see routing and load balancing systems classified according to the layer at which each does its work. In the context of HTTP, which is where we're doing most of our stuff in Knative-land, routers and load balancers are typically divided into two classes: Level 4 (L4) and Level 7 (L7).

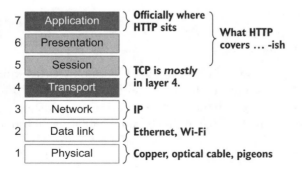

Figure 6.1   An OSI layer diagram seen here for the thousandth time in print!

Level 4 is the Transport layer. For us that means TCP, as this is the level 4 protocol that HTTP builds on. TCP works to present the illusion that bits stream into and out of ports without being interrupted or jumbled. Importantly, TCP has no idea what the bits *represent*. Its entire job is to get the bits from A to B.

Level 7 is the Application layer. In our context, this is HTTP. In HTTP, the system stops caring about bits. It has developed loftier interests in concepts such as paths, headers, status codes, and the like.[1]

This distinction matters because the deeper your semantic insight into the thing being routed, the more intelligently you can route it. A TCP-based load balancer can uphold policies such as "assign connections equally between these two hosts." But if one connection is basically quiet and the other is noisy, load is notably unbalanced. An HTTP-based router can, by contrast, enforce policies such as "assign requests equally between these two hosts." The unit of management is much closer to the unit of work, and better outcomes result.

This leads to an analogy: CloudEvents provide a "layer 7" for Eventing systems, roughly analogous to what HTTP provides for request-response systems. It defines a basic data model and maps these into particular formats and particular protocols.

CloudEvents have a two-part structure with data and attributes. *Data* is what you probably guessed: the part that systems squirt their payloads into. What is of more interest to us now is the *attributes*. These are roughly analogous to HTTP headers. Like HTTP headers, there is potentially an unlimited number, because anyone can add their own. But only a handful are standardized, which makes my job a bit easier.

6.2.1 Required attributes

To begin, there are four *required* attributes. These are found on every CloudEvent, without exception. If any of these attributes is missing, you don't have a CloudEvent.

- specversion—This signals the version of the CloudEvents spec that should be referred to for a given CloudEvent. At the time of writing, there's only one allowed value: 1.0.
- source—This is *where* the event occurs. The "where" here is a logical concept, not a physical one. For example, you might provide a Source that is something like abc-123.xht2kld.cdn.example.com. But most of the time, you'll want something more abstracted from the actual layout of machines and networks. It makes more sense for cdn.example.com to be the source, with particular machines identified in data as necessary.
- type—This is the *kind* of thing. For example, you might have com.example .cdn/flush as a type of CloudEvent for a caching service.

---

[1] These categorizations are strictly false, mind you. Modern HTTP squishes together concerns from the Application, Presentation, and Session layers, so it's really layer 7-6-5. And TCP has some things that are session concerns, which I guess makes it layer 4.5. This wasn't deliberate; the internet protocols mostly grew in splendid isolation from the work done by OSI architects. And OSI itself was a good example of the perils of standards politicking as it tries to smoosh together packet-based and connection-based networking concepts.

It's common practice to use reverse domain notation to scope this to your particular service. Slightly annoyingly, reverse domain notation (`com.example`) tends to be different from the normal-order domain notation (`example.com`) that's likely to show up in `source`, especially when those Source names happen to follow a Kubernetes convention.

- `id`—This is meant to be unique *per* source. Remember that Sources are meant to be logically, not physically, distinct. It's not enough to pick something that is unique per machine, per network, and so forth. This is a surprisingly tricky requirement but necessary to enable reliable downstream management of CloudEvents.

Use UUIDs

Use UUIDs for your `id` field; specifically, "version 4" UUIDs. UUID is a well-known format for conveying identities that are meant to be unique across the universe for all time. There are multiple variants. Of these, "version 4" is the one that involves randomly generating values. By and large, you can grab a standard library to create these, and then a whole bunch of tools will natively understand these: log parsers have matchers, databases have specialized types, and all that jazz.

It also helps you to avoid the temptation to rely on incrementing identifiers to establish event ordering by simply removing the incremental aspect. An identifier's only entire suitable role is to uniquely identify something. Anything else it does, any other meaning that can be derived or extracted, is a giant legacy and integration tar pit. Just say no to magic numbers and mystic strings.

6.2.2 *Optional attributes*

While mandatory, `specversion`, `source`, `type`, and `id` are not the only fields you can expect to find. There are also optional attributes in the core standard.

- `datacontenttype`—This is a Content Type/Media Type/MIME Type/slashy-namey-thingy type that you provide, identifying what kind of format `data` is in.

  The simplest, most likely case is `application/json`. In fact, it's considered so likely that a CloudEvent without a `datacontenttype` is assumed to be `application/json`. But it needn't be so. In theory, any valid Media Type can go here; there are hundreds of registered types, including the tragically underutilized `example/*` and `*/example` types. But for now, you're unlikely to see anything exotic.

- `dataschema`—This lets you point to a schema against which the CloudEvent's `data` can be validated. What goes in this field is up to implementers; let's all hope that everyone accepts that URIs are the best idea.

  This field is most helpful for basic future-proofing, because a CloudEvent can wind up being stored somewhere for a long time or being shuttled between software with widely out-of-sync versions. When you are responsible for creating CloudEvents, you should show courtesy to consumers by using this field.

At a higher level, this field is where folks building standards and APIs on top of CloudEvents will need to reach an agreement. For example, if Phriendly and Exampleomatic develop the "Common Automation Network Taskforce: Electrical Vendor Extension Nodes" standard (CANT:EVEN), they might need to upgrade it when one of them introduces a new device category. They might have begun with `dataschema: "https://example.org/cant-even/v1"`, but after Phriendly introduces a new line of devices for talking to houseplants, it becomes necessary to introduce `/v2` as well. Software that consumes the CANT:EVEN standard will then be able to know whether it will need to import `org.example.greenthumb`.

- `subject`—Subject is meant to be the "thing" that the event is about. You might wonder how this differs from `source`. After all, I can make the `source` value as specific as I like.

  The difference—at least, the intended difference—is that `subject` can identify particular instances or individuals in the population of the `source`. Loosely, `source` is like a programming language class or interface, but `subject` is the unique object. If my `source` is `hitgub.example.com`, my subject might be `/repos/123`.

- `time`—When the observed event occurred, according to whatever software created the CloudEvent, encoded in RFC 3339 format.

  That sounds great, but bear in mind: There are no timecops who go around ensuring that timestamps are in any way consistent. To start with, there are the classic problems like clock drift and misconfiguration to deal with (January 1, 1970 gets busier every day!). Then, there's the problem of people just putting the wrong format here. Or leaving out timezones. Or the problem of long delays during processing, meaning that the instantaneous point-in-time implied by a timestamp actually stands for an operation that took 45 minutes.

  But aside from these, you can also run into subtle policy differences. One Source might define the `time` as being "the time when I generated the CloudEvent JSON." If the CloudEvent is coming straight from the original observer, that might be OK.

  But CloudEvents don't need to be created by the original observer. Most won't, just as a matter of practicality, because the volume of existing software that won't be rewritten to directly emit CloudEvents is vast.[2] The designers of the CloudEvent standard explicitly assume that a lot of CloudEvents will be generated by agents, proxies, or other secondary observers. Which means that the

---

[2] `CLOUDEVENT-DIVISION`. might show up in time for COBOL's hundredth birthday, I guess, and be in widespread use by the bicentenniary. But let's not hold our breath for `MOVE payment TO EVENT payment-event` to be a common sight before then.

meaning of "time" is a matter of policy: does it represent a timestamp from the original occurrence, a first observer, or the CloudEvent-creating service?

Suppose, for example, that I built a system that converts log lines into CloudEvents. What should its `time` be? The timestamp in the log line? Or the timestamp of when the conversion occurred? The CloudEvents standard does not mandate which. You will need to check if you make time-aware or time-sensitive calculations.

6.2.3   *Extension attributes*

The attributes I've listed so far are part of the core specification. But there's also a variety of "Documented Extensions" that are available in secondary specifications. You're likely to see some mix of these in the wild, because these deal with common but not universal concerns.

- `dataref`—It won't be rare that you'd like to send big chunky things over a CloudEvent. Suppose, for example, that you decide to start wrapping newly baked binaries as CloudEvents. You could try squeezing a long binary into the `data` section as one of the fields, but that's a bit chancy and likely to be slow. And it might also be the case that while I am comfortable with having Cloud-Event *attributes* being visible as each one gets sent, I have security or privacy reasons for not carrying the *data* along with it.

  `dataref` lets you point to someplace else for the `data` field. For example, I might emit a NewCustomer event, which includes various personally identifiable information (PII). I'd like not to accidentally leak that, so instead of sending a `data` section, I push the PII into a trusted service and add a URL to `dataref`.

  Note that `data` and `dataref` are not mutually exclusive. You can have both, if you want. In fact, anyone handling a CloudEvent is able to perform a swap. You can turn a `data` into a `dataref` or convert from a `dataref` into `data`. If you have both, you can choose to drop one.

- `traceparent` and `tracestate`—Distributed tracing is useful and nifty and awesome, but it requires audience participation in order to be useful and nifty and awesome. These two keys are intended to carry tracing information according to the W3C Trace Context standard.

  We'll discuss tracing more in chapter 9, but I can preview the discussion here: You should support these in your own software. What "support" means is a sliding scale. Some libraries and SDKs can transparently inject basic trace data ("entered service Foo"), and you should take advantage of these whenever possible. Some libraries require you to do manual work to add traces. Sometimes, there is no relevant library and you'll need to add trace headers directly. But regardless of what you need to do, take the time to add these. You'll thank me later (no need to name your kids after me, though).

- `partitionkey`—Managing demand in large systems often relies on some way to divvy up the workload. The `source` and `subject` keys provide two such fields, for instance. I could send all of my `source: com.example.ping` events to one server and all the `source: com.example.bang` events to a different server. But what if my problem is actually that North Americans are so energetically pinging and banging that I need to subdivide their traffic?

  I could use `subject`, but that might not have the information I need to make sensible bucketing decisions—how do I bucket things like `subject: Lincoln`? Is it about the car, the person, the town, the company? This is where I use `partitionkey`. I could settle on values for various states, provinces, and territories and divvy up work that way. Or, I might split along timezones. Whatever makes the most sense.

  One word of warning: partition keys are how you learn that you don't really know your data. Abstractly, you want something that is *uniformly distributed*. But few things of interest are uniformly distributed. Don't be afraid to ask a data scientist to help you find efficient ways to cut up your data; it's pretty much what they do for breakfast.

- `rate`—A typical feature of metrics systems is the ability to *sample*. This is a fancy way of saying drop randomly chosen data points when there are too many to forward in a timely fashion.

  The `rate` attribute allows a CloudEvent to carry a signal of what the sampling rate was when it was created. It's meant to be interpreted as a ratio of all observations to the CloudEvent itself, including the CloudEvent. Putting that another way, if I make 10 observations and send 1 CloudEvent, its `rate` should be 10.

  This field is close to essential if your metrics system is using sampling to economize on traffic. Knowing the sampling rate makes it possible to estimate how uncertain a given measurement might be. Combined with the total number of measurements, it becomes possible to provide "good enough" approximations quickly.

- `sequencetype` and `sequence`—Sometimes, you just need a sequential numbering scheme to make sense of things. These two fields let you do that, but the definition is a bit scanty.

  The only defined `sequencetype` value is `Integer`. Once set, this means that `sequence` should be a signed, 32-bit integer, starting at 1, incrementing by 1 for each CloudEvent.

  Already I can hear some of you rejoicing—a way to evade my grumpy rule that you should use UUIDs for identity and nothing else. Bad news, I'm afraid: my ruling still stands. Resist the temptation to use `sequence` as a kind of pseudo-id. In fact, just resist the temptation to use it.

6.3   *A word about event formats and protocol bindings*

Something I've obscured so far is that, in theory, nothing about the CloudEvents spec *requires* it to be emitted as a JSON object. And nothing requires a CloudEvent to travel over HTTP. Instead, CloudEvents are meant to be mapped into something like JSON + HTTP in two ways: format and protocol.

JSON is an example of *format mapping*. The CloudEvents standard defines a specific JSON format, of the sort you're going to see a lot of in the coming chapters. There is also a format mapping for Apache Avro records as well, though, and more are likely to emerge.[3]

HTTP is an example of a *protocol mapping*. There are more of these currently defined: Kafka, AMQP, MQTT, and NATS. All of these are somewhat related to queueing systems or distributed log systems or whatever you prefer to use in diagrams. Yes, there are differences. For the purposes of CloudEvents, the differences are irrelevant. The point here is that if you have Kafka or RabbitMQ as your existing infrastructure for shipping events, then you can add CloudEvents to that mix smoothly. If you use NATS or MQTT, ditto.

Lots of protocols already have some kind of header/body or metadata/data separation. HTTP is again a useful example. The set of permissible HTTP headers is open by design, only a handful are predefined by IETF specs. A lot of tooling understands how to read and interpret headers, including previously unknown headers. You can imagine various proxies and routers acting on specialist headers. Consequently, adding and reading headers is trivial with any HTTP library worth its salt.

You needn't sit for the shocking news: you can use HTTP headers to carry Cloud-Event attributes. And this sets me up for an additional wrinkle in the CloudEvents protocol-mapping universe: *modes*. There are three of these: structured, binary, and batched.

6.3.1   *Structured content mode*

In the structured mode, your CloudEvent is completely self-contained. You map the event into one of the formats you chose, with its attributes included. By and large, this is what I've been showing you so far and is what you can see in the following listing.

> **Listing 6.5   JSON format: Structured content mode**

```
{
    "specversion" : "1.0",
    "type" : "com.example.type",
    "source" : "/example/source",
    "id" : "82C32673-0C78",
```

---

[3] I am a heretic on the matter of JSON. Blasting innocent electrons to smithereens in order to needlessly decode and re-encode text no human will ever look at is absurdly wasteful. By now, JSON probably merits its own line item in the global accounts of carbon dioxide emissions. Perhaps you are in the camp that "meh;" in which case, the engineering effort to use Avro instead of JSON may not seem necessary. But I urge you, *think of the electrons.*

```
    "time" : "2020-04-10T01:00:05+00:00",
    "datacontenttype" : "application/json",
    "data" : {
        "foo": "and likewise bar"
    }
}
```

Because this is wholly self-contained, I can squirt it over any old means of communication. To you and me, for example, FTP is dead, an historical concept that HTTP supplanted. But to most of the biggest financial institutions on earth, FTP is beyond death, beyond time and space and meaning and existence. Suffice it to say that structured content mode lends itself to adapting to existing modes of transmission that don't have the faintest understanding of, or interest in, CloudEvents as CloudEvents.

6.3.2 *Binary content mode*

But many protocols have some kind of separation between headers and bodies, between a control channel and a data channel. Sometimes, this is a physical separation (as in the phone system), but most often you're multiplexing together control signals and data somehow.

HTTP uses the simple approach: for each request or reply, the headers are sent before the body, with a blank line between the headers and the body. The set of headers is not limited to those in the relevant RFCs; it's open-ended by design to enable extensions. Sending a CloudEvent to a remote server in binary content mode via HTTP might look something like the following listing.

> **Listing 6.6   JSON format: Binary content mode**

```
POST /example/event HTTP/1.1
Host: example.com
Content-Type: application/cloudevents+json
ce-specversion: 1.0
ce-source: /example/source
ce-id: 82C32673-0C78
ce-time: 2020-04-10T01:00:05+00:00

{
    "foo": "and likewise bar"
}
```

In this case, I rely on setting `ce-` headers to carry the CloudEvent attributes. What previously lived under the `data` key is promoted to a top-level JSON object.

The pros here are that CloudEvents are now a bit easier to cleanly assemble. I can actually take any old JSON, smack it into the body, and smear CloudEvent headers over the top without modifying the original data (useful if you've signed it, for instance). And receivers of these HTTP exchanges can do Smart Things™ by reading the headers, without needing to delve deeply into the CloudEvent data itself. In theory, they can rewrite the headers if they wish.

Ah, but, now you're at the mercy of anything between you and the server. Maybe your proxies and firewalls will pass through CloudEvent headers unharmed. Maybe they won't. For largely internal systems, this should be fixable, but keep it in mind for future mystery bug hunts.

6.3.3   *Batched content mode*

Batching is an old and noble way to economize on resource usage. Every HTTP request, Kafka entry, MQTT message, etc., has some fixed overhead. By batching together multiple logical CloudEvents into one physical interaction with a protocol, you can amortize the overhead over all of the CloudEvents in the batch.

I include this mode mostly for completeness. If you need to improve efficiency at the cost of end-to-end latency, you can try different batching schemes to see what helps. But otherwise, I'm going to leave it here.

6.4   *A walkthrough*

In chapter 2, it didn't take me long to get to the hallowed "Hello world" moment. Getting there with Eventing will be a slightly longer way around. I'll start by turning to my trusty companion, kn, to tell me the current state of play, as the following listing demonstrates.

Listing 6.7   Whaddya know?

```
$ kn trigger list && kn source list && kn broker list
No triggers found.
No sources found in default namespace.
No brokers found.
```

Under the hood, these commands are groping around for Trigger, Source, and Broker records in Kubernetes. I haven't done anything yet, so there are none.

So far, not very enlightening. Especially because it's been a few chapters since I last committed these Triggers and Sources onto a page. Let's refresh: a Trigger combines information about an event filter and an event subscriber together; a Source is a description of something that can create events. Diagrammatically, it's something like that shown in figure 6.2.

Figure 6.2   A Source, a Trigger, and a Subscriber

That's at least how the configuration looks. In reality, Triggers don't really do anything in themselves. They're records that get acted on by a Broker, with potentially many

Triggers per Broker. You won't see Triggers running as standalone processes. So really, it's more like figure 6.3.

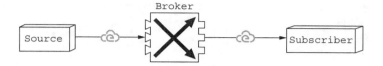

Figure 6.3   Now with added brokerage!

A Subscriber here is anything that Knative Eventing knows how to send stuff to. "Anything Knative Eventing knows how to send stuff to" is a sufficiently broad and nuanced category that I will simply forestall further discussion. Instead, I'm just going to bash my way through to that "Hello world" moment.

Let's work backwards, starting with a Subscriber. The simplest thing to put here is a basic web app that can receive CloudEvents and perhaps help us to inspect those. Luckily, helpful folks have already done so for us. Just as luckily, kn makes it easy to enjoy their work. I'm going to start by setting up a Broker and then adding the `cloudevent-player` as in the following listing.

Listing 6.8   Adding a Broker and installing `cloudevent-player` with `kn`

```
$ kn broker create default
Broker 'default' successfully created in namespace 'default'.

$ kn service create cloudevents-player \
    --image ruromero/cloudevents-player:latest \
    --env BROKER_URL=http://default

# ... log of service creation ...

Service 'cloudevents-player' created to latest revision
        ➥ 'cloudevents-player-skqwy-1' is available at URL:
        ➥ http://cloudevents-player.default.example.com
```

This is a handy little web app I can use to send and receive CloudEvents. If you open the URL, you should see a form and then some blank space. I'm going to go ahead and enter an event for you, send it, and then discuss a screenshot.

Figure 6.4 shows the CloudEvents player interface, which has a number of useful landmarks:

1 Here's the event ID. There's a handy autogenerator, just click the Loop icon (↻).
2 Here's an event type.
3 And the event source.

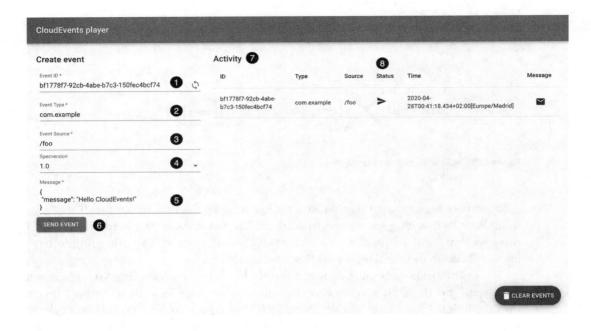

Figure 6.4   The CloudEvents player app

4   The `Specversion` can be altered, but shouldn't be. This made sense when CloudEvents was an evolving specification, but that's no longer the case.

5   The Message here is actually the `data` section of the message.

6   Clicking Send Event creates an event, which is sent to a broker (more in a second).

7   The Activity table shows events that have been sent or received.

8   The Status column gives a hint as to whether an event was sent or received. The arrow means Sent. An envelope, which we'll see in a second, indicates Received.

The residual question here is whether "Sent" actually has any meaning here. Sent to where? Right now, to nowhere. Like the tree falling in the unwatched forest or the right swipe on the dating app, it has been swallowed whole into the silent void, never to be heard from again.

I am, of course, being fast and loose with the truth here. The app has sent the event to the Broker. Specifically, to the `BROKER_URL` that I defined as part of the service.[4]

And that's as far as it got, because we hadn't defined a Trigger. Easily fixed as the next listing shows.

---

[4]   Assuming that one is available, of course. There are a number of sorts of Brokers and ways to wire those, which I'll cover in upcoming chapters.

Listing 6.9 Creating a Trigger with `kn`

```
$ kn trigger create cloudevents-player --sink cloudevents-player
Trigger 'cloudevents-player' successfully created in namespace 'default'.
```

Now head back to the CloudEvents player and try sending another event. You'll see that the event is both sent *and* received (figure 6.5).

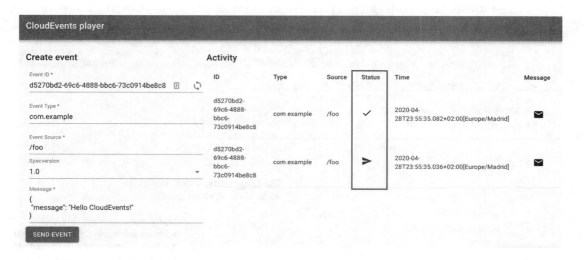

Figure 6.5 ECHO! Echo! echo!

The simple fact here is that I've cheated by making the CloudEvents player both the Source and Sink for events. Figure 6.6 shows the basic logic of how a CloudEvent created in the web UI flows back to the web UI. In part, this demonstrates that *any* software process can fill *either* the Source or Sink role. In this case, the CloudEvents player can do both.

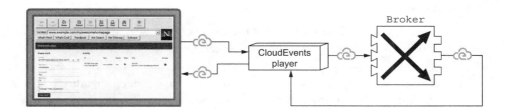

Figure 6.6 CloudEvents player is both Source and Sink.

The nomenclature of "sinks" and "sources" here is already widespread outside of Knative in lots of contexts, and its exact origin might be contested by armchair etymologists. But briefly: Sources are where events *come from*; Sinks are where events *go*.

I didn't explicitly define a Source, though. I only defined a Sink in the Trigger. This already hints at how flexible Eventing actually is, but also at the fiendish difficulty of smoothly introducing you to systems that can be assembled in just about any order.

Self pity aside, it's worth inspecting the gizzards more closely. Similar to Service and Route, kn provides `kn trigger describe` for such a purpose, as the following listing reveals.

Listing 6.10   Describing Triggers

```
$ kn trigger describe cloudevents-player
Name:          cloudevents-player
Namespace:     default
Labels:        eventing.knative.dev/broker=default
Annotations:   eventing.knative.dev/creator=jchester@pivotal.io,
            ➥  eventing.knative.dev/lastModifier ...
Age:           1h
Broker:        default

Sink:                                    The Trigger sets cloudevents-player
  Name:        cloudevents-player        as its Sink. So far so good.
  Namespace:   default
  Resource:    Service (serving.knative.dev/v1)     Many things can act as a Sink
                                                    without knowing it. Here, I created
Conditions:                                         a Knative Service and then made it
  OK TYPE                  AGE REASON               into a Sink. Does that mean that
  ++ Ready                 1h                       only Knative Services can be Sinks?
  ++ BrokerReady           1h                       Not at all. This is the magic of duck
  ++ DependencyReady       1h                       typing, which I'll discuss towards
  ++ SubscriberResolved    1h                       the end of the chapter.
  ++ SubscriptionReady     1h
                                         Some of our lovely friends:
                                         Conditions.
```

Right now the conditions are all ++, indicating a state of swellness and general good humor. As with other Knative conditions, `Ready` is the logical `AND` of all the others. If any other condition isn't OK, then `Ready` will not be ++. Looking a little closer at the other conditions

- `BrokerReady`—This signals that the Broker is ready to act on the Trigger. When this is false, it means that the Broker can't receive, filter, or send events.

- `DependencyReady`—Because I cheated and defined the CloudEvents player service as both `Source` and `Sink`, this doesn't have a deep meaning. This is really meant to tell you how a standalone source, such as `PingSource`, is doing.

  In non-cheaty-author situations, this is a handy field. It gives you a fighting chance of guessing whether stuff broke because you broke it or whether some external service broke it instead. If it's true, then you can eliminate outside forces of evil as a cause. If it's false, start limbering up whichever finger you use for pointing.[5]

- `SubscriberReady`—This is where the naming of things in Eventing starts to get squiggly. The practical point here is that `SubscriberReady` is about whether the *Sink* is OK. It's not a reference to the `Subscriber` field of a Trigger.

- `SubscriberResolved`—I've left this for last because it's the odd one out. `Broker-Ready`, `DependencyReady`, and `SubscriberReady` are all about the status of software that's running someplace else. That means it can change from time to time, due to the passage of Mars into the House of Jupiter under a blood moon or whatever else your postmortem picks as root cause for an outage.

  But `SubscriberResolved` is a once off. It refers to the business of resolving the subscriber (turning the Sink into an actual URL that can actually be reached). That happens right after you submit a Trigger. Eventing picks up the `Sink` and shakes it to see what's inside. It might be a directly hard-coded URL that you gave. It might be a Knative service. But it can also be a number of different things, such as a Kubernetes Deployment. All of these have some differences in how you get a fully resolved URL, but a fully resolved URL is what the Broker needs to do its job of squirting CloudEvents over HTTP.

  When it's OK, `SubscriberResolved` can be ignored. But if it's false, then your Trigger is wedged. You won't fix it directly by tinkering with the `Broker`, `Source` (aka dependency), or `Sink` (aka subscriber). To be sure, if those are misbehaving, fix these first. But you will still need to update the Trigger in order to get another go at URL resolving.

The conditions you see do go beyond a game of true-or-false, though. Each of these conditions has evil parallel universe relatives.

- `BrokerDoesNotExist`—This appears when there is no Broker. I have more than once forgotten to add a Broker to a namespace, and also more than once forgotten to check for this condition. It's possible for platform operators to configure Brokers to be injected automatically, but it's not the default behavior. In any case, if you see this, it means you need to use `kn broker create`.

- `BrokerNotConfigured`, `DependencyNotConfigured`, and `SubscriberNot-Configured`—These appear when you first create a Trigger. These represent that control loops take time to swirl: upon submitting records, it takes time to reconcile the desired world with the actual world.

  A lot of the time these will be the kind of thing you can miss if you blink. But if these hang around, something is wrong.

---

[5] Bear in mind that it might be wrong, and further, that tact can be as important as fact. In my consulting days, we used to run "Frenemy Tests" against external APIs as part of our overall testing and monitoring. It saved a great deal of panic, but it also created a great deal of drama. Few things are more insulting than historical data.

- BrokerUnknown, DependencyUnknown, and SubscriberUnknown—These are the Joker cards of conditions. By convention, an -Unknown condition literally means that Knative has no idea what's happening. The sister condition (e.g., Broker-Ready) isn't true, it isn't false, it isn't in the middle of being configured. It's just ... unknown.

  On the downside, if you see this, something weird is going on. On the upside, Knative at least has the manners to capture some details and log those. We'll see more when we get to chapter 9.

And speaking of stuff going wrong, what happens if I delete the Trigger? Let's look at the following listing to find an answer.

Listing 6.11   Deleting the Trigger with kn

```
kn trigger delete cloudevents-player
Trigger 'cloudevents-player' deleted in namespace 'default'.
```

So far, listing 6.11 looks innocuous. You don't get any warnings about the fact that your events now won't get delivered to cloudevents-player. Knative doesn't maintain an internal model of your system that can easily serve such a purpose. There are no foreign key constraints in the world of Kubernetes records. If the Trigger is gone, then it's gone. It's up to you to know if that's a desirable situation.

You can prove that we've broken the link. Generate new event IDs in the Cloud-Events player and mash the SEND EVENT button each time. All you'll see in Status is the Sent arrows. The events flow out, but do not flow back.

Going, going, gone

The practical upshot is that every event is on its own in the big, bad world because the Broker applies the Triggers it knows about, one event at a time, as these arrive. If an event arrives and there's a matching Trigger, loud hooray! If there isn't, silent horror!

This isn't unique to Knative Eventing, mind you. It's a common case. Distributed systems utilizing any kind of static analysis are few and far between. So much so that while I'm sure I could find one with some digging, I cannot think of any offhand.

Does it matter? No. In fact, this laxity facilitates loose coupling. You can add and subtract parts of your Eventing setup at will, which means that components added on day one probably don't need to know or care about components added on day two, insofar as both at least agree on CloudEvents as a common envelope format.

Does it matter? Yes. Agreeing on an envelope format is just the beginning. You will probably need to think about schema evolution as well.

But there's another reason why "looseness" matters. Suppose I have a source of events that's been nicknamed Old Faithful. One day it falls silent. Now, is that silence because Old Faithful has decided to retire? Or is it a network glitch? Or is the broker down? Or did someone inadvertently delete a Trigger? Inability to distinguish between failures of networking and failures of anything else is the Byzantine Generals problem and therein lies many species of hell.

There are a number of ways to deal with it at a lower level. By and large your infrastructure will handle these for you. But at a higher level, you need to remember that "a Trigger was deleted" is a potential cause for unnoticed degradation. It's easy to notice metrics when those blow up and easy to forget to check for boring old zeroes.

To prove my point, I can add the Trigger back.[6] The following listing demonstrates this.

Listing 6.12   Returning the Trigger

```
$ kn trigger create cloudevents-player --sink cloudevents-player
Trigger 'cloudevents-player' successfully created in namespace 'default'.
```

And when I return to `cloudevents-player` and send an event, I can see that it was both sent and returned (figure 6.7).

Activity

ID	Type	Source	Status	Time	Message
56235553-2dfb-4dd6-823f-4ecbe2432427	com.example	/foo	✓	2020-04-29T23:54:14.028+02:00[Europe/Madrid]	✉
56235553-2dfb-4dd6-823f-4ecbe2432427	com.example	/foo	➤	2020-04-29T23:54:13.991+02:00[Europe/Madrid]	✉
4c9f8629-d3ea-4b01-b57e-6ec5614e68b0	com.example	/bar	➤	2020-04-29T23:53:33.94+02:00[Europe/Madrid]	✉

Figure 6.7   After restoring the Trigger and sending a new CloudEvent

I can perform a similar magic trick by deleting the CloudEvents player and then adding it back. Deleting the Service also gives us a chance for some sightseeing of some Conditions that have turned false, as in this listing.

---

[6] "Add back" is a slight misnomer. It's the same name, but this is a new `Trigger` record.

Listing 6.13   Nothing up my sleeves

```
$ kn service delete cloudevents-player
Service 'cloudevents-player' successfully deleted in namespace 'default'.

$ kn trigger describe cloudevents-player
Name:          cloudevents-player
Namespace:     default
Labels:        eventing.knative.dev/broker=default
Annotations:   eventing.knative.dev/creator=jchester@pivotal.io,
               ➥ eventing.knative.dev/lastModifier ...

Age:           5m
Broker:        default

Sink:
  Name:        cloudevents-player
  Namespace:   default
  Resource:    Service (serving.knative.dev/v1)

Conditions:
  OK TYPE                   AGE REASON
  !! Ready                  2s  Unable to get the Subscriber's URI
  ++ BrokerReady            5m
  ++ DependencyReady        5m
  !! SubscriberResolved     2s  Unable to get the Subscriber's URI
  ++ SubscriptionReady      5m
```

You can see in listing 6.13 that SubscriberResolved is now false (!!). Consequently, the Trigger isn't Ready. This makes sense and is more or less what I would have expected. Now, let's reverse the procedure in the next listing.

Listing 6.14   Something up my sleeves

```
$ kn service create cloudevents-player \
    --image ruromero/cloudevents-player:latest \
    --env BROKER_URL=http://default

# ... log of service creation ...

$ kn trigger describe cloudevents-player
Name:          cloudevents-player
Namespace:     default
Labels:        eventing.knative.dev/broker=default
Annotations:   eventing.knative.dev/creator=jchester@pivotal.io,
               ➥ eventing.knative.dev/lastModifier ...
Age:           9m
Broker:        default

Sink:
  Name:        cloudevents-player
  Namespace:   default
  Resource:    Service (serving.knative.dev/v1)
```

```
Conditions:
  OK TYPE                  AGE REASON
  ++ Ready                  3s
  ++ BrokerReady            9m
  ++ DependencyReady        9m
  ++ SubscriberResolved     3s
  ++ SubscriptionReady      9m
```

Huzzah! Everything has returned to the status quo.

> **NOTE** One thing I should point out again is that these relationships aren't in any sense normalized. If I submit two Triggers with identical definitions, I will wind up with two copies of a CloudEvent being delivered. The Broker doesn't have any sort of de-duping logic to sniff these cases out. It's up to you to check for duplicate Triggers when you see duplicate events.

6.5 *The basic architecture of Eventing*

Before I wrap up the current chapter, I'm going to spend some time priming your mental cache of components. In chapter 2, I showed that in Serving I can nominate four kinds of records: Revision, Configuration, Route, and Service. The chapters about Serving were structured around these four with a special guest appearance by autoscaling. That made my job easy.

In Eventing, there are more kinds of records, subdivided into four major groups: Messaging, Eventing, Sources, and Flows. Added to these is a small but growing collection of *duck types*, which you can think of as shared interfaces that show up in multiple categories.

6.5.1 *Messaging*

This is about raw plumbing: the business of moving CloudEvents from one place to another. The primary record kinds are Channels and Subscriptions.

Channels are used to describe and configure systems like RabbitMQ, Kafka, and the like. You provide a Channel record to tell Knative about the availability of such systems, and hopefully, the Channel authors have provided additional tooling that knows how to fulfill the promise being made to Eventing.

For development convenience, Eventing bundles an "In-Memory Channel" (IMC) implementation. We used it earlier during our walkthrough, without needing to configure or install anything. That's a situation I like so much that I'll use the IMC for almost everything I demonstrate.

But your environment might be differently configured. Already, there are community Channel implementations for Kafka, GCP PubSub, and NATS Streaming. I'm sure more will show up over time. I'll discuss a selection of available Channel implementations in section 7.4.

Subscriptions are a less happy story. We saw something called subscriber previously. Not the same beast, it turns out. On a Trigger, the field *named* subscriber is not of the subscription *kind*. Much as a Knative Service melds together Configurations and Routes, the Subscription melds together Channels and Subscribers into a single unit.

I found this naming to be quite confusing; I am sure you did too. You might think of subscri*ber* as being "a process or address that can receive a CloudEvent" and subscri*ption* as "a bundle of channels within a subscriber." We'll no doubt stub our toes on this naming scheme again.

6.5.2   *Eventing*

It would be boring if all Eventing ever gave you was a way to define a substrate for shipping messages. That's why the examples mostly leaned on Brokers and Triggers. These belong in the "Eventing" subcategory of Eventing, or as I will now refer to it out of laziness, "Eventing."

The name here emphasizes that Brokers and Triggers are *most* of what you will interact with and think about as a developer. That you can talk about "Eventing Eventing" is just a bonus.

A third kind of record lurking under this category is the Event Type. These are the literal representation of CloudEvent attributes—the type, source, and so on. Most of the time, these will be invisible.

6.5.3   *Sources*

You'll recall that I described Sources as places where events flow *from*. In some sense, these belong in the "Eventing" category above. But in practice, these are broken out for two reasons.

The first is SinkBinding, which is also a mostly internal type. Its existence is entirely related to how Sources get wired into the wider world of Brokers, Triggers, Sinks, and so forth. It therefore lives in Sources with code that rely on it.

What code is that? Sources, of course. While a Source is a general interface that can be widely implemented, it's difficult to do anything or get a sense of the possible unless you have concrete examples out of the box. Knative Eventing provides three reference Sources: the PingSource, the ApiServerSource, and the ContainerSource.

PingSource has one purpose: it produces CloudEvents on a schedule you provide. It used to be called CronJobSource, a name which tended to cause confusion with the CronJob records available in vanilla Kubernetes. Unlike a CronJob, PingSource doesn't actually *run any jobs*. It just produces a CloudEvent. After roughing up a dictionary for naming ideas, the Knative Eventing team settled on "PingSource." It is a source of pings.

The ApiServerSource is a much more sophisticated example. It can observe changes made to raw Kubernetes records and convert these into CloudEvents. In a philosophical sense, this isn't really *necessary*. You can already use audit events or various tools and APIs to directly watch Kubernetes records. The point here is that ApiServerSource provides a fairly complete example of how you can wrap an existing event-ish system into a CloudEvents form, so that these can join the fun.

`ContainerSource` takes a bit more explanation. It's essentially a specialized adaptor. You provide a `PodSpec` to `ContainerSource`, and in exchange, it injects information about a `Sink` to which anything running in the Pod should send its information. Put another way, it's a simple wrapper for existing systems that can run on raw Kubernetes and learn how to send events to a URL provided externally.

Which leaves yours truly in the odd position of telling you to pay attention to Kubernetes so that you can take advantage of Knative, which was meant to excuse you from the burden of paying attention to Kubernetes. I get out of this corner by saying that while `ContainerSource` is useful as a reference implementation and for quickly adapting existing software, it should never be seen as the only option or the best option. Where you have a more specific source, you should use it.

Which leads me to another point: while Knative Eventing bundles these three Sources, there's no limitation on using third-party sources. There are several of these in various states of maturity, activity, and supportedness.

6.5.4 Flows

This is a little bit of icing on the Eventing cake. You can build arbitrary graphs of computation using Brokers and Triggers. But it can be tedious. More to the point, such a hand-assembled graph encodes the structure of computation, but not its meaning.

Flows comes with two types, `Sequence` and `Parallel`, to make this problem a little easier. The names are fairly descriptive of the types. `Sequence` provides a way to bundle sequential steps connected via CloudEvents sent over Channels. And `Parallel` provides a way to encapsulate basic fan-out and fan-in scenarios.

6.5.5 Duck types

These are odd ducks. I almost left this discussion out, but I've kept it for three reasons. First, a lot of the magic in Knative is achieved with duck typing. Second, the concept is spreading out of Knative into other projects and I expect you'll see more of it. Third, with due credit to its inventors (Matt Moore and Ville Aikas), it's a brilliant hack on the Go type system. It deserves a little bit of admiration.

In statically-typed languages like Java, the type of a variable is set once, when the variable is created. Anything inside that variable must be of the same type, or a subtype, as the name above the door. This *nominal typing* is good at detecting certain kinds of bugs at compile time. But it does rather lean on you, the programmer, to have defined all the relevant types before compilation time.

Static, nominal typing is not the only option for language designers. In a language like Ruby, there are variables holding objects, and objects have types. But what that type *is* can change from moment to moment as various merciless waves of metaprogramming sweep terrified victims ahead of them. You can *define* a type in Ruby without fuss. It has a shiny `class` keyword and so on. But until you call a method on an object, you don't know what will happen.

This leads to the term *duck typing*: if the object walks like a duck and quacks like a duck, then it's a duck. This is a *tremendously* useful capability for languages of this genre. It is also a *tremendously* agony-inducing capability for languages of this genre. I grew up with ducks and let me tell you, yes, they walk, and yes, they quack, but their truly distinguishing characteristic is an irrational urge to poop on verandas. As with ducks, so with Ruby: a watchful eye and judicious fencing are required to stop finding duck manure all over.

Golang is, basically, statically and nominally typed, but with a clever twist on nominal typing. In a language like Java, I can create a named interface and implement it with concrete classes. In Golang, I can also define an interface, but there's no concept of "implements." Instead, you can collect methods together onto structs. Any such collection with the same methods as an interface is considered to be that type.

This neatly solves most of the problems with the two abbreviated descriptions I gave of Java and Ruby types. Unlike Java, Golang does not require explicit statements of interfaces, so an interface can be added *after* a concrete type and still be picked up. Unlike Ruby, nominal type checking happens at compile time, so the terrible sensation of standing in something squishy first thing in the morning is less likely to occur.

But not is all well in Paradise, because the Golang type system distinguishes sharply between interfaces, which are entirely about *methods*, and structs, which are about *data*, with the ability to attach methods. At this point, code can define types that are either of a named interface or a particular struct. If you define the type by interface, you can put any conforming implementation into that variable. If you define the type as a particular struct, tough luck. You are stuck with it forever; you can't put any other type there, even if an interface existed that the struct would have satisfied.

A sample from my upcoming book, *Things Jacques Hates About Golang*

Fun fact: the Golang standard library is an inconsistent mix of interface-typed modules and struct-typed modules. Meaning, sometimes you can replace library calls with a test fake. And sometimes you can't.

Linguists sometimes debate whether language completely constrains our apprehension and comprehension of external reality, a long-running debate that can be found under the "Sapir-Whorf Hypothesis" in *The Encyclopaedia of Tedious Freshman Stoner Philosophy*. I am at last able to settle this debate once and for all: it is wrong. I speak only English and, after thoroughly ransacking the entire language, I am unable to procure any word which fully encompasses the depth and breadth of my spiteful rage about this design decision.

Why on earth would anyone *ever* choose to create a struct-typed variable when interface-typed variables are always possible to build? If I leave aside mere hatred of fellow programmers, there *is* one situation where this arises: subtypes where the primary extension or change is in the data model, not in the methods.

To be sure, you can embed structs into other structs. But then you're stuck with struct typing again, and may you prevail against all the forces of darkness, O Weary Traveler.

Knative's duck typing concept manages to break the evil spell and give you both the ability to have interface-typed variables *and* to have subtyping for data. The practical upshot is that Knative can define types like `Addressable`, which both have guaranteed data fields like a struct *and* guaranteed methods like an interface. Under the hood, this is achieved with a clever little trick involving casting types of static variables, so that the compiler will barf if you don't respect a desired duck type.

Suppose, for example, I am making an Icecream interface, where I can give a list of flavors and how many scoops I want. In the following listing, I show how this looks when serialized into YAML.

Listing 6.15 Icecream

```
icecream:
- flavor: vanilla
  scoops: 1
```

So far so good, but suppose I now develop a new type called Sundae, which includes, but is not the same, as Icecream. Duck typing allows me to cleanly embed the Icecream type into the Sundae type. When serialized it looks like the following listing.

Listing 6.16 Sundae

```
sundae:
  sprinkles: oreos
  topping: chocolate
  icecream:
  - flavor: vanilla
    scoops: 2
```

The punchline is this: I can write software that implements *just* Icecream, but it will be able to handle Sundaes as well, without needing to worry about sprinkles or toppings.

There's some useful documentation about duck typing, which is worth at least skimming. I also recommend the KubeCon talk that Matt and Ville gave on the topic.

Summary

- CloudEvents are a standard structure for events. These can be represented with multiple formats over multiple protocols.
- CloudEvents have attributes and data.
- Some attributes are required: `specversion`, `source`, `type`, and `id`, for example.
- There are also optional and extension attributes.

- The CloudEvents player is a useful debugging and development tool for working with Knative Eventing.
- You can use kn to list, describe, create, and update Sources and Triggers.
- Conditions on Triggers can show whether Brokers, Subscribers, or Sources are live and healthy.
- Eventing contains four major groups of components: Messaging, Eventing, Sources, and Flows.
- Much of the magic in Knative Eventing is due to the "duck typing" capability supported by Knative's implementation.

References

- Internet Assigned Numbers Authority, *Media Types*, http://mng.bz/Xd1G
- T. Taylor, "Example Media Types for Use in Documentation," *Requests for Comments: 4735* (IETF, October 2006), https://tools.ietf.org/html/rfc4735
- G. Klyne and C. Newman, "Date and Time on the Internet: Timestamps," *Requests for Comments: 3339* (IETF, July 2002), https://tools.ietf.org/html/rfc3339
- Sergey Kanzhelev, Morgan McLean, et al., "Trace Context" (W3C Editor's Draft, April 3, 2020), https://w3c.github.io/trace-context/
- The Avro Authors, "Apache Avro" (Apache Software Foundation), https://avro.apache.org/
- Gregor Hohpe and Bobby Woolf, *Enterprise Integration Patterns* (Addison-Wesley Professional, 2003)
- Matt Moore, Ville Aikas, and Eric Anderson (ed)., "Knative Duck Typing," (GitHub, April 7, 2020), http://mng.bz/yY8G
- Matt Moore and Ville Aikas, "Extending Knative for Fun and Profit" (KubeCon EU 2019), http://mng.bz/MXZ7

Sources and Sinks

Sources and their slightly less visible companion, Sinks, are the bread-and-butter concepts you use most often in Knative Eventing. Quickly revisiting: a *Source* describes a thing that can emit CloudEvents and a place (the *Sink*) where those events should be sent. Sources are the canonical way of describing how CloudEvents will move between points in a Knative Eventing design. Luckily, these are not super-complicated, so this chapter will be relatively brief.

7.1 Sources

In this section, I'm going to briefly look at the anatomy of Sources, then we'll poke one to see how it works. It's worth remembering that while *I* am putting "Source" and "Sink" on the same conceptual level, Knative's structure is that Sources are the top-level concept and that Sinks are a component of Sources.

7.1.1   *The anatomy of Sources*

Figure 7.1 is a representation of a Source, as seen by an X-ray machine. In figure 7.1, I've represented a Source as having two parts, but confusingly, only one is actually labeled 'Source'. That box contains Sink and CloudEvent-Overrides. Then underneath is the very helpful ??? box. We'll profit from ??? in a second, but first, what's the duck inside the octagon all about?

It's the "Ducktagon," a little icon for Knative duck types. My purpose here is to visually annotate the Source box as *being* a duck type; specifically, a Source. Knative's design is that any Kubernetes record having those two fields can be treated as a Source by Knative. More concretely, we can point our X-ray machine at PingSource (figure 7.2).

Figure 7.1   What's in the box?

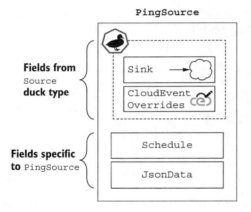

Figure 7.2   PingSource under the scope

My point here is that because PingSource contains Sink and CloudEventOverrides, it *is* a Source. Those two fields are used by Knative Eventing itself. The additional Schedule and JsonData fields are specific to PingSource.

Let me drive this home some more. *Anything with those two fields is a Source*, so far as Knative is concerned. The ContainerSource has these fields, so it is a Source. ApiServerSource has these fields; it too is a Source (figure 7.3).

This "is-a" relationship is not achieved through some sort of class inheritance mechanism; it's based purely on the fields present in the record. This makes it possible to extend Eventing without ever needing to modify the Eventing codebase or even to pull any Eventing code as a dependency.

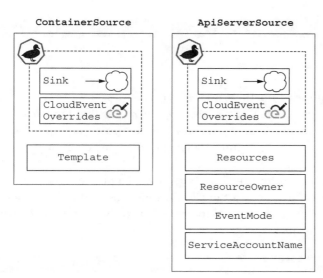

Figure 7.3 The other inbuilt Sources

7.1.2 *Using kn to work with Sources*

All good and well, but Sources are meant to be used, not dissected. Our trustworthy friend kn is standing by to help. Let's first prove that I am not lying about the Sources that are installed by default. I present in my defense the following listing.

Listing 7.1 Using kn `source list-types`

```
$ kn source list-types

TYPE               NAME                                       DESCRIPTION
ApiServerSource    apiserversources.sources.knative.dev
                       Watch and send Kubernetes API events to a sink
ContainerSource    containersources.sources.knative.dev
                       Generate events by Container image and send to a sink
PingSource         pingsources.sources.knative.dev
                       Send periodically ping events to a sink
SinkBinding        sinkbindings.sources.knative.dev
                       Binding for connecting a PodSpecable to a sink
```

Here are the three amigos of ApiServerSource, ContainerSource, and PingSource. As a reminder (or foreshadowing, if you're reading the book out of order), these represent a Source for Kubernetes API events, an adapter for existing software in a Kubernetes Pod, and a Source for sending CloudEvents on a regular schedule. Plus there's an interloper, SinkBinding, which I'll return to later.

You might have found list-types to be an odd subcommand name. My own first instinct is that list makes more sense. Is it aliased? Missing? Living in Panama under a false identity?

Listing 7.2   What does `kn source list` do?

```
$ kn source list
No sources found in default namespace.
```

Listing 7.2 reveals that none of my theories were correct (and I was *so* sure about the Panama thing). In fact, `kn source list` shows Source *records* that have been created and submitted, while `kn source list-types` shows what Source *definitions* have been installed. By a loose analogy to programming language concepts, `list` shows the objects, `list-types` shows the classes.

For working with `ApiServerSource` and `PingSource`, kn provides some convenient subcommands. I'll show off `ping` using the CloudEvents player that I installed in the previous chapter. The `describe` subcommand in the next listing follows conventions you should find familiar by now.

Listing 7.3   Creating and describing `ping-player`

```
$ kn source ping create ping-player
      ⇨ --sink http://cloudevents-player.default.example.com
Ping source 'ping-player' created in namespace 'default'.

$ kn source list
NAME          TYPE         RESOURCE                               SINK         READY
ping-player   PingSource   pingsources.sources.knative.dev
                      ⇨ http://cloudevents-player.default.example.com   True


$ kn source ping describe ping-player
Name:          ping-player
Namespace:     default
Annotations:   sources.knative.dev/creator=jchester@example.com,
                   ⇨ sources.knative.dev/lastModifier=j ...
Age:           2s

Schedule:      * * * * *

Data:          ⇠

Sink:
  URI: http://cloudevents-player.default.example.com

Conditions:
  OK TYPE                AGE REASON
  ++ Ready               2s
  ++ Deployed            2s
  ++ SinkProvided        2s
  ++ ValidSchedule       2s
  ++ ResourcesCorrect    2s
```

Generates a CloudEvent. It uses the charming Cron minilanguage, famous for being only slightly less murder-inducing than the Job Control Language of the mainframe era. The rule * * * * * is satisfied every minute.

Data is the actual JSON sent onwards to the Sink. More in a second.

There are, as always, some Conditions.

As you would expect, this is the HTTP(S) URI to which PingSource is meant to send the Data.

If you open the CloudEvents player, you'll see that `ping` events have begun to pile up (figure 7.4).

Activity

ID	Type	Source	Status	Time	Message
3f2f1bed-10d3-4d67-8a32-0e37329932f3	dev.knative.sources.ping	/apis/v1/namespaces/default/pingsources/ping-player	✓	2020-05-20T01:43:00.005+02:00[Europe/Madrid]	✉
094cab12-c68b-4090-9e2d-9186267f31e2	dev.knative.sources.ping	/apis/v1/namespaces/default/pingsources/ping-player	✓	2020-05-20T01:42:00.004+02:00[Europe/Madrid]	✉

Figure 7.4 CloudEvents piling up each minute

This gives me a chance to reiterate that every CloudEvent must have a unique ID (in this case, UUIDs), a type, and a source. PingSource follows the common idiom of using reverse-domain notation for the type and path notation for the source.

The `/api/v1` prefix in the Source field is another Kubernetism poking through. `namespaces/default` tells you which namespace to look in for the actual `PingSource` record. The name that I provided to `kn` hangs off `pingsources/ping-player`.

As an aside: these are idioms, not standards, nor requirements. Don't rely on string-splitting on `.` or `/` to suss out the internals of type and source. You'll just guarantee a future mystery.

It's all well and good that CloudEvents are *arriving*, but what are these *carrying*? Right now, nothing. Click the Message icon (✉) to look more closely at what I mean (figure 7.5).

The `root` here is not part of CloudEvents: it's how the CloudEvents player presents the CloudEvent JSON object. However `attributes` and `data` are definitely part of a CloudEvent, as are the attribute fields for `datacontenttype`, `id`, `source`, `specversion`, `time`, and `type`.

The `data` section is worth some comment. It's present, but its presence isn't necessary to make this a conformant CloudEvent. PingSource includes one anyway. I don't have strong feelings about whether that's better or worse than an implicitly "undefined" value; it really comes down to the idioms of how your preferred programming languages and libraries expose JSON to you.

Before I get to `extensions`, I am going to add some crunchy JSON to my pings using `kn`. Then I'll verify it was configured with both `kn` and the CloudEvents player as listing 7.4 shows.

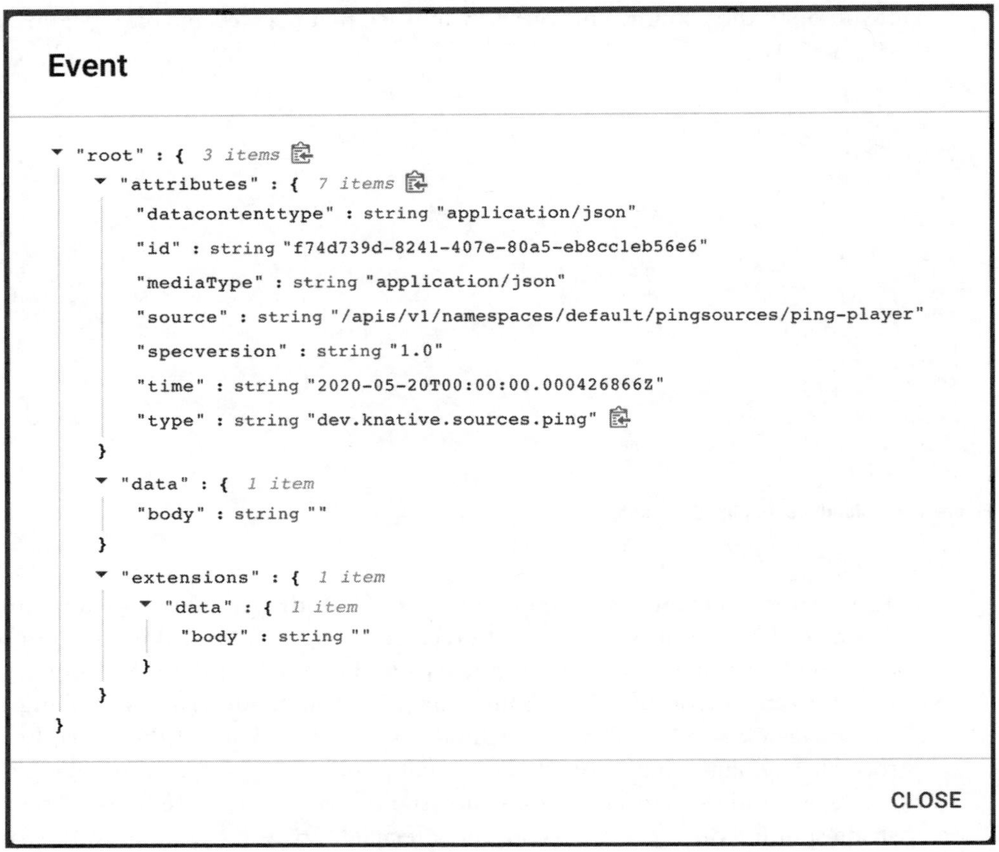

Event

```
▼ "root" : {  3 items 📋
    ▼ "attributes" : {  7 items 📋
        "datacontenttype" : string "application/json"
        "id" : string "f74d739d-8241-407e-80a5-eb8cc1eb56e6"
        "mediaType" : string "application/json"
        "source" : string "/apis/v1/namespaces/default/pingsources/ping-player"
        "specversion" : string "1.0"
        "time" : string "2020-05-20T00:00:00.000426866Z"
        "type" : string "dev.knative.sources.ping" 📋
    }
    ▼ "data" : {  1 item
        "body" : string ""
    }
    ▼ "extensions" : {  1 item
        ▼ "data" : {  1 item
            "body" : string ""
        }
    }
}
```

CLOSE

Figure 7.5   Looking more closely at a CloudEvent

Listing 7.4   Adding data and verifying using `kn`

```
$ kn source ping update ping-player --data '{"foo":"and likewise bar"}'
Ping source 'ping-player' updated in namespace 'default'.

$ kn source ping describe ping-player
Name:          ping-player
Namespace:     default
Annotations:   sources.knative.dev/creator=jchester@example.com,
          ➥ sources.knative.dev/lastModifier=j ...

Age:           2h
Schedule:      * * * * *
Data:          {"foo":"and likewise bar"}

# ... snip of Sink and Conditions
```

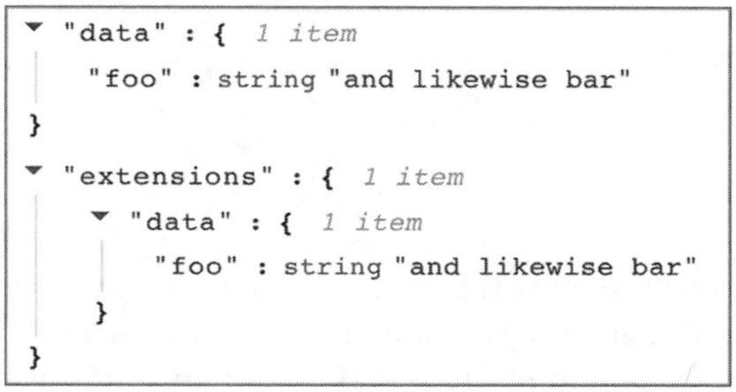

```
▼ "data" : { 1 item
     "foo" : string "and likewise bar"
  }
▼ "extensions" : { 1 item
     ▼ "data" : { 1 item
          "foo" : string "and likewise bar"
        }
  }
```

Figure 7.6 How it looks in CloudEvents player

You can see from both the `kn source ping describe` (listing 7.4) and the screenshot (figure 7.6) that my `PingSource` now includes {`"foo": "and likewise bar"`} in its CloudEvents `data` object. It is *not* put into a field called `data.body`. It's a direct child object of `data`. The `data.body` key you saw earlier is used by `PingSource` as a placeholder only.

So what about `extensions`? This is the serialized name for `CloudEventOverrides`, which you'll remember are part of any Source. These are more or less what they sound like. If you set an override, then Triggers will treat the overridden value as the actual value.

This is most useful for editing values to add context (for example, in a tracing framework). The presentation in figure 7.6 has a net effect of doing nothing. But if `extensions.data.foo` was no actually, `quux`, then a Trigger would treat that field as having that value.

Truthfully, I don't think you should use `extensions`. It's the vestiges of a previous scheme for adding flexibility in design, which has been largely superseded by duck types. I will leave it off from here on in.

7.2 *The Sink*

In my examples so far I've positioned the `Sink` as being a URI. It turns out that this is only *one* way to express "send my CloudEvents here." The other is to use a "Ref"—a reference to another Kubernetes record. Take the next listing, for example.

Listing 7.5 Updating my `PingSource` to use a Ref instead of a URI

```
$ kn source ping update ping-player --sink ksvc:cloudevents-player
Ping source 'ping-player' updated in namespace 'default'.

$ kn source ping describe ping-player
Name:         ping-player
Namespace:    default
Annotations:  sources.knative.dev/creator=jchester@example.com,
              ➥ sources.knative.dev/lastModifier=j ...
Age:          1d
Schedule:     * * * * *
Data:         {"foo":"and likewise bar"}
```

```
Sink:
  Name:       cloudevents-player
  Namespace:  default
  Resource:   Service (serving.knative.dev/v1)

# Snip of Conditions
```

If you compare listing 7.5 to a previous `describe`, you'll see that the Sink readout has changed. The subfield used to be `URI`, but now you have `Name`, `Namespace`, and `Resource`.

There's no `--sink-ref` or `--ref` argument to signal to `kn` that you're using a Ref instead of a URI. Your intention is derived from the syntax of what you pass in. If your argument starts with `http://` or `https://`, the assumption is that you want a URI. If instead it starts with `ksvc:`, the assumption is that you want a Ref.

What `kn` is showing you in the `describe` output is that it knows I've pointed it towards a Knative Service, because I asked for `ksvc:cloudevents-player`. I could also have used `service:cloudevents-player` as a more explicit alternative. Whichever you pick, just remember that a Knative Service is not the same as a Kubernetes Service.

Which is better? URIs are simpler to start with and allow you to target endpoints that live outside the cluster Knative is running on. But consider using Refs instead. A URI is just an address, what lies on the other side is (for good or ill) a blackbox. But a Ref is a Knative construct referring to a Knative Service. Knative knows how to open the box to peek at what's inside.

This is most useful when things go awry. Let's demonstrate by creating some unexpected havoc as uncovered in this listing.

Listing 7.6   No more service

```
$ kn service delete cloudevents-player
Service 'cloudevents-player' successfully deleted in namespace 'default'.

$ kn source ping describe ping-player

# ... Snip so we can get to Conditions

Conditions:
  OK TYPE               AGE REASON
  !! Ready              5s  NotFound    ◁── The Ready Condition is a top-level
  ++ Deployed           1d                  rollup of other Conditions.
  !! SinkProvided       5s  NotFound    ◁── The more diagnostic Condition is
  ++ ValidSchedule      1d                  that SinkProvided is !! (not OK). The
  ++ ResourcesCorrect   1d                  NotFound reason explains why.
```

This information is surfaced because Knative Eventing can go and see if the nominated Ref actually exists. That's not something it can do with URI. Think of Ref as being more like a phone number than an address. If I want to visit you, I can either just show up and hope you're at home (URI), or I can ring ahead before making that trip (Ref). Where possible, you are better served with Ref.

7.3   *The mysterious SinkBinding (and its sidekick, ContainerSource)*

PingSource is helpful for introducing the basics of working with Sources, but otherwise, there's not much to talk about. ApiServerSource does a *lot* more, but you might recall that I am trying to keep Kubernetes itself at arm's length from this book.

Or so I hoped, as it's now time to introduce SinkBinding, which is a kind of adapter plug for more or less "anything" that uses vanilla Kubernetes to run.[1] And time also to briefly point out why ContainerSource is sorta-kinda a special case of SinkBinding.

The basic problem is this: other software already exists in a state of genteel barbarism, unaware that Knative Eventing exists, providing no proper Sources that can be easily put to good use. It's true that Eventing comes most of the way to meeting in the middle, because it speaks HTTP and thinks in HTTP terms. But Eventing still requires some configuration to achieve that connection. It does not have autodiscovery or autoconfiguration of arbitrary HTTP endpoints as a capability or goal.

The SinkBinding provides a non-specialized recipe for configuring Eventing to interact with existing systems. It has two parts. First, it has a Sink. Second, it has a Subject. The Sink we already know reasonably well: it can be a URI or a reference (Ref) to a Knative Service, or even to a vanilla Kubernetes record such as a Pod or Deployment. The Subject is *also* a reference to a record, such as a Knative Service, Pod, or Deployment, using the Namespace, Name, etc., fields.

Note that Sinks and Subjects are *distinct* types. In particular, a Sink points to a *single* thing identified either by URI or by Ref. A Subject can only be identified by reference and can, in theory, refer to *any number* of matching records. Now, while this presents the possibility of performing fan-outs using SinkBinding, I'd like to shoo you away from it. The Broker is a better place for that sort of work to be done, while Parallels are explicitly designed to support fan-outs.

What does setting a Subject do that a Sink does not? After all, Knative Eventing can't read your code and do anything fancy to it. But what it *can* do is provide enough information for your code to do the right thing. In the case of SinkBinding, nominating something as a Subject causes Knative Eventing to inject a K_SINK environment variable into the software's container environment. The K_SINK variable is set to the URI of the Subject. By providing the K_SINK variable, Eventing enables the software inside the blackbox to target the Sink and send information directly to it.

For example, you might have a catalog microservice that typically POSTs updates to a shopping cart microservice. If you wanted to have Knative Serving take over this interaction, the first step would be to set your Subject to the existing shopping cart Service URL. Then you'd have the catalog POST to the address found in K_SINK. Later, you could change K_SINK to anywhere that makes sense—a Broker, for example.

---

[1] Other analogies that wound up on the cutting room floor: it's a Swiss Army knife; an escape hatch from Knative; a break-glass option for going around Knative; duct tape (not duck type!) for Knative Eventing to Kubernetes.

Bear in mind that SinkBinding is not meant to be the *best* solution for all Sources. It's mostly there to give you some help if you can't find a fully built Source to suit your needs. It might be that you need a gateway between a vendor API and your Eventing system. You want the integration, but the vendor hasn't bothered. This is where you bust out SinkBinding.

On the other hand, if the vendor comes to the table with a Source that does what you need, use it. First, because it's usually better to let someone else worry about bugs. Second, because SinkBindings are a bit like strings. A dozen SinkBindings could be about a dozen different things. Without inspecting these each manually, you won't know what kind of thing is being bound. But when I see PingSource and ApiServer-Source and so on, I know exactly what these are.

ContainerSource closely resembles a SinkBinding, but it is technically a distinct kind of thing. As its name suggests, ContainerSource is limited to dealing with one kind of thing: containers. More accurately, it lets you set the container for a given Pod.

I think that while ContainerSource is easy to first grasp, you should prefer Sink-Binding when you need to perform a quick adaptation of existing software without needing to write a full-blown Source. A SinkBinding is more general, for one thing. And it is more likely to stick around if ContainerSource is ever retired.

7.3.1   *Provisioning and binding are not the same*

The abstractness of SinkBinding gives me a useful jumping-off point to discuss a perennial source of confusion about Sources. When you create a Source, you are creating a record, stored somewhere in the bowels of Kubernetes. You are not necessarily creating anything else. In particular, how that Source record is interpreted is *up to the implementation* of the Source. It's one thing for me to turn up at a house with a piece of paper saying that I own it. It's another thing entirely as to whether anyone inside will believe me.

The underlying point is that provisioning a service and binding to the service are separate things that are often mixed up. When I *provision* a service, I am asking for some resource or service to be created from scratch, allocated from a pool, and so forth. Essentially, *provisioning* means "reserve some capacity for my exclusive use." That can mean a lot of different things. For example, "provision a database" might mean that I log into an existing MySQL system and type CREATE DATABASE. Or I might use Terraform to drive an Amazon RDS API, which will create an entire virtual machine on my behalf. Or perhaps I submit a ticket to a central IT services group. Or maybe I just sneakily install MySQL on the machine next to my desk.

In each case, I wanted to ensure that a service was available. And it's not just databases: I could be provisioning queues from RabbitMQ or topics from Kafka, buckets in blob stores like S3 or GCS, OAuth tokens for webhook callbacks, API gateway servers, accounts on a logging service provider … it goes on and on. That request might or might not include some reserved amount of underlying resources as well—in provisioning a database, I might also be requesting the exclusive use of a virtual machine.

When I *bind* to a service, I close the circuit between my software and something that has already been provisioned.[2] This is a nigh-universal requirement and it continues to be a fertile spring for reinvention. PHP files with hardcoded database credentials, JNDI, Open Service Broker API, Kubernetes ConfigMaps ... the names under which this concept has traded are as numerous as the folks who haven't heard of the previous names.

Taken together, provisioning and binding are like renting a car. You pick the type of car you want and book it, probably through a website. That's provisioning: A car is going to be reserved for your use. Then when you arrive to collect it, they give you car keys, a slab of fine print that would be challenging for ants to read, and a hand wave in the general direction of where to find it. You walk to the bay, get into the car, insert the keys, and drive off. That's the completed *binding*.

The distinction is important because Knative does not enforce any policy or lifecycle about provisioning or binding. You can normally *expect* that defining a Source will cause some sort of binding to occur; otherwise, these are not much use. But provisioning is the Wild West. Maybe your Source will provision something; maybe it won't. It will depend on the implementation.

`PingSource`, for example, is all-in-one. It both provisions a service (a little process that will run indefinitely to generate CloudEvents) and creates a binding (to the sink). But by contrast, `ApiServerSource` doesn't provision a Kubernetes API Server. It *only* does binding. For each Source you use, keep in mind that sometimes it will only do bindings, and sometimes both provisioning and binding.

7.4 *Other Sources*

By themselves, `PingSource`, `ApiServerSource`, and `ContainerSource` don't give you much to work with. Mostly, as first-party Sources, these enable you to kick the Eventing tires immediately after installation. But that's about it. You'll need more for your day job.

There are a few places to look for more Sources, which I'll describe in brief. The place to look up a more centralized, more complete list is in the Knative Eventing documentation "Knative Eventing Sources" page (https://knative.dev/docs/eventing/sources/).

First is Knative's own `eventing-contrib` repository (https://github.com/knative/eventing-contrib). This is a relatively loose directory of third-party Sources provided by a number of contributors. Looking at it now, while I write, I can see Sources covering a variety of integrations. For example: CephFS, CouchDB, Github and GitLab, Kafka and NATS Streaming, plus a few others. As this is a designated sandbox for Eventing Sources, you can expect that list to grow over time.

For AWS-centric situations, TriggerMesh provides a growing collection of Sources (https://github.com/triggermesh/aws-event-sources). TriggerMesh supports some other Sources as well. Make sure to poke around their Github org to see what's being worked on.

---

[2] It might not have been provisioned because I asked for it, by the way. I might be sharing a database between two apps, for example.

Whereas AWS is represented by TriggerMesh's third-party Sources, Google has been working on providing first-party Sources (https://github.com/google/knative-gcp), as well as other integration points (e.g., Channels) which I've yet to discuss.

Azure is, at writing, unrepresented among Eventing Sources. I expect that to change rapidly—Azure was the first of the hyperscalers to announce first-class CloudEvents support (http://mng.bz/6g05). It seems like a short hop from there to providing broad support for Eventing Sources as well.

Other large vendors are starting to dip their toe into this space. VMware has an experimental Source for vSphere (https://github.com/vmware-tanzu/sources-for-knative).[3]

This informal list isn't fully exhaustive, and it won't remain accurate for long. I expect more first-party and third-party Sources will emerge over time. You'll need to keep an eye out for things you want or need. Right now the best ways to do that are (1) periodically revisiting `eventing-contrib` and (2) reviewing the documentation after each release.

Summary

- All Sources contain `Sinks` and `CloudEventOverrides`. Any record with these fields is recognized as a Source by Knative Eventing.
- Each Source adds fields relevant to its use. For example, `PingSource` adds fields for `Schedule` and `JsonData`.
- `kn` can be used to create, update, and list Sources.
- Out of the box, Eventing installs four Source types: `PingSource`, `ApiServerSource`, `ContainerSource`, and `SinkBinding`.
- Other Sources are available for installation, including Sources for Github and Gitlab, Kafka, Google Cloud Platform, and others.
- Sinks can be targeted with either a direct URI or by providing fields that identify a Kubernetes record (name, namespace, and so forth).
- `SinkBinding` and `ContainerSource` are general-purpose adapters, enabling you to integrate with existing systems for which there is no Source provided.

References

- Matthew Dixon, Karen Freeman, and Nicholas Toman, "Stop Trying to Delight Your Customers" (*Harvard Business Review*, July-August 2010), http://mng.bz/1raX
- The CloudEvents Primer Authors, "JSON Extensions," *CloudEvents Primer*, V1.0, http://mng.bz/PPNw

---

[3] An earlier vSphere Source was developed by TriggerMesh, but their focus has apparently moved towards AWS.

Filtering and Flowing

8

This chapter covers

- The Broker
- Triggers and filters
- Sequences
- Parallels

In the last chapter, I focused on the hard-wiring approach to Eventing. Now I want to look at some of the luxury features. These basically fall into two basic categories.

The first is *brokering and filtering*, creating a middleman to make the shipment of CloudEvents from one place to another simpler and more reliable. I've already spent a fair amount of time on the basics in previous chapters, but there are a bunch of additional capabilities around error-handling that I can at last reveal to you. I'll also make a small detour into the lower-level guts of Eventing: Channels.

The second category of luxury features is *flows*, higher-level abstractions over the wiring of Sources, sinks, and so forth. These go last because these build on many of the topics we've discussed so far in chapter 7. I suspect that in time these will grow to be a larger and larger part of your systems.

Together, these luxury features can save you a fair amount of boilerplate. The goal is to express your intent at a higher level, after all, and to do so somewhat efficiently.

Brokers, Triggers, Sequences, and Parallels provide higher abstractions that you can use to move CloudEvents to where these are needed with a minimum of hassle.

8.1 *The Broker*

But first, the Broker. Sources and Sinks are all very well, but have an essential difficulty: brittleness. If a Source or Sink disappear or isn't available, your lovely event-driven architecture becomes uneventful rubble. As required by law and custom, Knative solves this problem by introducing indirection via the Broker.

> **About the name**
>
> "The Broker" is a slightly misleading title. For starters, Knative Eventing ships with an inbuilt broker, the "multi-tenant broker," more often called the "MT Broker." Why specify it as "multi-tenant"? As befits all confusing names, the answer is "History." In the early days, there was just "the" Broker. You needed a copy running for every namespace where you used Eventing. The practical upshot is that Eventing could be fairly wasteful on large clusters with many apps running side-by-side, separated by Kubernetes namespaces.
>
> Then came the multi-tenant Broker, which was forked from the original Broker and modified so that it could deal with Eventing workloads spread across multiple Kubernetes namespaces. The overhead of running a Broker instance could then be amortized over many Triggers. Eventually, the original Broker code was removed and the MT Broker became "the" Broker.
>
> But it's not "the" Broker either. It's "a" Broker, the one that ships by default with Knative Eventing. But it's permissible to write third-party brokers that follow a spec. These too are brokers, on a level footing with the inbuilt Broker. You might note that we first saw this pattern with Sources: there are a few built in, but nothing prevents you from using others, if that suits your purposes.
>
> Perhaps this sounds a little like a "Who's The Architect-iest?" duel fought out in front of a whiteboard. But at least one third-party broker implementation exists: for GCP, optimized to run in that environment. I expect others will follow in time. For now, I use the MT Broker, because that's what Knative installs for you. And for convenience, I will just refer to it as "the Broker."

A Broker in Knative land serves two major purposes:

- It's a sink, a place where CloudEvents can be reliably sent by Sources.[1]
- It gives life to Triggers. It applies their filters to incoming CloudEvents and forwards these to subscribers when filters match.

---

[1] The quacker fans among you will be pleased to learn that there's a duck type involved: `Addressable`. A conforming Broker is `Addressable`, meaning that it can be used as a sink or subscriber by other components. But this point of trivia won't come up much, except for implementers of Brokers. That's why, instead of discussing this in the main text, you and I needed to duck outside for a quack chat.

As a developer, you ideally don't need to set up a Broker yourself. Knative will install one for you with some basic default settings, intended for development. Once installed, a Broker listens for Triggers that are submitted or modified.

How can you verify this? By creating a Trigger and then looking more closely. The next listing shows how.

Listing 8.1 Looking for the Broker

```
$ kn trigger create example-trigger \
    --filter type=dev.knative.example.com \
    --sink http://example.com/

Trigger 'example-trigger' successfully created in namespace 'default'.

$ kn trigger describe example-trigger

Name:          example-trigger
Namespace:     default
Labels:        eventing.knative.dev/broker=default        ◁──┐
Annotations:   eventing.knative.dev/creator=jchester@example.com,
               ⇒ eventing.knative.dev/lastModifier ...
Age:           1m
Broker:        default                  ◁─────────────
                                                            
Filter:                                  ◁──────
  type:        dev.knative.example.com

Sink:
  URI:  http://example.com/

Conditions:
  OK TYPE                 AGE REASON
  ++ Ready                1m
  ++ BrokerReady          1m
  ++ DependencyReady      1m
  ++ SubscriberResolved   1m
  ++ SubscriptionReady    1m
```

The eventing.knative.dev/ broker=default label that Eventing adds to help it identify which triggers belong to which brokers

The Broker: default field is a friendlier presentation of the same information.

The filter itself, where the Broker gets its instructions on picking and sorting CloudEvents

8.2 *Filters*

Triggers include filters. When I created `example-trigger` earlier, I stapled a simple filter to it: `type=dev.knative.example.com`. This says "let through any CloudEvent with type of `dev.knative.example.com`."

Eventing's filtering rules are strict: exact matches *only*.[2] There are no partial matches, no `startsWith` or `endsWith`, no regular expressions. You *can* filter on multiple CloudEvent attributes, but this too is quite strict: *all* the fields must match. These are `ANDed`, not `ORed`.

---

[2] This was true as of writing. There are discussions afoot to allow for some sort of general expression language, but these were preliminary.

Suppose I decided to do all my triggering based on the `type` and `source` attributes of CloudEvents. The following listing shows how I can set up a series of triggers and their filters with kn. Then figure 8.1 illustrates how these Eventing filters look.

Listing 8.2   Filtering all some of the things

```
$ kn trigger create trigger-1 \
    --filter type=com.example.type \
    --sink example-sink
Trigger 'trigger-1' successfully created in namespace 'default'.

$ kn trigger create trigger-2 \
    --filter type=com.example.type \
    --filter source=/example/source/123 \
    --sink example-sink
Trigger 'trigger-2' successfully created in namespace 'default'.

$ kn trigger create trigger-3 \
    --filter type=com.example.type \
    --filter source=/example/source/456 \
    --sink example-sink
Trigger 'trigger-3' successfully created in namespace 'default'.

$ kn trigger create trigger-4 \
    --filter type=net.example.another \
    --sink example-sink
Trigger 'trigger-4' successfully created in namespace 'default'.

$ kn trigger create trigger-5 \
    --filter type=net.example.another \
    --filter source=a-different-source \
    --sink example-sink
Trigger 'trigger-5' successfully created in namespace 'default'.
```

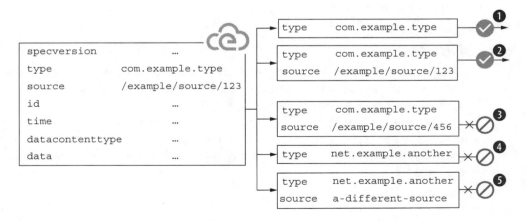

Figure 8.1   Examples of filters for a CloudEvent

Now, suppose I have a CloudEvent with `type: com.example.type` and `source: /example/source/123`. What happens? The answer is that only *exact matches* will pass through the filter defined by a Trigger. Anything that doesn't completely and entirely match gets ignored for that Trigger. And that's what you can see in figure 8.1:

1 Matches because the CloudEvent's `type` is `com.example.type`.
2 Matches because the CloudEvent's `type` is `com.example.type` *and* the source is `/example/source/123`.
3 Fails because even though the CloudEvent's `type` is `com.example.type`, its source is not `/example/source/456`.
4 Fails because the CloudEvent's `type` is not `net.example.another`.
5 Fails because the CloudEvent's `type` is not `net.example.another` and/or its source is not `a-different-source`.

This strictness is a mixed blessing. On the upside, it's strict. In distributed systems, folks all too frequently allow today's convenience be borrowed at high interest rates from tomorrow's bugs and security holes. And, if you have highly specific filters, downstream systems are less likely to be accidentally overloaded by traffic with unexpected new fields or changes in demand.

The downside is that it's inexpressive. If you like, you can try stringing multiple triggers together using De Morgan's Law or Karnaugh maps and other things flung at inattentive Computer Science students, mostly in vain. And yes, you can combine filters using multiple ANDs to behave like ORs, but I recommend against it. First, for mere sanity. The odds of creating infinite loops is quite high when all the pieces of one are widely spread out. Second, for performance. Knative Eventing very much treats Triggers as black boxes. It won't sense that you intend to combine multiple filters into a single predicate in the way that, for example, a database query planner can. Each filter will be applied and then a message sent or not sent to a subscriber. Each such hop imposes delay and adds variability to the overall system you are working on.

You have three choices. One is to wait for Eventing to acquire a more expressive filtering system. Another is to perform some amount of filtering at the receiving end, meaning that some fraction of incoming CloudEvents is basically wasted. The third option is to inject additional information at the origin, against which simple filters can be applied.

You can filter on broadly "anything" in a CloudEvent. As I've already shown, you can add filters for `source` and `type` attributes. You can add filters for the other required attributes (`specversion` and `id`). You can also add filters for optional attributes (`datacontenttype`, `dataschema`, `subject`, and `time`). And you can add these for extension attributes (like `dataref`, `partitionkey`, and so on).

Note what's missing from this list: filtering on the *body* of the CloudEvent. Only *attributes* are watched by a filter. For folks coming from previous generations of event-y systems, this won't be a shock. Routing on metadata, headers, whatever you like to call those, is the norm. "Content-based routing" is less common.

You might be quite determined to do something like this anyway. For example, you might have a customer ID that you use to shard requests into different regions (European traffic goes to Europe, US traffic to the US, etc.). There's no standard CloudEvent attribute for `customerID`. What do you do?

> **WARNING**   When working with CloudEvent attributes, keep in mind that embedding any kind of personally identifiable information (PII) into attributes is risky. Earlier I used `customerID` as a possible field to transmit, possibly via `subject`. That's usually going to be OK. Much *less* likely to be OK is someone's name, email address, phone number, national or public identification number, etc. You don't know in advance where CloudEvents will wind up or what systems are traversed. That makes "right to forget" difficult to implement unless you use opaque identifiers instead of PII in your CloudEvents.

The first option is to DIY. Add some service, function, or gateway somewhere into the flow of CloudEvents and perform content-based filtering there. It is my suspicion that many readers will at this point fling the book over their shoulder in the rush to get to their keyboard, but please, reconsider. Do-it-yourself is also maintain-it-yourself-forever.

The second option, which is often the best option, is to find the most similarly defined attribute and use that. For example, it seems reasonable to use `subject` or `partitionkey` for distinguishing between customers. That is assuming, however, you're not using those attributes already.

The third option is to add an attribute. This is a special case of DIY, for which my previous warning about book-flinging applies, but less strongly. Using a CloudEvent attribute instead of something embedded into the CloudEvent body has the advantage that future CloudEvent-aware systems will play more nicely with it, and code dedicated to attributes will probably see more optimization than the code that handles the body.

8.2.1   *Filtering on custom attributes*

A quick example is in order, but all I have time for is a fiddly example. The tools I've used so far (kn and the CloudEvents Player) don't let me show what I'd like to show, so I will need to drop down to a lower level of abstracton. I'll create CloudEvents manually and directly, `POST`ing these to the default broker.[3]

To do this, I must first create a forwarded port. I'll use the magic spell in the following listing.

---

[3]   Originally, I wrote the examples using `curl`, but switched to using HTTPie (at the command line, `http`). While it's true that `curl` is close to omnipresent, it's not close at all to being omnibenevolent. HTTPie is a nicer all-around experience.

```
Listing 8.3  Forwarding a port
```

```
# In the first terminal
$ kubectl port-forward \
        service/broker-ingress 8888:80 \
        --namespace knative-eventing

Forwarding from 127.0.0.1:8888 -> 8080
Forwarding from [::1]:8888 -> 8080
```

Essentially, kubectl now maps my localhost port 8888 to port 8080 of the Broker's ingress component.[4] Slightly confusingly, I asked for port 80 and got 8080 instead. This has to do with how Kubernetes handles networking, and happily, it doesn't matter to the discussion. But now you know.

Having now established a forwarded port in one terminal, I can directly send HTTP requests to the Broker from another terminal. The following listing shows this transmission.

```
Listing 8.4  Sending a CloudEvent with http
```

Indicates the magic port-forwarded URL for the broker. First, localhost:8888 sends traffic to the kubectl port-forward we ran earlier, which then forwards it to the Broker ingress component running inside the cluster. The /default/default path tells that Broker ingress which Broker it's dealing with: the default Broker, in the default namespace. (You needn't memorize this, it won't be on the final exam.)

```
# In a second terminal
$ http post http://localhost:8888/default/default \

    Ce-Id:$(uuidgen) \
    Ce-Specversion:1.0 \
    Ce-Type:com.example.type \
    Ce-Source:/example/source \

    message="This is an example." \
    --verbose

POST /default/default HTTP/1.1
Accept: application/json, */*;q=0.5
Accept-Encoding: gzip, deflate
Ce-Id: 4F4912F1-6F92-42A6-8FB5-35DA62D2520A
Ce-Source: /example/source
Ce-Specversion: 1.0
Ce-Type: com.example.type
Connection: keep-alive
Content-Length: 34
Content-Type: application/json
Host: localhost:8888
User-Agent: HTTPie/2.1.0
```

Every CloudEvent is meant to have a unique ID. For convenience, I use uuidgen to cook one up; you might need to install it on your OS.

The Ce-Specversion, Ce-Type, and Ce-Source HTTP headers map to specversion, type, and source attributes, respectively. See the discussion on binary content mode in chapter 6 for more on how the headers are used.

Here I use HTTPie's key=value syntax for setting JSON keys.

---

[4] Not to be mistaken for a Kubernetes Ingress component.

```
{
    "message": "This is an example."
}
```

The key=value syntax is automatically transformed into {"key": "value"} for me by HTTPie.

```
HTTP/1.1 202 Accepted
Content-Length: 0
Date: Wed, 24 Jun 2020 23:00:55 GMT
```

If sending a CloudEvent is successful, the broker responds with a 202 Accepted status. This indicates that it processed our CloudEvent. It's not a 200 OK because, by default, the Broker won't itself be generating any kind of response. It's just accepting the CloudEvent on your behalf.

Most of this response is recognizably what we provided in our command. So far, not super interesting. For one thing, how will I know if things go *wrong*? And how will I know things go *right*?

Port forwarding woes

One thing to note here is that the port-forwarding command isn't meant to be a robust connection. If I close the terminal, or put my computer to sleep, or log out, etc., then the port-forwarding connection is dropped. When that happens, you'll see hairy and unhelpful messages like this one:

```
http: error: ConnectionError:
    HTTPConnectionPool(host='localhost', port=8888):
    Max retries exceeded with url: /default/default
    (Caused by NewConnectionError(
        '<urllib3.connection.HTTPConnection object at 0x10f1411c0>:
    Failed to establish a new connection:
    [Errno 61] Connection refused'))
    while doing a POST request to URL:
    http://localhost:8888/default/default
```

It's easily fixed. Run the port-forward command again (listing 8.3), and the connection is reopened.

The main mistake that the Broker can alert you to is *malformed* CloudEvents. Suppose I left out the Ce-Source header that would be mapped to the required source attribute as in this listing.

Listing 8.5   What happens when Ce-Source is missing?

```
$ http post http://localhost:8888/default/default \
    Ce-Id:$(uuidgen) \
    Ce-Specversion:1.0 \
    Ce-Type:com.example.type \
# Ce-Source is missing!
    message="This is an example."

HTTP/1.1 400 Bad Request
Content-Length: 28
```

```
Content-Type: text/plain; charset=utf-8
Date: Wed, 24 Jun 2020 23:15:00 GMT

{
    "error": "source: REQUIRED"
}
```

The `400 Bad Request` status means that I messed something up. Helpfully, the body of the response tells me what went wrong: `"error": "source: REQUIRED"`. Note, however, that you don't get an error key per mistake. Multiple errors are instead concatenated into a single string. For example, if I knock out both the `source` and `type`, I get `"error": "source: REQUIRED\ntype: MUST be a non-empty string"`. I'm not precisely sure why these error messages have inconsistent style, but I do know these are not well-suited to robust, automatic interpretation by monitoring systems. Watch for the `400`s. You'll need to dig a bit when these surface.

Now, how do I know things went *right*? Well, at a surface level, the `202 Accepted` status is sufficient. It tells you "Yes, I have the CloudEvent, and it was well-formed, and I am now going to do *something* with it."

But that's only one hop of the journey. I am, after all, trying to show you how to filter on an attribute of your own creation, which means finding some way to see CloudEvents emerging on the other side of the Broker. I hope that by now you expect that I will use a Trigger, pointed to the CloudEvents player. Almost. I will instead point to a different "show me stuff" system called Sockeye, which reveals a slightly lower-level view than the CloudEvents player does.[5]

Let's install Sockeye and add a Trigger to send events there in the next listing.

Listing 8.6 Setting up and wiring Sockeye

```
$ kn service create sockeye --image docker.io/n3wscott/sockeye:v0.5.0
# ... usual output

$ kn service describe sockeye
Name:        sockeye
Namespace:   default
Age:         10s
URL:         http://sockeye.default.example.com    ◁── The URL for
                                                         Sockeye
Revisions:
  100% @latest (sockeye-rnjhs-1) [1] (10s)
        Image:  docker.io/n3wscott/sockeye:v0.5.0 (pinned to 64c22f)
```

---

[5] "But Jacques," you exclaim, "aren't you a software-making kind of person yourself? Why not write your own thing for the book?" I considered this, but decided against it. I wanted to try and use the tools that already existed when I wrote this book because I knew that I would absolutely *dive* down any rabbit holes I found. I have ADHD. I'm treated for it, but even so, writing the book, the whole book, and nothing but the book, is really hard.

```
Conditions:
  OK TYPE                     AGE REASON
  ++ Ready                    10s
  ++ ConfigurationsReady      10s
  ++ RoutesReady              10s
```

Creates a filter, requiring source to equal com.example.sockeye

```
$ kn trigger create sockeye-source \
    --filter type=com.example.sockeye \
    --sink sockeye
Trigger 'sockeye-source' successfully created in namespace 'default'.
```

There, we've set up everything. Next, I navigate to the URL for Sockeye and take a look-see. As you can see in figure 8.2, it's fairly spartan to begin with.

Figure 8.2   Nothing to see here

So, in the following listing, I'll send Sockeye a CloudEvent (making sure to be one that matches my Trigger filter).

Listing 8.7   Sending a CloudEvent that will appear in Sockeye

```
$ http post http://localhost:8888/default/default \
    Ce-Id:$(uuidgen) \
    Ce-Specversion:1.0 \
    Ce-Type:com.example.sockeye \
    Ce-Source:cli-source \
    message="This is an example."
```

```
HTTP/1.1 202 Accepted
Content-Length: 0
Date: Thu, 25 Jun 2020 21:48:39 GMT
```

And now, when I look at Sockeye, I can see my message. It did indeed get filtered and forwarded based on the `type` attribute.

But I could already show that with the CloudEvents player. How can I filter on a *custom* attribute? Easy! Watch this:

Listing 8.8   Filtering on a custom attribute

```
$ kn trigger create sockeye-example-attr \
    --filter example=fooandbarandbaz \          ⟵   Sets the attribute to
    --sink sockeye                                    example with a value
                                                      of fooandbarandbaz

Trigger 'sockeye-example-attr' successfully created in namespace 'default'.

$ http post http://localhost:8888/default/default \
    Ce-Id:$(uuidgen) \
    Ce-Specversion:1.0 \
    Ce-Type:com.example.type \              HTTP header for the attribute
    Ce-Source:/example/somethingelse \      to be sent over Binary content
    Ce-Example:fooandbarandbaz \      ⟵     mode, prefixed with Ce-
    message="El zilcho"
```

```
HTTP/1.1 202 Accepted
Content-Length: 0
Date: Thu, 25 Jun 2020 21:54:37 GMT
```

The key is that when creating a Trigger, I can use `--filter` for *anything*. Having done that, I can prove that it worked by returning to Sockeye (figure 8.3).

8.2.2 *Nice things that Eventing adds for you*

Look again at figure 8.3 and you'll notice that I was not the only one adding attributes to the CloudEvent. Knative Eventing also adds attributes to CloudEvents that it processes:

- `traceparent`—A defined CloudEvents Extension attribute that I discussed in chapter 6. Adding it here ensures that downstream systems will have tracing information to hang their hat on.
- `time` and `knativearrivaltime`—In the default Broker, `knativearrivaltime` is set when the CloudEvent *first* arrives at one of its two components: the Broker ingress. It's "the moment that Eventing first saw the CloudEvent." The `time` attribute is added in a lower layer: the CloudEvents SDK that Eventing

Figure 8.3   Something to see here

relies on. It's set when the CloudEvent is sent from the Broker to the Subscriber. And it's only there as a stopgap. If I provide my own value for `time`, it will be left alone.

You may be tempted to subtract `knativearrivaltime` from `time` to deduce some measure of processing time. Please don't. For one thing, the processes involved might be running on different machines with clocks that disagree, meaning any such timing will be suspect. For another thing, Eventing records metrics for this exact purpose, as I'll show in the next chapter.

8.3 Sequences

Given enough time, you can use Sources (and Sinks) to wire everything together. But that's inconvenient, so you can use Brokers and Triggers to do it more simply. But at some point, that too becomes a hassle: remembering to provide the right collection of Triggers and being careful to set these up in the correct order. And further, Brokers can become a choke point in your architecture. The answer to this problem is to more directly move traffic from place to place without passing through the central hub. Sequences are the annointed way to fulfill this goal.

Why not just skip the Broker? Well, for one thing, it is a simple and flexible way to get started. Then, as time goes on, you will start to see "desire paths" in your architecture.

You may have seen desire paths in real life, possibly without knowing the name. A beautiful paved path cuts a straight, geometrically pleasing line across a lawn. But around it are the curving naked dirt tracks created by pedestrians walking where they *want* to walk, not where the landscape architects thought they *ought* to work. Wiser institutions wait for the desire path to emerge and *then* pave it.

I raise this analogy because distributed systems are not totally dissimilar. There is the path you thought demand would take through your systems, and there is the path that actually emerged in usage. Using the Broker and Triggers is a good way to find the desire path; once found, it can be swapped for a Sequence.

Another reason to use the Broker/Trigger approach first is that, as of this writing, kn doesn't support Sequences (or Parallels). While I can use it for some of what follows, for the actual Sequences, I will use kubectl.

8.3.1 A walkthrough

I'm going to build a simple Sequence to demonstrate three main points: how Cloud-Events get into a Sequence, how these move through a Sequence, and how these leave the Sequence. I'll be building something like that shown in figure 8.4.

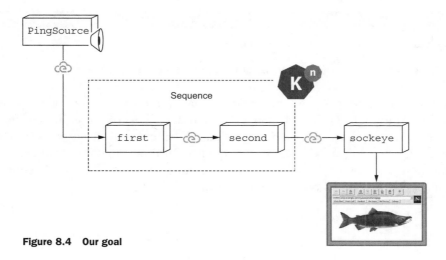

Figure 8.4 Our goal

I assume that you still have Sockeye running, but that you *don't* have a `PingSource` right now. I'll show why in a second. But first, let's drop to some shiny, pretty YAML and look at the Sequence itself, which the following listing shows.

Listing 8.9   Your first `Sequence`

```
apiVersion: flows.knative.dev/v1beta1        kind: Sequence tells Kubernetes what
kind: Sequence                               we're talking about. It then delegates that
metadata:                                    to Knative Eventing for further work.
  name: example-sequence        Everything, even a
                                Sequence, needs a name.

spec:
  steps:        The spec.steps block is the only compulsory part of a Sequence definition.
                It's the truly sequential bit of Sequences, representing a list of destinations
                to which Eventing will send CloudEvents, using YAML's array syntax. Order
                is meaningful: Eventing will read it from top to bottom.

    - ref:                                            The ref here is not accidental. This is the
        apiVersion: serving.knative.dev/v1            same type of record used for sinks (a Ref).
        kind: Service                                 You can either put a URI here or manually
        name: first-sequence-service                 fill out the identifying Kubernetes fields
    - ref:                                            (apiVersion, kind, and name). The latter is
        apiVersion: serving.knative.dev/v1            one thing that kn does for you in other
        kind: Service                                 contexts.
        name: second-sequence-service
  reply:                                      The spec.reply section is also a Ref, but
    ref:                                      only one Ref is allowed here. Unlike
      kind: Service                           spec.steps, this is not an array. You can
      apiVersion: serving.knative.dev/v1      again choose between a URI or Ref.
      name: sockeye
```

What does this get us? Let's ask, in our next listing.

Listing 8.10   Unreadiness revealed

```
$ kubectl get sequence example-sequence
NAME                READY    REASON                  URL                   AGE
example-sequence    False    SubscriptionsNotReady   http://example.com    8s
```

What I can see in listing 8.10 is that the Sequence is not ready, because `Subscriptions-NotReady`. You might fairly and (spoiler!) accurately guess that the Subscriptions in this case are my two Services: `first-sequence-service` and `second-sequence-service`. I have quite rudely defined a Sequence for things that don't yet exist. I will create these now, using a simple example system provided by Knative Eventing for examples like this one (shown in the next listing).

Listing 8.11 Creating the sequential services

```
$ kn service create first-sequence-service \
  --image gcr.io/knative-releases/knative.dev/eventing-contrib/cmd/appender \
  --env MESSAGE='Passed through FIRST'
# ... usual output

$ kn service create second-sequence-service \
  --image gcr.io/knative-releases/knative.dev/eventing-contrib/cmd/appender \
  --env MESSAGE='Passed through SECOND'
# ... usual output

$ kubectl get sequence example-sequence

NAME                READY   REASON   URL                  AGE
example-sequence    True             http://example.com   8s
```

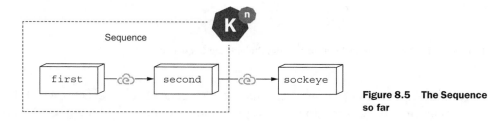

Figure 8.5 The Sequence so far

Figure 8.5 shows where we are so far. What's left is to add `PingSource` as in the following listing.[6]

Listing 8.12 PingSource for Sequence

```
kn source ping create ping-sequence \
    --data '{"message": "Where have I been?"}' \
    --sink http://example-sequence-kn-sequence-0-kn-channel.
      ➥ default.svc.cluster.local

Ping source 'ping-sequence' created in namespace 'default'.
```

Now, if I go to Sockeye, I can see the CloudEvents as those arrive after passing through the Sequence (figure 8.6).

---

[6] You may notice that the `--sink` argument has a whopping great URI passed into it, but my `kubectl get sequence` output from earlier said the URL was `http://example.com`. This was because fitting the `kubectl` output onto the page seemed more important than perfect accuracy.

Figure 8.6   How the CloudEvent looks after passing through the Sequence

Note the appending of `Passed through FIRSTPassed through SECOND`, which I've left in its original buggy form to lend a righteous aura of truly production-grade software to the example. This is the evidence that Knative Eventing shipped the CloudEvent via the two steps defined in the Sequence.

One last point before I move on to a rigorous dissection of Sequences: you don't need Sources to drive a Sequence. The Sequence satisfies the `Addressable` duck type in Knative Eventing. In short, anything that can squirt CloudEvents at the Sequence will work. Such as, for example, the Broker in the following listing.

Listing 8.13   Brokers and Sequences

```
$ kn source ping delete ping-sequence # a bit of tidying up

$ kn trigger create sequence-example \
    --filter type=com.example.type
    --sink http://example-sequence-kn-sequence-0-kn-channel.
      ➥ default.svc.cluster.local

Trigger 'sequence-example' successfully created in namespace 'default'.

$ http post http://localhost:8888/default/default \
    Ce-Id:$(uuidgen) \
    Ce-Specversion:1.0 \
    Ce-Type:com.example.type \
    Ce-Source:/example/pewpew \
    message="PEW PEW!!! "
```

Figure 8.7 presents the evidence. We asked the Broker to filter on `type: com.example`
`.type` and send it the URI for our Sequence. Then it popped out on the other side of
our Sequence and into Sockeye. Figure 8.8 shows what happened diagrammatically.

Figure 8.7 Fishing out our directly created event

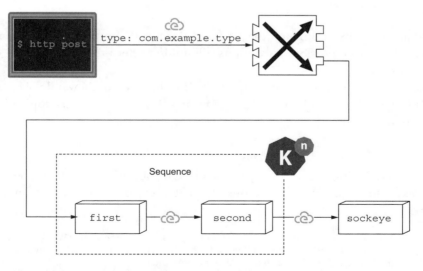

Figure 8.8 The Broker can send CloudEvents to Sequences.

The point here is that you don't need a Source to use Sequences. Anything that can send a CloudEvent over HTTP to a URI can be used to kick off Sequences.

8.4   *The anatomy of Sequences*

And now to pick the bones. The Sequence has three main, top-level components. These include the `steps` and `reply`, which you've already seen, plus `channelTemplate`, which you haven't.

8.4.1   *Step*

What I showed you in the walkthrough was that *steps* contain *destinations*. These are the same stuff as a Sink on a Source. You can either provide a URI, or you can provide some lower-level Kubernetes fields (the Ref) to identify what it is you're addressing.

Suppose I have a Knative Service called `example-svc-1`, which answers to the URL `https://svc-1.example.com`, plus another `example-svc-2`. Then I can define steps for each using either a URI or a Ref, as this listing shows.

> **Listing 8.14   URL take the low road and I'll take the high road**

```
---
apiVersion: flows.knative.dev/v1beta1
kind: Sequence
metadata:
  name: example-with-uri-and-ref
spec:
  steps:
    - uri: https://svc-1.example.com
    - ref:
        apiVersion: serving.knative.dev/v1
        kind: Service
        name: example-svc-2
```

Note that I can mix and match the URI and Ref formats in the same Sequence. My general advice from previous encounters still holds: prefer the Ref to the URI for reasons of flexibility.

And now for a little foreshadowing: the URI or Ref are not the whole of a step. You can also attach error-handling configurations in a `delivery` section, a topic I'll return to later in this chapter.

8.4.2   *Reply*

I have mixed feelings about the `reply` field.[7] On the one hand, it's something you *should* explicitly signal your intentions about. Either your Sequence is intended to

---

[7]   The concept of the reply is inspired by the Reply pattern in Gregor Hohpe's and Bobby Woolf's encyclopaedic *Enterprise Integration Patterns (EIP)* (Addison-Wesley, 2003). In the 1990s, there was an algal bloom of patterns catalogs in the wake of the "Gang of Four." As with most algal blooms, the net result was that oxygen ran low and a lot of it stank. But there are gems in the patterns literature worth mining for, and EIP is a rich orebody indeed.

swallow everything, or it's intended to return an output of some kind to some destination. The presence or absence of `reply` can signal this intention fairly well.

But that's part of my concern: it's only a signal, only a hint. Nothing here is really enforceable, so it's still going to rely on you and your peers being mindful about when it gets used. I expect linters will make this more visible in the future; for now, keep it in mind.

Should you even use `reply`? Yes and no. The case for "yes" is that you should consider it good practice to emit *something* from *every* Sequence. Even if all that gets emitted is a CloudEvent that says "yep, I'm done here." It's far easier to diagnose silent failures when failures cause silence. And if you have in fact adopted that rule, then there needs to be a final place to send that CloudEvent. A `reply` makes that intention explicit, and you can, for example, develop policies like "all Sequences reply to the same place," or "all Sequences that handle Foometreonics without producing anything new must reply with a status to the Foometreonics metrics controller."

Of course, there are many flows in which a reply is what you wanted in the first place. This comes about when you are creating Sequences programmatically, instead of manually laying out everything in advance. While a fixed architecture of Sequences can all reply to the same destination, a Sequence generated by process *X* should probably reply back to process *X*.

There is one small downside to the `reply` versus its `step` sibling. You can't set any `delivery` configuration on it. Put another way: `reply` doesn't provide fallback mechanisms in the way that `steps` can.

8.4.3 *ChannelTemplate and Channels*

I've largely avoided any in-depth discussion of Channels in the book, because I have wanted to focus your attention on higher-level, everyday concerns of developing, wiring, and updating functions or apps. There is a level at which the Channel is an irrelevancy. It's just "a way" that your CloudEvents move from place to place.

A nice argument, as far as it goes. Details matter and, in the evil, backwards, upside-down, topsy-turvy, reversi-blinky, dunky-dorey-flibby-fizzy-bang-y world of distributed systems, details matter even more. In a single-machine system, you didn't need to worry about function calls failing about 1% of the time or just not returning, or returning gibberish, or returning an incompatible type. By and large, things Just Worked, thanks to decades of investment in CPUs, RAM, operating systems, filesystems, compilers, linkers, and on and on. But add a network and a whole bunch of independent machines, and suddenly, it all goes to hell, or at least somewhere adjacent to hell (real estate agents will be here any second to rename it "Distributed Damnation Heights").

So Channels *matter*. You will need to think about these at least once or twice when designing systems based on Knative Eventing. In particular, you'll need to pay attention to the exact guarantees that your Channel implementation offers and decide whether these matter to your users (not you: *your users*).

So what does the ChannelTemplate actually look like? An awkward question for me to answer, because "it depends." Eventing imposes little structure on a ChannelTemplate as the following listing shows.

Listing 8.15   The simplest `channelTemplate` I can remember

```
apiVersion: flows.knative.dev/v1beta1
kind: Sequence
metadata:
  name: example-sequence-in-memory
spec:
  channelTemplate:
    apiVersion: messaging.knative.dev/v1beta1
    kind: InMemoryChannel
    spec:
        # ... anything goes!
  steps:
    # ... steps, etc
```

A ChannelTemplate, embodied here as a `channelTemplate` field on the Sequence, only *requires* that two subfields be set: `apiVersion` and `kind`. These are the ordinary Kubernetes fields of the same name. In the example YAML in listing 8.15, you can see that these sit directly under `spec.channelTemplate`.

But `spec.channelTemplate.spec` can be anything, so far as Eventing is concerned. The reason is that all Eventing does is to scoop out the ChannelTemplate and turn it into a Channel record. Which is what, I suppose, one *would* expect from a template. The `apiVersion` and `kind` fields tell it what kind of the record the template needs to be submitted as. The `channelTemplate.spec` is not validated by Eventing. Instead, `spec` validation is delegated to whatever Channel implementation is installed for that `kind`.

And so, in the example, the `kind: InMemoryChannel` means that Eventing delegates the Channel here to the in-memory Channel that I've used throughout this chapter. But it needn't be so. For example, I might decide to use the Kafka Channel adapter as in this listing.

Listing 8.16   The metamorphosis into `KafkaChannel`

```
apiVersion: flows.knative.dev/v1beta1
kind: Sequence
metadata:
  name: example-sequence-with-kafka
spec:
  channelTemplate:
    apiVersion: messaging.knative.dev/v1alpha1
    kind: KafkaChannel
    spec:
        numPartitions: 1
        replicationFactor: 1
  steps:
    # ... steps, etc.
```

Unlike `InMemoryChannel`, the `KafkaChannel` *does* need a spec. Here it carries configuration information about the connection to a Kafka broker, which you'd not see on an `InMemoryChannel`. And the same is true for other kinds of Channel implementations—their `specs` are going to be specialized for that particular Channel implementation. I'm sorry. You will need to read some docs.

The more cunning sort of developer is now wondering: If I edit my services to use a KafkaChannel, will I get a Kafka broker and so on? The answer is "no," or at least, "no, unless your platform engineers installed it for you." This goes back to my discussion in the previous chapter about provisioning versus binding.

Setting a `channelTemplate` field tells Eventing to perform the binding dance for you, but it won't necessarily provision a Kafka broker. Someone needs to have (1) installed Kafka and (2) installed some kind of software that knows how to read and act on `KafkaChannel` records (much as Knative controllers know how to read and act on Service, Route, Source, Trigger, etc., etc.). The YAML in listing 8.16 will do neither; it's purely a declaration of the binding you want to exist.

So the cunning developer is out of luck, but what about the lazy developer? Is the ChannelTemplate compulsory on my Sequences? Happily, the answer is "no." If you choose not to provide a ChannelTemplate, one is provided on your behalf. Out of the box, Knative Eventing appoints `InMemoryChannel` for you, but platform engineers can override that default for either a namespace or for an entire cluster.

My expectation is that *in general,* as a developer, you won't be setting `channel-Template` often. Consider that you might want to use different Channel implementations and/or different Channel settings in different situations. It might be fine to use `InMemoryChannel` for a development environment, but less acceptable in production. If you manually set a `channelTemplate`, you'd need to either maintain two versions of the record or add some kind of ChannelTemplate ... template ... to your CI/CD infrastructure. Leaving out `channelTemplate` entirely rescues you from this fate.

8.4.4   *Mixing Sequences and filters*

You can mix and match Sequences with Broker/Trigger setups in basically any combination you please. This is again due to the magic of duck typing: a Broker can be a destination for a Sequence `step` or `reply`, and a Sequence can be a destination for a Trigger.

Your mix between these two should reflect the degree to which you have specialized your Sequences. Put another way: Put your stable, well-worn pathways into Sequences. Put Brokers and Triggers either in front of your Sequences (on the principle that filtering sooner is more efficient) or directly after your Sequences (on the principle that a Sequence need not care where its results wind up, but you do). In *theory,* you can have the Broker as a step inside a Sequence, but down this path lies confusion and madness; any bugs in your filter definitions will cause half-baked Sequence executions to pile up and place pressure on the overall system.

Effectively, I'm arguing that Brokers still wind up as a switchboard for your architecture, but that the switching is now between Sequences, not individual Services. As a particular Sequence→Broker→Sequence pathway becomes heavily used, you can consider whether to update it to become Sequence→Sequence, or even whether to combine the two Sequences into a single Sequence.

8.5   *Parallels*

Parallels resemble Sequences, but there are some ergonomic differences. Let's look at the next listing.

Listing 8.17   Seems familiar

```
---
apiVersion: flows.knative.dev/v1beta1
kind: Sequence
metadata:
  name: example-sequence
spec:
  steps:
    - uri: https://step.example.com
---
apiVersion: flows.knative.dev/v1beta1
kind: Parallel
metadata:
  name: example-parallel
spec:
  branches:
    - subscriber:
        uri: https://subscriber.example.com
```

In Sequence, each entry in the spec.steps array is a destination—a URI or Ref, as desired.

In Parallel, the top-level array is spec.branches. It's not an array of destinations. It's an array of branches.

Each branch has one required field: a subscriber, which is a destination. Again, you can use a URI or Ref here.

So why the extra level of indirection via `subscriber`, between `spec.branches` and `uri` or `ref`? It exists because a branch can actually carry quite a bit of optional configuration:

- `filter`—A specialized destination that can pass or reject a CloudEvent. Much to my chargrin, it's *not* the same as filters in a Trigger.
- `reply`—It's our old friend, Reply, but you can set one for each and every branch if you like.
- `delivery`—I'm still holding this over until later, but it's the same type as the one found in a `step`.

The two meanings of "filter"

The filter in Parallel is not the same as a filter on a Trigger. It's just a completely different, completely unrelated thing. It's an unfortunate naming choice.

Instead of being a rule that's applied by a Broker or Broker-like system, a Branch's filter is a *destination*. It's a URI or Ref to which a CloudEvent is sent by Eventing and then whatever lives at that destination has to give a thumbs up or thumbs down.

If you squint a bit, the combination of filter and subscriber is a lot like a two-step Sequence. The CloudEvent flows to the filter, then from the filter onto the subscriber.

But realistically, the filter and the subscriber are both fully-fledged processes; anything the filter can do, the subscriber can, and vice versa. In terms of expressing developer *intention*, it's a nice separation and resembles guarded clauses. But the overhead of routing through a process to get a pass/fail decision can prove to be fairly hefty.

When should you use a filter on Parallel branches? My view is that you shouldn't, with one exception. If your subscriber is an expensive or limited resource, you will want to shed as much unwanted demand *before* you reach it. For example, I might be running a system where I want to send some small fraction of CloudEvents to an in-memory analytics store for further analysis. Rather than inserting everything coming off the wire, I would prefer to shed load *before* reaching the database. In this scenario, the filter is a useful ally.

8.5.1 A walkthrough

The simplest thing you can do with a Parallel is to pretend it's a Sequence. I'm going to demonstrate by recreating a single-step Sequence in the following listing. Note carefully that indentation is meaningful and also annoyingly finicky.

Listing 8.18   The contents of `parallel-example.yaml`

```
---
apiVersion: flows.knative.dev/v1beta1
kind: Parallel
metadata:
  name: example-parallel
spec:
  branches:
  - subscriber:            <──  The subscriber is in
      ref:                       the same branch
        apiVersion: serving.knative.dev/v1    definition as ...
        kind: Service
        name: first-branch-service
    reply:                 <──  ... the reply.
      ref:
        kind: Service
        apiVersion: serving.knative.dev/v1
        name: sockeye
```

I hate to belabor this point, but the indentation is important. The `reply` is not part of the `subscriber`—it's a peer to it.

Now I can create a trio of Service (for `subscriber`), a Trigger (to manage the flow of CloudEvents into the Parallel), and the Parallel itself as does the following listing.

Listing 8.19   Setting up a Service and a Trigger

```
$ kn service create first-branch-service \
  --image gcr.io/knative-releases/knative.dev/eventing-contrib/cmd/appender \
  --env MESSAGE='FIRST BRANCH'
```

```
# ... service creation output

$ kn trigger create parallel-example \
  --filter type=com.example.parallel \
  --sink
  ➥ http://example-parallel-kn-parallel-0-kn-channel.
  ➥ default.svc.cluster.local
Trigger 'parallel-example' successfully created in namespace 'default'.

$ kubectl apply -f parallel-example.yaml

parallel.flows.knative.dev/example-parallel created
```

Note that I used `kn` where I could, resorting to `kubectl` where I must. What do I expect to happen next?

Recapping: I have a Trigger to send matching CloudEvents to the Parallel's URI. The Parallel sends that CloudEvent on to the Service I created, which appends FIRST BRANCH to whatever CloudEvent message passes it by. Then the CloudEvent should pop up in Sockeye.

Let's poke things in the following listing. Then we can see what comes out in Sockeye (figure 8.9).

Listing 8.20   Poking the Parallel

```
http post http://localhost:8888/default/default \
  Ce-Id:$(uuidgen) \
  Ce-Specversion:1.0 \
  Ce-Type:com.example.parallel \
  Ce-Source:/example/parallel \
  message="Here is the Parallel: "
```

Figure 8.9 shows that I got a Sequence-like outcome. But doing what Sequence already does is not what Parallels were built for. I want to fan-out identical copies of the CloudEvent to multiple `subscribers`. It's not hard, as this listing shows.

Listing 8.21   Sending to multiple branches

```
---
apiVersion: flows.knative.dev/v1beta1
kind: Parallel
metadata:
  name: example-parallel
spec:
  branches:
  - subscriber:
      ref:
        apiVersion: serving.knative.dev/v1
        kind: Service
        name: first-branch-service
    reply:
      ref:
```

```
          kind: Service
          apiVersion: serving.knative.dev/v1
          name: sockeye
  - subscriber:
      ref:
          apiVersion: serving.knative.dev/v1
          kind: Service
          name: second-branch-service
    reply:
      ref:
          kind: Service
          apiVersion: serving.knative.dev/v1
          name: sockeye
```

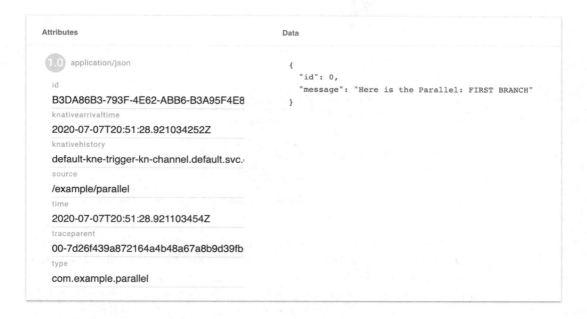

Figure 8.9   Receiving the CloudEvent in Sockeye

In listing 8.22, I've decided to add a new `second-branch-service` as a `subscriber`. But both branches still `reply` to the sample place—Sockeye. Conceptually, it looks like that shown in figure 8.10.

Listing 8.22   Updating my example

```
$ kn service create second-branch-service \
  --image gcr.io/knative-releases/knative.dev/eventing-contrib/cmd/appender \
  --env MESSAGE='SECOND BRANCH'
```

```
# ... service creation output

$ kubectl apply -f parallel-example.yaml

parallel.flows.knative.dev/example-parallel configured

$ http post http://localhost:8888/default/default \
  Ce-Id:$(uuidgen) \
  Ce-Specversion:1.0 \
  Ce-Type:com.example.parallel \
  Ce-Source:/example/parallel \
  message="Here is the Parallel: "
```

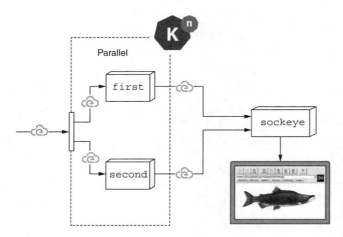

Figure 8.10   The conceptual model of Parallels

Figure 8.11 shows the outcome: two copies. In this case, the Parallel made two copies of the CloudEvent and sent those to each of the branches (fan-out). Then those branches sent their reply to the same instance of Sockeye (fan-in).

You might be unconvinced that this is what actually happened. To prove it, I will create a second Sockeye service and have one of the branches reply to it. I'll use some fancy kubectl trickery to avoid boring you with almost identical YAML (see the next listing).

Listing 8.23   Adding a second Sockeye and updating the Parallel

```
$ kn service create sockeye-the-second \
    --image docker.io/n3wscott/sockeye:v0.5.0

# ... service creation output

$ kubectl patch parallel example-parallel \
  --type='json' \
  -p='[{"op":"replace", "path":"/spec/branches/1/reply/ref/name",
            "value":"sockeye-the-second"}]'

parallel.flows.knative.dev/example-parallel patched
```

```
$ http post http://localhost:8888/default/default \
    Ce-Id:$(uuidgen) \
    Ce-Specversion:1.0 \
    Ce-Type:com.example.parallel \
    Ce-Source:/example/parallel \
    message="Here is the Parallel with parallel replies: "
```

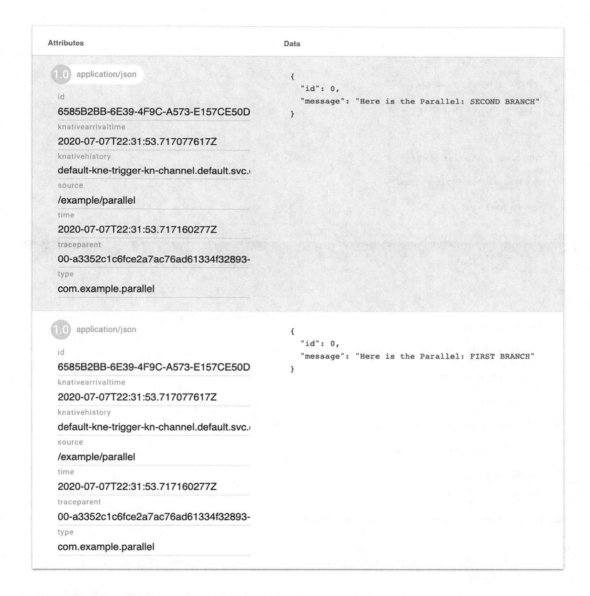

Figure 8.11   Parallel CloudEvents in parallel

I've opened both `sockeye` and `sockeye-the-second` in two browser windows (figure 8.12), I can see that the Parallel did in fact send the CloudEvent to two different `reply` destinations.

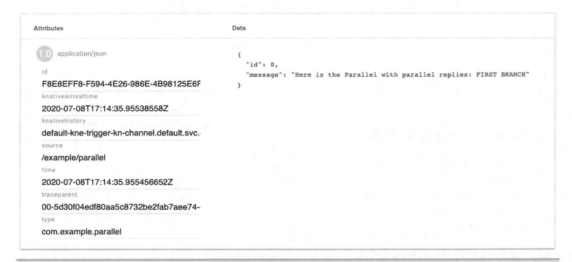

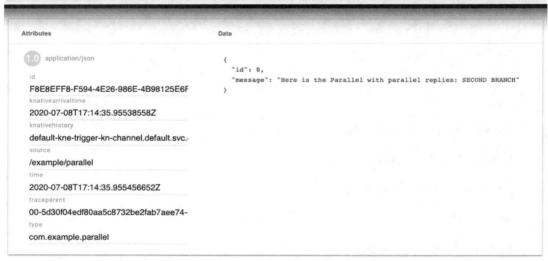

Figure 8.12   Receiving the CloudEvent in two Sockeyes

I hope that you notice that these two CloudEvents (figure 8.12) are close to being identical.

But I should apologize, because my example here is not very well behaved. I now have two CloudEvents with identical `id`, `source`, and `type` fields; any conforming implementation is within its rights to treat these as the same logical CloudEvent, even though these are physically distinct. When working with Parallels, you need to take this into consideration when you have a fan-in. For example, if one branch does some kind of conversion to a different CloudEvent, you are largely in the clear. But if you are merely adding to a CloudEvent, as I did in listing 8.23, you need something stronger. Either you should be `filtering` so that logical duplicates don't arise, or you should be changing one of `id`, `type`, or `source` according to what makes the most sense.

You might now be wondering whether you will need to laboriously provide a `reply` for every branch. The answer is "no," for two reasons. First, you just might not care about the fate of a CloudEvent sent to a branch's `subscriber`. You can leave `reply` out entirely; CloudEvents are delivered as HTTP requests, but no HTTP reply is expected or dealt with. Second, you can provide a single top-level `reply` for the whole Parallel. This acts as a default for *every* branch. You can override on any branch by providing a `reply` specific to that branch, but otherwise, anything coming out is sent on to the top-level `reply`. That means I can rewrite my YAML to be slightly shorter, as in this listing.

Listing 8.24 A simpler fan-in

```
---
apiVersion: flows.knative.dev/v1beta1
kind: Parallel
metadata:
  name: example-parallel
spec:
  reply:
    ref:
      kind: Service
      apiVersion: serving.knative.dev/v1
      name: sockeye
  branches:
  - subscriber:
      ref:
        apiVersion: serving.knative.dev/v1
        kind: Service
        name: first-branch-service
  - subscriber:
      ref:
        apiVersion: serving.knative.dev/v1
        kind: Service
        name: second-branch-service
```

You may note that in listing 8.24, I have placed `reply` above `branches`. To be clear: it doesn't make any difference to Knative Eventing. I'm doing that because it's less likely to cause failures due to confusing indentation. If you put `spec.reply` below `spec.branches` in a YAML file, the visual difference between "this `reply` belongs to this branch" and "this `reply` belongs to this Parallel overall" is slight. It can be easily missed in an editor or during a code review.

As with Sequence, it's possible to set the `channelTemplate` field on a Parallel at the top level. And like Sequence, it's possible to place `delivery` settings, in this case, on each branch. Which means I must at long last reveal what the hell I'm talking about.

8.6   *Dealing with failures*

> *A popular bumper sticker states that phenomena can and will spontaneously occur. (The bumper sticker uses a slightly shorter phrase.)*
>
> —Timothy Budd

Marcus Aurelius was a fairly calm and collected person, as far as Roman Emperors go, and he took the time to explain his reasons for remaining calm. But he only had to deal with powerful and warlike enemies, crushing economic difficulties, and a psychopathic son. He never had to deal with distributed systems. Or even the un-distributed kind, come to that. Had this been the case, his famous *Reflections* might have been *Rants* instead.

Yes, things fail. They fail so much. So often. It's maddening. And it has been so for decades (some of my favorite laments are *A Critique of the Remote Procedure Call Paradigm* and *A note on distributed computing*). Eventing provides allowances for failure by implementing some common patterns: retries, retry backoffs, and dead-letter destinations.

What I'm going to describe now is the `delivery` type. It can be found in either a Sequence step or in a Parallel branch. The following listing demonstrates this.

Listing 8.25   Sequence steps and Parallel branches with `delivery` settings

```
---
apiVersion: flows.knative.dev/v1beta1
kind: Sequence
metadata:
  name: example-sequence-delivery
spec:
  steps:
  - uri: http://foo.example.com
    delivery:
      # ... TBD!
---
apiVersion: flows.knative.dev/v1beta1
kind: Parallel
metadata:
  name: example-parallel-delivery
spec:
  branches:
  - subscriber:
      uri: http://bar.example.com
    delivery:
      # ... also TBD!
```

So what's *in* a delivery field? Basically, it covers two things: retries plus backoffs, and dead letters. I'll use a Sequence as my running example because it's slightly less busy, but the discussion applies just as well to Parallels.

> **NOTE** All the `delivery` configurations I will discuss are optional. You can, in theory, have an empty `delivery` block. It will parse and pass validation, but it will look silly.

8.6.1 Retries and backoffs

Failure is inevitable and, in a distributed system, failure becomes close to normal. Retries are a simple coping tactic for failed operations. You typically don't want to do it forever, so a first stop in retry logic is to cap the number of times an operation is retried as this listing indicates.

Listing 8.26 Delivery retries

```
---
apiVersion: flows.knative.dev/v1beta1
kind: Sequence
metadata:
  name: example-sequence-delivery
spec:
  steps:
    - uri: http://foo.example.com
      delivery:
        retry: 10
```

A `delivery.retry` field is a simple integer. It's defined as the minimum number of retries attempted, in addition to a first failed attempt to deliver a CloudEvent. In the YAML example in listing 8.26, I have `retry: 10`. If everything goes wrong, there will be *at least* 11 requests made, not 10.

It can be *more than* 11, because Channel implementations are allowed to deliver a CloudEvent more than once. This may come as a surprise. It's common for various queue or message systems to have "at-least-once" guarantees. It's much less common for these to provide "at-most-once" guarantees. "Once-and-only-once" guarantees, which is the intersection of the two, is arguably impossible, depending on how one defines the problem. This is partly why CloudEvents encourage you to provide unique id, source, and type fields—to help downstream systems to sanely ignore re-deliveries. Especially since retry might be causing deliveries which are *successful*, but where the delivery result is incorrectly considered to be *failed*. In that scenario, retries cause the same CloudEvent to be sent multiple times.

Speaking of problems with retries, you probably don't want to try again instantly. Done poorly, these lead to "retry storms," where hapless upstream systems get mashed into paste by rampaging mobs of impatient downstream systems. Systems that are buckling under load are notoriously bad at having spare non-buckled capacity to communicate their general state of buckled-ness. When a system is merely teetering on the edge of overload, overly aggressive retries will just push it over.

Hence the need for backoffs, configured with `backoffDelay` and `backoffPolicy`. The `backoffDelay` is a duration expressed in a simple format (e.g., "10s" for 10 seconds). The `backoffPolicy` describes how that duration will be used.

If I set `backoffPolicy: linear`, retries are made after fixed delays. If I have `backoffDelay: 10s`, retries are attempted at 10 seconds, 20 seconds, 30 seconds, and so on.[8]

If I set `backoffPolicy: exponential`, retries take twice as long between each attempt. With the same `backoffDelay: 10s`, attempts are made at 10 seconds, 20 seconds, 40 seconds, and so on. The `backoffDelay` provides a base value that is raised by a power of 2 on each attempt—1x, 2x, 4x, 8x, ..., etc.

8.6.2   *Dead letters*

All the retries may be for naught, however. One option might be to just give up entirely and let the CloudEvent evaporate into thin air. For some use cases that is perfectly fine. Losing a metric point now and then is *OK*, if your use case is to summarize single points into statistics, because the presence or absence of one data point won't affect results enough to be worth worrying about. But if you're losing a lot of Cloud-Events, or if you're using CloudEvents to encode information where the individual event has a high independent value ("the server has crashed with a stack overflow," "the customer added a hat to their shopping cart"), then accepting silent lossiness is not ideal.

More likely than either of those, to be honest, is just plain old bugs. You made changes that work in testing but somehow glitch in production. Two versions of the software are running during deploy, and versions from v1 → v2 are working fine, but from v2 → v1 (which you don't test because oops) are silently failing. You spin up an ancient log and replay it to recover an old record, but the schema changed and there's a weird bug in version 22.7 of the DangNabbit.io proxy, and you forgot to sacrifice the right goat, and now every 121st message vanishes, but you don't notice it because your software rolls up in multiples of 120 ... you get the idea.

The `deadLetterSink` is an additional guardrail against unforeseen problems like these. You nominate a place where, if all regular delivery attempts fail, a CloudEvent will wind up. And then, I hope, you have monitoring turned on to annoy you the first time that ever happens, because dead letters are a Big Bad Red Flag that you need to investigate. And you should also, periodically, inject a known bad CloudEvent to see if it does, in fact, wind up in the dead letter sink.

The dead letter pattern isn't perfect. The sink can be down, or it can be the victim of sudden hammering when some high-demand service vanishes and it begins to receive everything. But it's invaluable as a safety net. When it's there and when it's

---

[8]   If you're using `linear`, consider picking a prime number duration—11 seconds instead of 10, 997 milliseconds instead of 1 second, etc. Prime numbers are less likely to be coincidentally synchronized across many backoffs than are non-prime numbers.

working, you get the *real* CloudEvent that failed to get somewhere, which gives you more clues as to *why*.

8.6.3 *The bad news*

There's a small fly in the `delivery` ointment: it's meant to be interpreted and acted on by Channel implementations, but it's *optional* for these to do so. As of this writing, only the `InMemoryChannel` actually does so. Not my favorite state of affairs, but I expect it will change rapidly as Eventing becomes more widely used and supported.

Summary

- Brokers are responsible for two things: acting as a sink for CloudEvents and for acting on Triggers.
- Channels are responsible for transporting CloudEvents between Knative Eventing components such as Sources, Brokers, and Sequence steps or Parallel branches.
- Triggers have filters that are exact matches on particular attributes.
- Sequences can wire multiple linear steps without needing to route everything through the Broker.
- Sequences have steps, replies, and ChannelTemplates.
- You can use Triggers to enter a Sequence.
- Parallels can fan-out and fan-in a CloudEvent to multiple services without needing to route through the Broker.
- Parallels have branches, channelTemplates, and replies.
- Branches have filters. These are not the same as Trigger filters.
- Branches can have a `subscriber` and a `reply`.
- Failure policies can be described on Parallel branches and Sequence steps using `delivery`.
- Delivery can have retries, backoff delays, backoff policies, and a dead letter sink.
- Delivery does not, however, have to be implemented by a channel. Only the `InMemoryChannel` implements delivery configuration at time of writing.

References

- Matt Moore, Grant Rodgers, et al., "Knative Broker Specification," http://mng.bz/yYoq
- Andrew S. Tanenhaum and Robbert van Renesse, "A Critique of the Remote Procedure Call Paradigm" (Department of Mathematics and Computer Science, Vrije University, 1987)
- Jim Waldo, Geoff Wyant, et al., "A note on distributed computing" in *International Workshop on Mobile Object Systems* (Springer, Berlin, 1996). Originally published as SMLI TR-94-29, "A Note on Distributed Computing" (Sun Microsystems Labs, Inc. Tech Reports, 1994). Available online: http://mng.bz/MX1n

From Conception
to Production

What I've spoken about so far is Knative-as-Knative. But software doesn't exist in a vacuum—it has to be made and run. To wrap up the book, I'd like to touch lightly on the basics of what comes next in the real, day-to-day work we have to do. Pivotal Tracker calls these "Chores": things you need to do to make things tidier around the place, so that you can move faster in the future.

We tend to neglect these as a profession. In the kitchens of Michelin-starred restaurants, perfectionist chefs are taught to obsess over *mise en place*—"Everything in its place." Before cooking a dish, they want every knife, every herb, every surface, every ingredient, every utensil, every pan, every gas burner, everything, to be clean and sharp and fresh and in the same place as it always is.

Right now you have your software, on to which I imagine you have lavished all the attention and love that you can muster. And you've now learned about Knative, which is a system that can launch, run, scale, and wire together your software.

Now it's time to talk a little bit about the connective tissue. The first is getting your software into Knative. The second is observing its behavior. I've talked about how *you* are the controller that sits above Knative and your software (figure 9.1). Well, here's the part where I describe two arrows: getting your software into production (actuation) and seeing how it behaves in production (sensing).

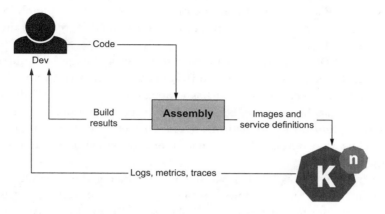

Figure 9.1 You are in the loop too.

9.1   *Turning your software into something runnable*

Let's first look at the business of converting source code into a container image. A common practice is to use a Dockerfile and hang everything off the `latest` tag. I am not a fan. My views are that you can't trust registry tagging, and you should at least consider alternatives to Dockerfiles.

What alternatives? There are many. But before I arbitrarily pick the one that by pure coincidence I have previously worked on, I will take a moment to insist that you *always use digests.*

9.1.1   *Always use digests*

This is important and will take some time to explain. Stay with me.

Deep down, a container image is a bag of tarballs, sticky-taped together with some JSON. When you hand over a Service to Knative to run, it delegates down to Kubernetes to run. Kubernetes, in turn, delegates down to its "kubelet" agents to run. The kubelet agents will, in turn, turn to an actual container runtime, such as `containerd`, to actually truly run the software.

The most important input given by the container runtime is a reference to the container image that it should run. As I've noted before, a single image can be referred to in many ways. But ultimately, the runtime needs to convert the reference into a URL, fetch metadata about the image, then fetch the blobs that contain the image's actual contents.

So far so good, but fetching blobs isn't free. So container runtimes will typically maintain a local cache of images and layers. If a runtime has fetched `example/foo` before, it won't bother dialing out when asked again to run a container using the example/foo image. It picks up what it has on disk and uses that.

Here is the problem: example/foo is a name that doesn't have an exact, stable meaning. From moment to moment, it can refer to different images, depending on which system you ask. Each container runtime in your cluster can completely disagree about which image is example/foo:latest. And these can *all* disagree with the registry that you just pushed to.

But there's more! Different names can refer to the same image (as in identical, byte-for-byte), but still be considered to be different by container runtimes. So when the container runtime checks to see if it has example/foo in its cache, there is *no guarantee whatsoever* that the example/foo in its local cache is the same as the one in the registry it is configured to fetch things from. In fact, you have no guarantees about what it means whatsoever. All you've had to enforce consistency, up until now, is lucky timing.

Kubernetes tried to make this less painful by introducing the imagePullPolicy configuration item, which Knative allows you to set. In particular, it lets you set this to Never (uninteresting for our purposes), to IfNotPresent, or to Always. At face value, these should be enough. But they are not.

Setting IfNotPresent collides with the problem of names being mutable. It ensures that, over time, a cluster will wind up with multiple versions of an image in circulation, because different Nodes will fetch from the registry at different points in time.

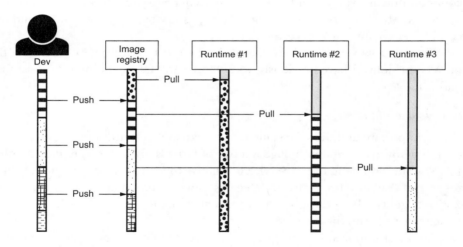

Figure 9.2 Without digests, this nightmare will eventually be yours.

So how about Always? It still doesn't solve the inconsistency problem, because it's only applied when containers are being launched from the image. If a copy of your software runs for a long time on node #1, then later a second copy is launched on node

#2, you can still wind up with inconsistent versions. And, of course, `Always` means you enjoy no gains from caching.

Figure 9.2 lays out a scenario where, at the end, there are *five different versions* of an image in circulation. It's easy for the developer's mental model to be far out of sync with the actual state of the cluster. This scenario can occur whether you use `Always` or `IfNotPresent` policies, depending on the exact order of events.

The *only* way out of this mess is to use fully-qualified (also called "digested") image references, which means image references that include a digest (e.g., `@sha256:abc-def123…`). Unlike any other form of reference, an image reference with digest refers to one, and only one, container image. That reference is immutable and exact. What it refers to today, it will refer to tomorrow, next week, next year. That's because it's based on the image *itself*, the actual and exact bytes. It doesn't rely on a registry definition. It can be computed from the image. Change one bit and the digest becomes radically different.

> **NOTE** "What about tags?" you ask. "What's wrong with `example/foo:v1.2.3` if my CI system is generating trustworthy image tags?" The problem is that tags are mutable. There's no guarantee that `v1.2.3` will be the same image tomorrow. In fact, tags can be *deleted*. Basically, relying on tags is begging for bitrot.

For folks using raw Kubernetes, fully-qualified image references plus `IfNotPresent` are both safe and efficient. But that requires you to exercise discipline in how you use Kubernetes resources like Pods or Deployments. Kubernetes itself enforces no policy about the image references you provide; it basically pipes those directly to the container runtime and leaves any dire consequences to rest upon your immortal soul.

Knative takes an important step towards sanity on your behalf: If you submit a fully-qualified image reference, it will use it. If you don't, Knative will *create one for you*. That is, it will resolve a loose reference like `example/foo` into a fully-qualified one like `docker.io/example/foo@sha256:2ad3…` whenever a Revision is created.

This is critical to ensure that Revisions are consistent and stable. It ensures that every running copy of a Revision uses an identical container image. And it ensures that if you use that Revision again in the future, you will still get the same container image.

However, I think you can and should go further. Anywhere that you create an image, or define a record with an image reference, *you* should *always* use the fully-qualified version. That's because the gap between "an image was created" and "the image is used" can be quite wide. Knative can't see backward into your CI/CD pipeline. When it resolves an image reference, it can only see what is in a registry at that instant. That might or might not be what you think it is. But if you use the fully-qualified reference, you are guaranteed to get the exact image you expect.

9.1.2   *Using Cloud Native Buildpacks (CNBs) and the pack tool*

Maybe you have built a container image before, and maybe you haven't. If you have, you probably used a Dockerfile. My views on Dockerfiles are unflattering. I recognize that these are easy to start with and almost universal in their usage. But these are also arguments for Bash, that plucky platoon of hacks masquerading as a programming language. Dockerfiles are like the first stage of a Saturn V rocket. They got things off the ground, but they aren't the destination. I want to stretch you a little.

There are numerous alternatives in circulation. My favorite is Cloud Native Buildpacks. I opened this book with the Onsi Haiku Test:

```
Here is my source code.
Run it on the cloud for me.
I do not care how.
```

To me, buildpacks were always the bedrock of this promise, because these meet you at the *code*. Deployment artifacts come and go, but there will always be code. Learning to write a Dockerfile requires a short tutorial to begin with, and then a fair few longer tutorials to create safe, efficient, secure images.

But to use buildpacks, historically, you just typed git push heroku or cf push and that was *it*. In fact, that is *still* it. All the clever optimizations and security mechanisms are done for you.

So I like buildpacks. And the easiest way to use Cloud Native Buildpacks (CNBs) is the pack CLI.

Listing 9.1   `helloworld.go`

```go
package main

import (
    "fmt"
    "net/http"
)

const page = `
<!DOCTYPE html>
<html>
<head>
    <title>Hello, Knative!</title>
</head>
<body>
    <h1>Hello, Knative!</h1>
    <p>See? We made it!</p>
</body>
</html>
`

func main() {
    fmt.Println("OK, here goes...")
```

```
    http.HandleFunc("/", func(w http.ResponseWriter, r *http.Request) {
        fmt.Fprintf(w, page)
    })
    http.ListenAndServe(":8080", nil)
}
```

Suppose I have a simple, single-file Go program, like the one in listing 9.1. All it does is write a fixed chunk of HTML into the response of any HTTP request. And I must begrudgingly accept that Go makes it easy to write quick-n-dirty programs like this one. No frameworks and no needing to select an HTTP library. Just import from the standard library and you're off to the races.

Each buildpack can understand how a given language ecosystem looks. In the case of Go, a buildpack can rely on the convention that the `main()` function in the `main` package will be what needs to be run at launch. And then it does the rest for you in terms of turning that into an efficient, reproducible container. Listing 9.2 shows how a `pack build` looks.

Listing 9.2 Tightly packed

```
$ pack build eg --path ./

tiny: Pulling from paketo-buildpacks/builder
f83c9afda5ef: Already exists
b839abbd6cba: Already exists
96914eecdef7: Already exists
14b23dd2b80a: Already exists
4e4e7b1ce15e: Pull complete
849c3a63fdbf: Pull complete
4c2d02b49fab: Pull complete
001fccc4ad38: Pull complete
ea92060a149b: Pull complete
1d8713b8430e: Pull complete
0c33a3ac2707: Pull complete
7c29e2eef350: Pull complete
5e64e68d5e00: Pull complete
7bec636aa549: Pull complete
f3452e1989b0: Pull complete
3e71995b619f: Pull complete
07cdcccb0c6c: Pull complete
7fc970a75c69: Pull complete
89732bc75041: Pull complete
Digest: sha256:da8da3bcce3919534ef46ac75704a9dc
   618a05bfc624874558f719706ab7abb1
Status: Downloaded newer image for gcr.io/paketo-buildpacks/builder:tiny
tiny-cnb: Pulling from paketobuildpacks/run
Digest: sha256:53262af8c65ac823aecc0200894d37f0
   c3d84df07168fdb8389f6aefbc33a6d7
Status: Image is up to date for paketobuildpacks/run:tiny-cnb

===> DETECTING
paketo-buildpacks/go-dist  0.0.193
paketo-buildpacks/go-build 0.0.15
```

> Here pack uses Docker to run a builder image that contains buildpacks and all the machinery needed to run those. Docker then fetches paketo-buildpacks/builder to use for the rest of its work. Docker's output is piped through pack.

> The first step in running buildpacks is detection to identify which buildpack to run. Each buildpack looks at the source code and says whether it can do something with it. In this case, the paketo-buildpacks/go-dist and paketo-buildpacks/go-build buildpacks have raised their hands.

Checks to see if there are any previous build outputs that can be reused. I've used pack on this machine before, so common layers created by /go-dist and /go-build are already present.

```
===> ANALYZING      <
Previous image with name "index.docker.io/library/eg:latest" not found
Restoring metadata for "paketo-buildpacks/go-dist:go" from cache
Restoring metadata for "paketo-buildpacks/go-build:gocache" from cache
```

If the analyze step identifies that there are previously built layers that don't need to be rebuilt, the restore step picks these up for use in the rest of the build.

```
===> RESTORING      <
Restoring data for "paketo-buildpacks/go-dist:go" from cache
Restoring data for "paketo-buildpacks/go-build:gocache" from cache
```

The build step is closest to what you'd do yourself, either by hand or in a Dockerfile. It picks a language or compiler version, runs a build command, and calculates what command is needed to run the executable it creates. This output varies according to language ecosystem. If you provide a Java project with Maven, for example, there's often quite a lot of output around fetching dependencies and running the build. It also needs to create a fairly detailed command to effectively configure the JVM for efficient use of a container environment.

```
===> BUILDING       <
Go Distribution Buildpack 0.0.193
  Resolving Go version
    Candidate version sources (in priority order):
      <unknown> -> ""

    Selected Go version (using <unknown>): 1.14.6

  Reusing cached layer /layers/paketo-buildpacks_go-dist/go


Go Build Buildpack 0.0.15
  Executing build process
    Running 'go build -o
      /layers/paketo-buildpacks_go-build/targets/bin -buildmode pie .'
      Completed in 1.18s

  Assigning launch processes
    web: /layers/paketo-buildpacks_go-build/targets/bin/workspace


===> EXPORTING                                          <
Adding layer 'launcher'
Adding layer 'paketo-buildpacks/go-build:targets'
Adding 1/1 app layer(s)
Adding layer 'config'
*** Images (9d6e49ea8c1b):
      index.docker.io/library/eg:latest
Reusing cache layer 'paketo-buildpacks/go-dist:go'
Adding cache layer 'paketo-buildpacks/go-build:gocache'
Successfully built image eg
```

Once building is complete, the export step gathers together all the layers that were restored, along with any new or updated layers that were built, and assembles those into the final container image.

By default, `pack` gives you a fairly chatty account of its activities. When run using a Docker daemon, it also passes through any output given by Docker.[1] Its chattiness lets me point out a few landmarks in listing 9.2.

The result of the command I gave in listing 9.2 is a container image I can run with a local Docker daemon using `docker run -p 8080:8080 eg`. That's because at the end of the process, the image has been added to Docker's local cache of images. But that's no good for Knative, which lives somewhere else and relies on registries to store and serve up container images.

That's solvable, though, using the `--publish` option. As the name suggests, it causes `pack` to publish a built container image to a registry. Having done that, it becomes possible to use `kn` to run it as the following listing proves.

Listing 9.3 Build it, run it, see it

```
$ docker login --username <your username>
Password: <your password>
Login Succeeded

$ pack build <your username>/knative-example -path ./ --publish
# ... build output
Successfully built image <username username>/knative-example

$ kn service create knative-buildpacked \
  --image <your username>/knative-example
Creating service 'knative-buildpacked' in namespace 'default':

# ... Service creation output

Service 'knative-buildpacked' created to
 ➥ latest revision 'knative-buildpacked-rfplb-1' is available at URL:
http://knative-buildpacked.default.example.com
```

Upon clicking the URL, you'll see our jaunty greeting. As proof I didn't fool you, try editing it (may I suggest some knock-knock jokes?) and running through this cycle again.

> ### Some more dev-friendly tools
> There are developer-oriented tools that can reduce this cycle to a single command. Some of the ones I know of are
>
> - ko (https://github.com/google/ko), which can take a Kubernetes YAML template and a Golang project and handle all the steps of rendering the YAML, building an image, putting the image into a repository, and applying the YAML. One of

---

[1] It may seem odd that I am describing Cloud Native Buildpacks, for which "it isn't Docker!" is a prime marketing point, while saying that the reference CLI tool is using a Docker daemon to do its thing. The point here is that the daemon isn't strictly necessary to run buildpacks, but it's handy for local development when available (some companies forbid Docker on their workstations). When building on clusters, however, buildpacks can run *without* needing access to a Docker daemon, or to other container runtimes. This is a huge security win.

(continued)

ko's nicest features is that the YAML it writes contains fully digested image references.

- kbld (https://get-kbld.io/) is similar to ko, but is not specialized for Golang. Instead, it can use either Dockerfiles or Cloud Native Buildpacks to perform its build steps. Like ko, kbld renders fully digested image references.
- Tilt (https://tilt.dev/) and Skaffold (https://skaffold.dev/) are two tools that aim to provide a complete environment for developing container-based applications. These each do what ko or kbld do, but more as well. For example, both support live update functionality so that you don't have to run any commands while you iterate on your code. Skaffold supports Cloud Native Buildpacks as a first-class feature.

The real beauty of CNBs is less about this first run experience and more about the long term gains. Some of it is due to security—having a standard means of assembling images makes it easier to audit what's running inside the box.

But it also improves performance for building *and* running. For building, it's possible for CNBs to replace only layers of an image that need replacing, without needing to rebuild everything else. Dockerfiles don't have this property. Changing any layer invalidates all the layers that follow. This shows up most strikingly when upstream images are updated. Have 100 images that start with FROM nodejs? Then you live in fear of each new version of that image, because it will force 100 rebuilds … if indeed you even have a way to *tell* that you need to run 100 rebuilds. But a Cloud Native Buildpack can simply "rebase" the container image you already have onto the new base layers. No rebuilds required. The update can be done in seconds.

And it's faster at runtime too. Different images can have identical layers that are shared, and container runtimes are smart enough to take advantage of that to cache more efficiently. Using buildpacks means that images are more alike than not. These have more layers that are exactly identical. Rather than having 50 different variants of Ubuntu floating around, you only have one. Caches are more likely to be warm, network traffic is reduced, and disk space less bloated.

9.2   *Getting your software to somewhere it runs*

I'm going to assume now that you have built the image and pushed it. How does it get into a running Revision? One way is to use kn. That works well for development, but less so for production. What I want now is a means to go from "I have a shiny new container image" to "it's rolling out progressively." I'll work through a simple example here.

I'll use Concourse (the self-described "Continuous Thing-Doer") for the simple reason that it's awesome and I like it better than alternatives. Some folks prefer Spinnaker, Tekton, the thousand or so projects that have some kind of joint custody over the name "Argo," or self-flagellation with Jenkins. What I outline should be broadly adaptable to each of these.

I could do all of this with kn and the various commands I covered in chapter 4. However, I'm going to demonstrate doing most of the CI/CD shuffle with YAML, because otherwise, I won't be invited to give conference talks.

Which now brings me to a fork in the road. My aim in this book has been to use kn as much as possible. The interactivity is a boon for learning and playing, but not without cost. Each change you make through kn is in some sense lost. You run the command, but without your own working memory or discipline to check before every action, drift can emerge between *your* desired world and the desired world as Knative understands it. For example, other teammates may be using kn on the same Service as you. Or, more prosaically, you used it yesterday and forgot about a change that you made. And today, you plough ahead with a faulty mental model.

The way around the sins of interactivity is to separate the business of defining the desired world from the act of expressing it to the system. That's where YAML comes back in force. While you can and should use kn for development work, or to quickly and easily inspect a Knative system, for production work, you should instead be using tools that directly submit chunks of YAML. For example, instead of kn update service, you would edit your service-whatever.yaml as required and then use kubectl apply. For a developer iterating at a terminal, this is pure overhead. But for a team working together to modify production systems, it becomes essential for general sanity.

I'm going to do the simplest, dumbest progressive deployment scheme that I can manage.[2] I will have a Service that has two traffic tags: current and latest. Each time the Service's image changes, I will pull it down and edit the Service to use the new image. That will trigger the creation of a new Revision. I'll modify the Service again to redirect 5% of the traffic to it. I'll wait a short while and then check for reachability. If that succeeds, I'll edit the Service a third time to make the new Revision into the current Revision. See figure 9.3 for a sequence diagram.

Figure 9.3 has a lot of arrows, but that's just because I'm showing the bits where I meticulously push everything through a Git repository. In the figure

1. A new version of an image is uploaded to a registry.
2. The deployment system detects the new image version's availability.
3. The deployment system fetches the existing YAML of the Service from a Git repository. It changes the image key to point to the newest version of the image.
4. The modified YAML is pushed back into the Git repository.
5. The push back into the repo is a new commit, so another deployment system job lights up to handle it.
6. It's a simple job: apply the YAML to the cluster (here called "Knative").
7. Knative sees that the Configuration has changed. That means it needs to create a new Revision.
8. It also sees that the YAML includes updated traffic, directing 5% to the latest Revision.

---

[2] Pray for me, because my natural urge is to Do It Right in a thousand-page thunderclap of minutiae.

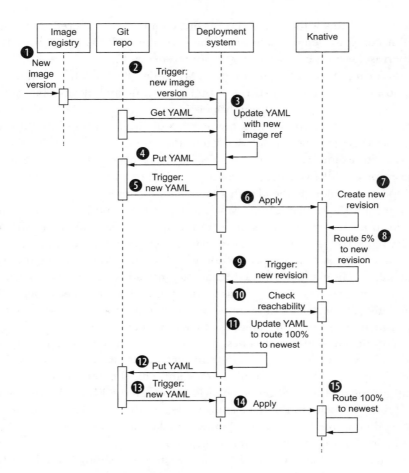

Figure 9.3   Sequence of deployment

9   The deployment system wakes up again when Knative finishes stamping out the new Revision.

10   It checks the direct reachability of the new Revision.

11   If the new Revision is reachable, the YAML gets updated again. This time the newest Revision is tagged as `current` and set to receive 100% of traffic. The `latest` tag is set to 0% traffic. The previous Revision is just dropped from the traffic block altogether.

12   The newest revision of the YAML gets pushed back into the repo, and …

13   That triggers …

14   Another apply operation.

15   Knative updates its Routes from the new YAML and now the whole waltz is complete.

Be aware that this is a toy example

Some caveats are in order: I left out a lot of things you'd need for a Serious, Grown-Up Deployment System. For one thing, I didn't define any kind of rollback here, although you can imagine one at the reachability check. For another thing, I skipped directly to routing 5% traffic to the newest Revision without checking reachability *first*. Nowhere does the system pause to let the newest Revision warm up, I don't check for errors, and so on and so forth.

But these are the humdrum problems. The exciting problem is that this approach leads to "race conditions." If two images are pushed in rapid succession, you could have two different pipelines churning. But the actual Knative Service is a shared resource. If you scribble on this diagram places where the later image goes ahead of the earlier image, your toe hairs will turn gray and ominous tones will tone ominously. You can deal with this by having some lock on the Service, so that only one image version at a time can proceed through the flow.

For reasons of space, I won't go into a full example of this flow with Concourse, or Tekton, or Argo, or Jenkins, or whathaveyou, but I can at least provide you with an example repo (https://github.com/jchesterpivotal/chapter-9-example). The thrust is to provide short scripts for the two main transformations that are needed. First, I need something to render a YAML template. Second, I need something that can check reachability.

If you don't have at least three tools that somehow process YAML, hand in your Cloud Native Architecture merit badge at the next meetup. The most common approach is text templating, which is easy to start with, but which typically leads to utter and entire madness, because YAML has significant whitespace. You *could* just render JSON in a single line, which is technically valid YAML, minus whitespace issues. But that would be uncool.

Less common, but more protective of sanity, are higher-order tools that treat YAML as a kind of compilation target. There are many of these as well. People I trust have sung to me the virtues of Dhall (https://dhall-lang.org/), Pulumi (https://www.pulumi.com/), and CUE (https://cuelang.org/), but I haven't used any of those. Myself, I use ytt (https://get-ytt.io/), because it's relatively simple and so am I.[3]

> **NOTE** By way of disclosure, I work (as of this writing) for the same company—VMware, via the Pivotal acquisition—that sponsors the development of ytt, kapp, and kbld. Did I choose these out of corporate loyalty? Not really, no. I picked ytt because I like it better than Helm or Kustomize. I picked kapp because it recreates and reimagines many of the things I liked about BOSH, a powerful tool that remained obscure. But it is fair to say that I was *aware* of these tools because these were first developed by people I have some connection to.

---

[3] Strictly ytt refers to the actual command-line tool; the embedded language is a restricted Python dialect called Starlark (https://github.com/bazelbuild/starlark). Informally, it's probably not an important distinction for you or me, unless you're already using Starlark for another purpose as well.

The following listing shows the template I will use to generate my Service.

Listing 9.4   A `ytt` template for a Knative Service

Loads ytt's data library. In turn, that searches for various kinds of inputs (command-line flags, environment variables, or files) to snapshot at the start of execution. A key gotcha is that in order to refer to a variable through data, it needs to first be loaded from a file. I give an example of such a file in listing 9.5.

This line loads the JSON library.

```
#@ load("@ytt:data", "data")

#@ load("@ytt:json", "json")

#@ resource = json.decode(data.read("resource.json"))
---
apiVersion: serving.knative.dev/v1
kind: Service
metadata:
  name: knative-example-svc
spec:
  template:
    spec:
      containers:
        - name: user-container
          image: #@ data.values.digested_image
    traffic:
    - tag: current
      revisionName: #@ resource['status']
        ['latestReadyRevisionName']

      percent: #@ data.values.current_percent
    - tag: latest
      latestRevision: true
      percent: #@ data.values.latest_percent
```

Loads a file (here resource.json), representing my existing Service. In my Concourse pipeline, this file is created by a Kubernetes resource performing a get on my behalf. But you could achieve largely the same with kubectl get ksvc knative-example-svc -o json > resource.json. The json.decode() converts the JSON file into a key-value structure (aka dictionary or hash).

Updates the image itself. As I showed in chapter 3, this is a change that leads Knative Serving to spit out a new Revision. The key is that I provide the fully digested image reference myself. By putting it here, I guarantee that the exact image intended is the exact image that will be deployed.

Pulls out the latestReadyRevision value from the existing Service. At the first pass, this will be the last version of the Service that was sent to Serving for processing. More to the point, it's the most recent Revision that's actually working. I tag it as current.

I have a percentage target for current and ...

... a percentage target for latest.

In listing 9.5, I provide variables that ytt will inject into my template. The fact is that I want to set *all* of these at the command line. But to do so, I need to define their existence in a file. To me it seems like a silly gotcha, but I haven't dug deeply into why it's this way. It, at least, provides a kind of requirement to provide a declarative form of the variables somewhere in a repo.

Listing 9.5   values.yaml for the template

```
#@data/values

---
digested_image: '[ERROR! Image missing!]'
```

Tells ytt that what follows is usable for data. This little incantation is actually detected by the load("@ytt:data", "data") in listing 9.4.

Sets broken defaults to force me to override these variables. If I didn't, it would be too easy to create a system that appears to do what I want, but which subtly ignores some configuration I thought I was setting. I've had too many multi-day bugs that came to some helpful default being set somewhere in a codebase. Never again. Obnoxious failures are a better option than silent deceptions.

```
current_percent: -111

latest_percent: -999
revision_name: '[ERROR! Revision name missing!]'
```

← **A variation on theme. The percentage variables are numerical, so using an ERROR! message here is not ideal. Instead, I set impossible values that I know Knative Serving will reject. I use III and 999 because these are visually distinct and obviously out of place.**

So now I have my template.yaml and my values.yaml. I can use `ytt` to render this into a final output provided by the following listing.

Listing 9.6 Using `ytt` is easy as 1-2-3

```
$ ytt \
  --file template.yaml \
  --file values.yaml \
  --file resource.json \
  --data-value-yaml
    ➥ digested_image='registry.example.com/foo/bar
    ➥@sha256:ee5659123e3110d036d40e7c0fe43766a8f071
    ➥68710aef35785665f80788c3b9' \
  --data-value-yaml current_percent=90 \
  --data-value-yaml latest_percent=10
```

← **Uses the --file flag to pass in the files that will be needed: the template file, the values file, and a resource file (representing the JSON representation of my existing Service).**

← **Here I use --data-value-yaml to pass individual values into ytt. One for the image reference and one each for traffic percentages.**

```
apiVersion: serving.knative.dev/v1
kind: Service
metadata:
  name: knative-example-svc
spec:
  template:
    spec:
      containers:
      - name: user-container
        image: registry.example.com/foo/bar
          ➥@sha256:ee5659123e3110d036d40e7c0fe43766a8f071
          ➥68710aef35785665f80788c3b9

  traffic:
  - tag: current
    revisionName: knative-example-svc-q6ct6
    percent: 90
  - tag: latest
    latestRevision: true
    percent: 10
```

← **By default, ytt spits out the rendered YAML into STDOUT. I did that here so you can see the results, but for the next step, you would need to pipe the output into a file. Something like ytt ... > service.yaml.**

In listing 9.6, a design principle of `ytt` is that you need to give it everything it will need *before* it does anything. There's no file access, no network access, no clocks. Nothing is added which might make the template non-deterministic. Of course, this might seem boilerplate-y, especially if you start working with directories with many files. In that case, you can flip over to passing directory paths instead of file paths as I did with the `--file` flag.

In a proper CI/CD situation, the next step is to commit the change to a repository. This establishes a log of intentions over time, as I discussed early in chapter 3. If you're following a multi-repo approach, then put these into a separate, special-purpose repository.

Listing 9.7 shows the commands I've settled on for use in commit-as-part-of-CI tasks. It's more involved and verbose than what I do at a local workstation. Like a trial lawyer, I am asking `git` to state information "for the record"—in this case, gathering logs that can help me with bug fixing or historical understanding in the future.

Listing 9.7   Committing changes in a chatty fashion

Assuming I ran ytt ... > service .yaml in a previous step.

```
$ git add service.yaml
$ git status --verbose
```

Here I ask for a verbose status. By itself git status only shows me the first part of this information (which branch I am on, whether I am up to date, and which files are going to be part of a commit).

```
On branch master
Your branch is up to date with 'origin/master'.

Changes to be committed:
  (use "git restore --staged <file>..." to unstage)
      modified:   service.yaml

diff --git a/services/rendered/service.yaml
    b/services/rendered/service.yaml
index 040a075..c94aee9 100755
--- a/services/rendered/service.yaml
+++ b/services/rendered/service.yaml
@@ -9,10 +9,10 @@ spec:
     spec:
       containers:
       - name: user-container
-        image: registry.example.com/foo/bar
                @sha256:ee5659123e3110d036d40e7c0fe43766a8f0716871
                0aef35785665f80788c3b9
+        image: registry.example.com/foo/bar
                @sha256:43e8511d2435ed04e4334137822030a909f5cd1d37
                044c07ef30d7ef17af4e76
    traffic:
    - tag: current
-     revisionName: knative-example-svc-2415l
-     percent: 100
+     revisionName: knative-example-svc-n9rfd
+     percent: 90
    - tag: latest
      latestRevision: true
-     percent: 0
+     percent: 10
```

By using --verbose, I also get a diff of the changes that are staged. I could achieve something similar by using git diff --cached, but to future devs it probably looks too magical. git status --verbose gives me everthing I want here, especially the before-and-afters as it was seen at the time.

```
$ git commit -m "Update rendered service YAML." \
             -m "This commit is made automatically."
```

Using multiple -m flags removes any need to understand heredoc sorcery.

```
[master 606a816] Update rendered service YAML.
 1 file changed, 2 insertions(+), 2 deletions(-)

$ git --no-pager log -1
```

This command spits out the commit as I would see it in a log, without getting stuck in less. CI/CD systems vary on how terminal-y their runtime environments are, so it's useful to force the issue with --no-pager.

```
commit 606a8168e12356789ee016843dbcabcf24c79127 (HEAD -> master)
Author: Jacques Chester <jchester@example.com>
Date:    Thu Aug 20 18:57:32 2020 +0000

    Update rendered service YAML.

    This commit is made automatically.
```

When using `git status --verbose`, the information printed duplicates the Git repository itself, doesn't it? Yes, it does, but only if the `git push` to the repo is successful. It could fail or error out and I'd have no independent way to know what was *meant* to happen. And, of course, nobody has ever made a force push that they later regretted, right?

At the end of listing 9.7, I have a commit that can be pushed into a repo. In the example Concourse pipeline, I use `git-resource` to do this, but you can use a script or whatever other system makes sense to you. My goal is to *record my intent*, which in this case is twofold:

- Change the current exact container image to a different exact container image
- Split traffic so that only 10% of traffic flows to the `latest`

Having pushed my YAML into a Git repository, the next step is to do something with it. Opinions vary on what comes next. Some vendors sell tools that perform a `git pull` *inside* of each cluster, then turn to the API Server to apply whatever was pulled. Other vendors instead sell tools that perform a `git pull` *outside* of clusters, which then turn to the API Server to apply whatever was pulled.

A surprising amount of light and heat attends to this distinction, probably because "push-based GitOps vs. pull-based GitOps" is, for folks involved, connected to their meal ticket. I myself like the external push approach. It allows me to use a single tool like Concourse, Tekton, Jenkins, or whatever for all my "things-happen-in-some-kind-of-order" needs. More importantly, it does not depend on the stability of the target cluster. GitOps from within a cluster cannot dig you out of a misbehaving cluster—you'll need to do that from the outside if things go bad. But if you're going to do so, why not smooth the road you will wind up on anyhow?

The main counterarguments are about scale and security. For *scale*, the idea is that many clusters pulling from Git are more scalable than a single system pushing to many clusters. I don't fully disagree, actually, but I note that you can quickly reach thresholds at which GitHub or GitLab become unwilling to cooperate. It's also the case that you can scale the pushing apparatus pretty easily. And again, you'll need that capability if you roll out a change that wedges *all* your clusters, so why not prepare it now?

Which leaves *security*—that your central system will need too many privileges for too many things. Again, I partially agree, but at a per-cluster level it's a wash. Kubernetes does allow some fine-grained slicing and dicing with its RBAC stuff, but in practice, many folks become impatient and slather `cluster-admin` everywhere (a tip: don't). You need to treat secrets as special anyhow, you need to manage your portfolio of sensitive key material anyhow, so … why not prepare it now?

In any case, I will demonstrate the "push" approach. Broadly, this just means that I'm going to use `kubectl apply`. If you were wondering whether I would use `kn`, the answer is no. Or, more precisely, not for *applying the change*. First, slinging YAML explicitly is the province of `kubectl`; `kn` is meant for interactive use. Second, `kn` likes to take a little extra control of your Services. In particular, it takes control of Revision names itself, rather than letting Knative Serving pick one automatically. This turns out to play poorly with a YAML-based approach. You can't cross the streams.

This is *fine* in CI/CD land. You're not doing anything interactive. Precision control of settings is a good tradeoff against convenience if your changes are automated and repeatable. In theory, I could have my CI/CD pipeline take charge of Revision names for me. A lot of places have naming schemes that make that capability necessary. I won't demonstrate it here though.

Now I'll apply the YAML and then look at what I have in listing 9.8. The interesting part of that listing is that I've split traffic between two Revisions, distinguished by their digest.

Listing 9.8   Applied YAML

```
$ kubectl apply -f service.yaml
service.serving.knative.dev/knative-example-svc configured

$ kn service describe knative-example-svc
Name:          knative-example-svc
Namespace:     default
Annotations:   example.com/container-image=registry.example.com/foo/bar
Age:           1d
URL:           http://knative-example-svc.default.example.com

Revisions:
   90%    knative-example-svc-8tn52 #current [7] (4m)
          Image:  registry.example.com/foo/bar
            @sha256:e1bee530d8d8cf196bdb8064773324b2
            435c46598cd21d043c96f15b77b16cb3 (at e1bee5)

   10%    @latest (knative-example-svc-vlsw6)
            #latest [8] (4m)
          Image:  registry.example.com/foo/bar
            @sha256:c9951f62a5f8480b727aa66815ddb572
            34c6f077613a6f01cad3c775238893b0 (at c9951f)

Conditions:
   OK TYPE                AGE REASON
   ++ Ready               2m
   ++ ConfigurationsReady 4m
   ++ RoutesReady         2m
```

> The current tag now receives 90% of traffic. It's the previous Revision, the one that I already know works.

> Here's the full image definition for current.

> Sets @latest to 10%. That's traffic flowing to …

> … the newest Revision.

In a Canary rollout or progressive rollout, you would now be monitoring the rate of errors being returned to end users. No point releasing something new if it's not working for your customers. And you might get fancy and monitor performance as well, to see if there are any unwanted regressions.

But, in the interests of space, I will just tap on the front door to see if anyone is home (the fancy name is "reachability test"). At my own workstation I like to use HTTPie's `http` command, but for CI/CD purposes, `curl` is more traditional and so widely available that I use it in the following listing.

Listing 9.9   Knock knock!

```
$ curl \
  --verbose \
  --fail \
  http://latest-knative-example-svc.default.example.com

Begin
* Rebuilt URL to: http://latest-knative-example-svc.default.example.com/
*   Trying 198.51.100.99...
* Connected to latest-knative-example-svc.default.example.com
  ➥ (198.51.100.99) port 80 (#0)

> GET / HTTP/1.1
> Host: latest-knative-example-svc.default.example.com
> User-Agent: curl/7.47.0
> Accept: */*
>
< HTTP/1.1 200 OK
< content-length: 159
< content-type: text/html; charset=utf-8
< date: Fri, 21 Aug 2020 21:54:46 GMT
< x-envoy-upstream-service-time: 3291
< server: envoy
<

<!DOCTYPE html>
<html>
<head>
    <title>Hello, Knative!</title>
</head>
<body>
    <h1>Hello, Knative!</h1>
    <p>See? We made it to the end!</p>
</body>
</html>
* Connection #0 to host latest-knative-example-svc.default.example.com
  ➥ left intact
```

How did I know the URL? Through the magic of convention. In chapter 4, I discussed that Knative Serving creates routable names for tags. I know that whatever lives at @latest will be reachable at **latest**-whatever-whatever.

The `curl` command is fairly taciturn, so using `--verbose` shows me the full exchange. As with `git status --verbose`, this leaves some historical clues in my logs that can be vital later on. The `--fail` flag tells `curl` that if it gets an HTTP 4xx or 5xx error code, it should exit with a non-zero exit code. Not using `--fail` is an easy gotcha in a CI/CD scenario. You expect the task to blow up if the target is unreachable, but `curl` takes the view that it won't pass judgement on HTTP error codes unless you tell it to.

In a CI/CD system I'd go through the same cycle of edit-YAML, commit-YAML, push-YAML, pull-YAML, apply-YAML. If I use the same commands as previously, the logic automatically promotes `latest` to `current`. I can set the traffic percentage to 100%. Tada, I've completed my rollout!

Deployment by traffic percentage is different from deployment by instances

I will bring up again that Revisions and Services provide a toolkit for rolling out changes that are divided by *traffic*, not by *instances*. Nowhere in my description is anything like "20 instances `current`, 2 instances `latest`." Instead, I tell Knative to send percentages of traffic, after which the Autoscaler is responsible for providing the right number of instances. Any given request has a *set* probability of being routed to one or the other. If instead rollouts are based on instances, the probabilities depend on at least two factors: the ratio of instances and the relative performance of instances.

This is one of those "the-hairsplitters-aren't-crazy" moments. Splitting traffic by percentage has two big benefits. The first is granularity. If I have three instances behind the `current` tag and two instances behind `latest`, then in a purely random selection, I have a 60% chance of one and 40% of the other. But what if I want to try out the new Revision without risking so much of my traffic on it? In this scenario, it will be difficult to get below 33% going to `latest`, all things being equal. If I have 100 instances, this wouldn't be a problem, but a lot of the time, you won't have 100 instances lying around.

Which leads to the second advantage of traffic splitting by percentages: it controls the variable of changed performance between Revisions. If I had a 3:2 split of `current` to `latest`, and `latest` is struggling to keep up with demand, there isn't much I can do. But if the split is by traffic, then I can at least hope that horizontal scaling by the Autoscaler will get me out of a tight spot.

An idea I would like you to think about is that the combination of these key features—autoscaling and percentage routing—acts like a pump for variability. If instances are fixed, then variability in your software's performance is seen by end users. If the autoscaler is allowed to work, then it will pump variability away from users back into the Kubernetes cluster, which is better suited for absorbing it.

9.3 *Knowing how your software is running*

Now I have a thing that's running. But is the thing doing the thing I think it does?

This is the problem of monitoring, or observability, or whatever your vendor has taught you to call it. Yes, there are differences and nuances that folks on Twitter go to the mats over. I will use all these terms interchangeably in order to most fairly share out causes of annoyance. First, what *is* monitoring?

Monitoring is like a fire department. You don't need it. Until, one day, you need it very much indeed.

At this point, one learns that (1) you don't have what you need to fight fires, and (2) it is difficult to get what you need to fight fires when *everything is on fire*. It only took hundreds and hundreds of years for various civilizations and nations to sort out the whole firefighting business; with any luck, we brave developers should be able to knock that down to around 50 years, plus or minus a century for flamewars.

Put another way: make inspectability, probeability, monitorability, instrumentability, observability, what-the-hell-ability a part of your design. Nag product managers and tech leads. Be merciless. And read! There are dozens of excellent books on this topic; I enjoyed *Practical Monitoring* and *Site Reliability Engineering*.

It is the current fashion to say that there are "three pillars of observability": logs, metrics, and traces. I feel that this is a post-facto rationalization invented by vendor marketing rather than some inevitable structure arising from fundamental physical laws. But it's also how most tools fit themselves into the market and how most folks have learned to think of things. Logs and metrics are the oldest; traces have only really emerged out of necessity.

The story of logs, metrics, and traces in Knative is really just the story of logs, metrics, and traces *for Kubernetes*. Knative doesn't guarantee to provide any particular mechanism for these, but it does try to provide standards-ready facilities. For example, Knative's own components create logs, gather metrics, and plumb through traces. But those logs and metrics and traces won't be *kept* anywhere centrally accessible by Knative. Someone else needs to set up the infrastructure.

This problem is largely delegated to vendors who rebundle Knative into some sort of commercial offering. That's because vendors tend to include some sort of monitoring tool into their offerings, so they add the adaptors to pipe stuff into their tools. Hopefully, your platform engineers have installed and configured *some* sort of monitoring tool. Likely, they have for their own needs, but do check to see if they offer observability tools to you as well.

It's worth noting something here: Knative's own components are good citizens, publishing all kinds of information that can be slurped into various tools and systems. But Knative can't magically fit those onto *your* software. For deep insight, you still need to write logs, emit metrics, and add spans to traces. In particular, you may need to add instruments that show what the *user* is experiencing in terms of their own goals. Sure, the front page loads fast, but how long does it take for an insurance application to trigger a confirmatory email? How long between a stockout at the retail store and a warehouse order?

Nevertheless, the information that Knative collects automatically is still helpful, so I'm going to spend some time doing an introductory tour. I'll be using some widely used tools (Kibana, Grafana, and Zipkin) because these were the easiest for me to set up. Any resemblance to a tool endorsement, living or dead, is purely accidental.

9.3.1   *Logs*

First, I'm going to look at Kibana for logs (figure 9.4). This is Kibana's most general, simplest view, Discover.

1 Here you can enter search queries. The syntax is relatively simple for basic `variable: value` sorts of searches. A blank search means "I want to see everything."

2 This histogram shows how many log entries were received in each time bucket. It's mostly helpful for showing patterns once you begin to narrow your search.

3 Here's the detail view for each log entry. Knative takes great care to log things out in a common JSON format, which makes it easy for logging systems to parse and extract fields. You can see the result here, which is that Kibana marks field names in **bold**.

4 What field names, you might ask? Here's where you can see every field name that has so far been encountered by Kibana.

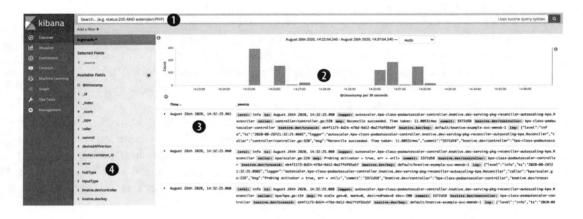

Figure 9.4   The default Kibana "discovery" screen

This is not even skimming the surface, of course. By clicking into fields or particular log entries, I can perform all manner of drilling down. Many tools will show an interface like this one, but I don't think a parade of fast decaying screenshots is the best use of your time.

What I *will* do is talk about what Knative logs on your behalf. As I noted before, Knative keeps solid logs of its own activity. It also emits logs for stuff flowing to and from your Revisions. Most importantly, every log entry is liberally slathered with additional data and context. For example, it adds a `commit` field that identifies the exact version of Knative being used.

Table 9.1 is a list of some Knative-provided fields you can use to narrow your search. Not all fields are available in all logs.

Table 9.1 Some available logging fields

Field name	What it's for
`knative.dev/key`	The namespace and name of the Service or Revision. For example, if my `foo-example-svc` Service is in the `bar-example-ns` namespace, the `knative.dev/key` will be `bar-example-ns/foo-example-svc`. You'll probably use this more than anything else when debugging.
`knative.dev/name` and `knative.dev/namespace`	These seem like they cause confusing overlap with `knative.dev/key`. The main difference is that these are fields set by Knative's components when emitting their logs. When it's about something *you* provided (a Service, a Revision, etc.), you'll see the `/key` instead.
`knative.dev/traceid`	As the name suggests, this is where Knative propagates traces. It's mostly used by tracing systems like Zipkin. But for quickly narrowing to "just this one request, please," it can quickly narrow logs as well.
`knative.dev/kind` and `knative.dev/resource`	The sort of *thing* that's being talked about—a Service, a Revision, and so on. Truthfully, these carry similar information. I prefer `/kind` but `/resource` seems more widely used.
`knative.dev/operation`	This comes from the `webhook` component, acting in its admission control role. The permissible values are `CREATE`, `UPDATE`, `DELETE`, and `CONNECT`. This is useful for diagnosing permissions errors. Also a possible filter for stuff you'd like to copy into independent auditing logs.
`knative.dev/controller`	Where individual Reconcilers identify themselves in logs. I know the name is confusing, but remember what I said in chapter 2: `controller` is a process, Reconcilers are logical processes (e.g., `route-controller` or `kpa-class-podautoscaler-controller`).

If you or your platform engineering team have enabled request logging, you will get additional fields you can look at under the `httpRequest.*` keys. Out of the box, you get `latency`, `protocol`, `referer`, `remoteIp`, `requestMethod`, `requestSize`, `request-Url`, `responseSize`, `serverIp`, `status`, and `userAgent`. It also prints any `X-B3-Traceid` headers it sees on incoming requests.

9.3.2 *Metrics*

Knative instruments quite a few things for metrics collection, so if you have a place where the metrics drain to, there's a lot to work with. As before, the data falls into two broad categories: metrics about Knative itself and metrics about things running *on*

Knative. Both are useful to suss out whether bottlenecks are in Knative or in what you're running on it.

Lots of folks use Grafana to plot metric values over time. Figure 9.5 shows metrics gathered for the HTTP requests of a Revision under load. Figure 9.6 shows how Reconcilers are behaving during the same load test.

Figure 9.5   A Grafana dashboard of HTTP request behavior

As with logging, metrics are collected with additional labels to identify what they're about. When we talk about "100 requests per second," the question is 100 requests to *what*? Is that to the whole cluster, to one Revision, to one instance of one Revision? The labels added to metrics make it possible to drill down or roll up your data as needed.

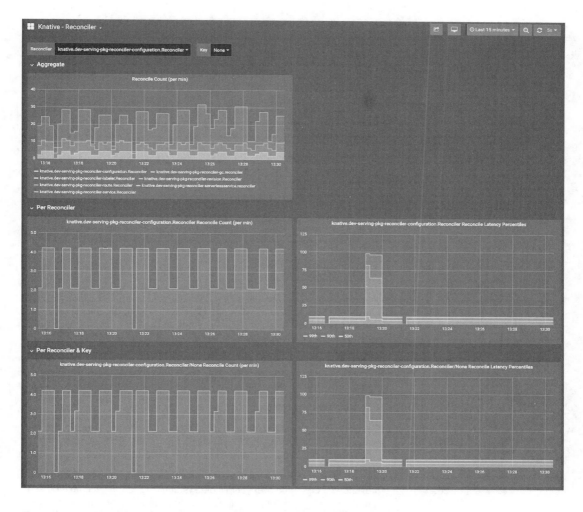

Figure 9.6 A Grafana dashboard that shows Knative Serving Reconciler behavior

Table 9.2 describes metrics labels that can be used to group metrics values. Tables 9.3, 9.4, and 9.5 describe various metrics that are collected by default.

Table 9.2 Labels you can see from metrics

Label name	What it's for
`project_id`, `location`, and `cluster_name`	Identifiers pulled from the underlying cloud provider. On GCP, for example, `project_id` is your project ID (amazing, I know). Similarly, `location` is used for things like availability zone. The `cluster_name` is the provider used for the cluster that Knative is running on top of.
	Right now these are best supported on GKE; hopefully, other providers will catch up.

Table 9.2   Labels you can see from metrics *(continued)*

Label name	What it's for
namespace_name	The namespace where the subject lives. If you're using namespaces to divvy up clusters, this will be an essential key.
container_name	Knative Serving typically names your container user-container, and Queue-Proxy is under queue-proxy. This is useful when trying to distinguish between metrics provided by each.
pod_name	The underlying Kubernetes Pod that represents a Revision instance. These change because of autoscaling. Pods spun up for Revision instances will come and go. This can be useful for live investigations but not as useful for reviewing historical data.
service_name, configuration_name, and revision_name	Set by Knative Serving, these are the most useful all-round keys to partition your metrics, because (ideally!) your collection of Services and Revisions is related to some kind of underlying user problem.
response_code	Serving sets this—literally the HTTP response code. Useful to drill on a particular status code.
response_code_class	Serving sets this as one of 1xx (informational), 2xx (successful), 3xx (redirects), 4xx (client errors), or 5xx (server errors). Grouping like this is helpful to get the "big picture" of whether things are OK or not. A user suddenly faced with 501 or 503 isn't very interested in the distinction. In terms of detecting errors quickly, neither should you.
response_error	An error *label*, rather than a status code. Mostly nice for quick eyeballing. It won't show up for non-error situations (such as a 200).
response_timeout	This boolean indicates whether the request timed out.
trigger_name and broker_name	Eventing sets these to help you group metrics for different Triggers and Brokers. They're useful for seeing how particular components are behaving.
event_type and event_source	Eventing sets these as well. They're useful for seeing the effects of an event type or source over your whole system. You can also combine these with broker_name or trigger_name to understand how an event type or source is affecting particular processes.

Table 9.3   Request metrics

Metric name	What it's for
request_count	The number of requests as seen by the Queue-Proxy.
app_request_count	The number of requests as seen by your process. This figure typically lags behind request_count because of queueing.
request_latencies	Request-response latency distribution as seen by the Queue-Proxy.
app_request_latencies	Request-response latency distribution as seen by your process. This has the same distribution buckets as request_latencies.

Table 9.3   Request metrics *(continued)*

Metric name	What it's for
queue_depth	How many requests are waiting in the Queue-Proxy to be processed. This is the connecting number between request_count and app_request_count. See chapter 5 for a discussion of how these bits fit together.

Table 9.4   Knative Serving metrics

Metric name	What it's for
request_concurrency	The number of concurrent requests as seen by the Activator. This number is useful in live investigations, but don't try to base trend alerts on it. If you remember chapter 5, the Activator is sometimes on the data path and sometimes off the data path, so this metric can swing a lot without reflecting a shift in arriving demand.
request_count	The count of requests as seen by the Activator. The caveat about the Activator coming and going applies.
request_latencies	A distribution of request latencies as seen by the Activator. Not to be confused with the metric collected on Revisions of the same name—you can distinguish by checking whether the metric has labels for a Revision or not. The distribution has the same buckets as request_latencies and app_request _latencies gathered for Queue-Proxy and your software. But bear in mind, the caveat about the Activator coming and going applies.
panic_mode	Whether the Autoscaler is panicking: 0 is stable, 1 is panic.
stable_request_concurrency or stable_request_per_second	The Autoscaler's count of concurrent requests or requests-per-second over the stable window. The former is the default metric used for decisions, but the latter can be used as well (see chapter 5).
panic_request_concurrency or panic_requests_per_second	The Autoscaler's count of concurrent requests or requests-per-second over the panic window.
target_concurrency_per_pod or target_requests_per_second	The target concurrency or RPS level that the Autoscaler aims for.
excess_burst_capacity	The current calculated value for Excess Burst Capacity (see chapter 5).
desired_pods	The current calculated number of Revision instances that Autoscaler thinks should be running, based on its configuration and metrics. You can compare this to metrics gathered about request latencies, concurrency, and so on to see if the Autoscaler behaves the way you want it to.

Table 9.4 Knative Serving metrics *(continued)*

Metric name	What it's for
`requested_pods`, `actual_pods`, `not_ready_pods`, `pending_pods`, and `terminating_pods`	The figures gathered by the Autoscaler from Kubernetes as part of its decision-making process. These are useful for diagnosing bottlenecks in the Kubernetes cluster itself. For example, if you see `pending_pods` rising fast, or `terminating_pods` isn't falling, something ugly is happening and you should investigate further.

Table 9.5 Knative Eventing metrics

Metric name	What it's for
`event_count`	This shows up for Triggers and Brokers. It's a count of events handled. Be wary about overreliance on this, because it resets to zero if the Trigger or Broker are restarted or recreated.
`event_dispatch_latencies`	Also shows up for Triggers and Brokers. On a Trigger it measures the time spent dispatching an event to a sink. If it begins to rise, investigate the sink. On a Broker, it measures time spent dispatching to a channel. If it rises, investigate your Channel implementation.
`event_processing_latencies`	Broker only. This reflects the time spent in processing by the Broker itself. If it rises, you may be under heavy load.

Serverless or memoryless?

Knative, especially Knative Serving, is quite ephemeral. Revisions instances live and die by the whim of autoscaling, with ever present gravity tugging the count to zero.

This means that if you don't set up some kind of logging, metrics, or tracing infrastructure, you will have close to zero idea what the hell is going on when everything is going to hell.

A "gotcha" that easily arises is that the Prometheus metrics system, probably the most used such system in Kubernetes clusters, works by periodically scraping the systems it monitors. Like a lot of things that were designed before scale-to-zero, this betrays the invisible assumption that all processes are long-running and that exiting is abnormal. Out of the box, Prometheus scrapes every 20 seconds. Revision instances can be shut down within 60 seconds or so, meaning that you won't get many metrics out of your instances before they vanish.

The argument for this scraping design is that the load on central metrics systems is too high otherwise. My own view here is that the problem is one of the economics of externalities. If developers can vomit up logs and metrics without paying any cost, they absolutely will do so. A better fix, in my view, would have been to turn logging and metrics into *blocking* operations. The polling approach, instead, creates a lowest denominator outcome. Badly behaved systems are still badly behaved, but systems that really need high frequency are punished.

> The practical upshot is that you have two options. One is to increase scraping frequency. The other is to install and configure the Prometheus `pushgateway` (https://prometheus.io/docs/practices/pushing/). I don't feel ready to say which you should choose.

9.3.3 *Traces*

Traces are criminally underutilized. Logs inform, but are often wasteful and ill-structured. Metrics indicate, but show aggregates instead of single stories.

Traces can fill both roles. Anything you can put into a log or a metric can be put into a trace, *and* you get a strongly sequential history, *and* you get timing breakdowns.

So what's the problem? The problem is that traces need cooperation to really shine. Each trace needs to be plumbed through systems that understand what they are used for and how to propagate one. A trace is only as good as the participants.

Out of the box, Knative produces traces for HTTP requests passing through Serving and for CloudEvents flowing around Eventing. This is useful for diagnosing where the work is getting stuck, especially if you cross-reference with metrics that measure queue lengths or concurrency.

What *is* a trace, exactly? Basically, it's a tree structure that represents how a given request moves through a distributed system. The root of this tree is "the trace." Within traces are spans. Spans can contain other spans. For example, if you have a web server talking to a database, then you might see a trace with two spans: one representing time inside the web server, which contains a span representing time spent sending a query to the database and then receiving a result back.

In figure 9.7 I use the Zipkin tool to examine the history of my browser trying to retrieve a `/favicon.ico` from my toy server. Note that Jaeger is a popular alternative.

1 In the figure, along the top I get headline statistics: how long the entire trace took, how many services were identified, how many levels deep the trace gets to, and how many spans were there overall. Most of the time, you'll be most interested in duration, but do note that depth can be very enlightening. Or very depressing.

2 Here Zipkin shows me the components that were identified, along with the number of appearances in the trace. The `activator-service` we know; the long name next to it includes information about the Service (`knative-example-svc`) and the Revision (`-zcgsl-1`).

3 The time line is automatically scaled to the total trace time.

4 The top four spans all occur inside the Activator. This reveals an important point: no law requires you to only create spans when crossing a network boundary. You can absolutely create these inside your own code.

5 Because Knative Serving has a Queue-Proxy, I can see spans for a request being sent to the Revision, being received by the Queue-Proxy, and then handled by

my process. I didn't add anything to the trace in my code, but if I did, it would show up below this span.

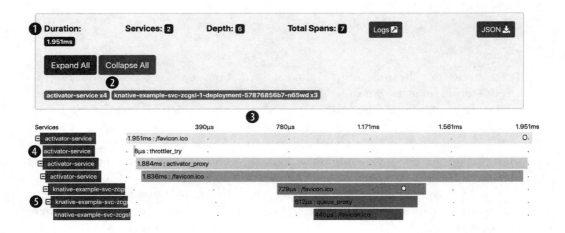

Figure 9.7   The trace for /favicon.ico

This is all very well, but I did claim you could use traces to capture information normally given to logs and metrics. Zipkin doesn't show these at its top-level trace view, but you can click any of the spans to see a detail view (figure 9.8).

The detail view reveals that more or less arbitrary data can be attached to spans. Here, for example, I can see the exact timestamps of when the span began and ended and how many bytes it was. Also attached are values for HTTP host, path, method, and so on.

For Serving, Knative adds spans you've already seen, showing the flow of HTTP requests. For Eventing, spans are added for movements across Channels. By default, you will get attributes attached for CloudEvent ID, type, and source. This is *tremendously* helpful for debugging event flows in your system.

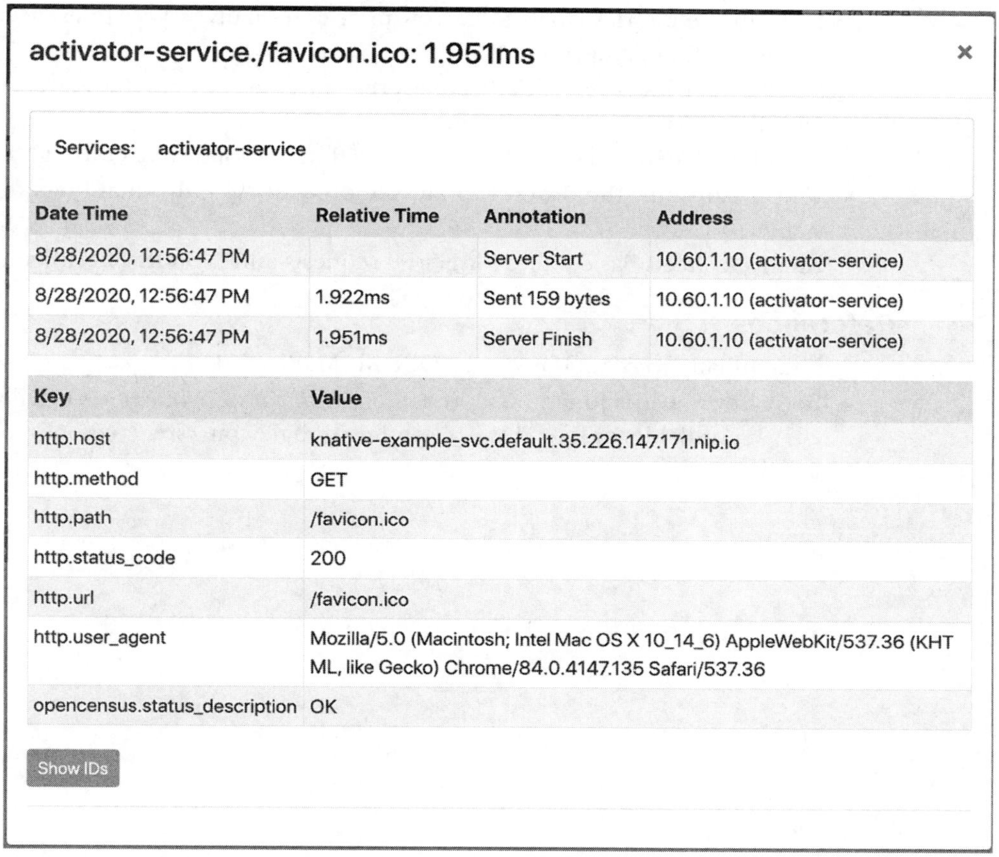

Figure 9.8   A span detail view

Summary

- You can use `pack` and Paketo Buildpacks to build efficient images without needing to maintain a Dockerfile.
- You can automate the rollout of Services by using tools that edit and commit YAML to a repository.
- Always use image digests in your Service YAML! Automation makes this easy.
- `ytt` is a simple and powerful tool for safely templating YAML.
- Knative is monitoring-friendly: it provides rich logs, metrics, and traces out of the box. However, it does not install or manage *infrastructure* for collecting logs, metrics, or traces. You will need to install or bind to such systems.
- You can use log field names to narrow logs to individual Services or Serving Reconcilers.

- You can use metrics labels to narrow metrics in many ways: namespace, Service name, revision name, etc.
- Serving metrics cover HTTP request-response data, as well as Autoscaler data and decisions.
- Eventing metrics can show the timing and flow of CloudEvents through Eventing.
- Traces can show the order, causality, and details of individual flows through a system.
- Knative collects basic traces for HTTP requests and CloudEvent flows.

References

- Mike Julian, *Practical Monitoring* (O'Reilly Media, 2017)
- Betsy Beyer, Chris Jones, et. al. (eds). *Site Reliability Engineering* (O'Reilly Media, 2016). Available online: https://landing.google.com/sre/sre-book/toc/index.html

appendix
Installing Knative
for Development

A.1 Installing kubectl and kn

I use `kubectl` in a few places to peek behind the Knative curtain. There are many ways of installing it (https://kubernetes.io/docs/tasks/tools/install-kubectl/) on different operating systems. My daily driver is MacOS, so I used `brew install kubectl`.

Installing `kn` is slightly less convenient at this time of writing. You need to head to Github and download the binaries that are compiled for MacOS, Windows, or Linux, then install these yourself.

My installation process looks like the following listing.

Listing A.1 Installing `kn`

```
$ pushd $HOME/Downloads        ◁──  I use pushd to switch
                                    to my Downloads
                                    directory.

$ curl \
    https://github.com/knative/client/releases
    ➥ /download/v0.17.0/kn-darwin-amd64 \     ◁──

    --location

  % Total    % Received % Xferd  Average Speed   Time    Time     Time  Current
                                 Dload  Upload   Total   Spent    Left  Speed
100   641  100   641    0     0   1950      0 --:--:-- --:--:-- --:--:--  1954
100 46.4M  100 46.4M    0     0  14.6M      0  0:00:03  0:00:03 --:--:-- 19.7M
```

This URL varies according to the version of the client and the OS you're downloading for. You can always visit the kn releases page (https://github.com/ knative/ client/releases) to see what's available (look for "Assets").

GitHub downloads include an HTTP redirection. The --location parameter tells curl that I want to follow redirects.

```
$ install kn-darwin-amd64 /usr/local/bin/kn
```

The install command is a handy little utility. It both moves files and marks those as executable.

```
$ kn version
Version:       v0.17.0
Build Date:    2020-08-26 11:08:52
Git Revision:  8fcd25c3
Supported APIs:
* Serving
  - serving.knative.dev/v1 (knative-serving v0.17.0)
* Eventing
  - sources.knative.dev/v1alpha2 (knative-eventing v0.17.0)
  - eventing.knative.dev/v1beta1 (knative-eventing v0.17.0)

$ popd
```

popd takes me back to the directory I originally came from via pushd.

A.2   *Installing Knative*

What I'm about to discuss is *a* way to install Knative. It is not necessarily the *only* way. The installation instructions on the Knative website are more general and cover more alternative options than I do. Your mileage may vary.

During writing I used plain GKE (but neither of the two Knative-based Cloud Run offerings). This isn't an endorsement as such. In its early life, Knative was not comfortable running in a local environment like Minikube, and I just happened to have access to a corporate account on GCP already.

Other folks have reported using Minikube (https://minikube.sigs.k8s.io/docs/) and KinD ("*K*ubernetes *in D*ocker": https://kind.sigs.k8s.io/) for local development. If you have a somewhat beefy system, then using Minikube or KinD will be snappier for development than a remote cluster option like GKE. It also means you can perform development in a disconnected environment, like a laptop.

For KinD, at this time of writing, these comprehensive instructions (https://github .com/retgits/springonelabs2020) from a SpringOne conference workshop were effective. For Minikube, Carlos Santana's `knative-minikube` (https://github.com/ csantanapr/knative-minikube) is helpful and frequently updated.

A challenge while writing has been that Knative moves pretty quickly. By an agreed release policy (http://mng.bz/NYaN), official numbered releases of Serving and Eventing are cut every 6 weeks, with occasional shifts to allow for holidays. Releases of kn trail Serving and Eventing by one week. When I started writing, Serving was on v0.2.1. As I write, it's at v0.17.1. By the time the book is printed, it will be at least v0.20.

Knative sets a minimum version of Kubernetes as its target. At writing, it requires v1.16 versus the current Kubernetes release version at writing, which is v1.19. If your vendor is struggling to remain three versions behind current releases, have a sharp word with them.

The biggest change in Knative's installation process since the early days is that Istio is no longer a hard dependency. Knative still leans towards Istio; it just doesn't lean *on* it. This is advantageous for small installations for development purposes, because Istio carries a lot of functionality that Knative does not use. In particular, Knative only really needs some kind of Ingress capabilty. Other service mesh capabilities like fault injection or automatic retries are not required by Knative. Istio also used to be much more resource hungry, which is how I originally wound up using GKE instead of Minikube or KinD.

As you might have guessed, while I was writing the book, I switched from Istio to another option: Kourier. Kourier is developed exclusively for Knative. There are other built and tested alternatives (Contour, Ambassador, Kong, and Gloo). I'd tried Kourier first, it worked, and so that's as far as I got in weighing the alternatives. That said, the folks behind the Contour, Ambassador, Kong, and Gloo alternatives have been fairly active and approachable. If you have an existing relationship with one of those, then by all means I encourage you to use their offerings. And, of course, if your clusters already have Istio set up, that's what you should use.

Throughout my writing, I've used the `kapp` (https://get-kapp.io/) tool to install, configure, and update Kourier and Knative. I am a huge fan of `kapp`. First, it avoids a lot of the pain I'd encountered with Helm 2 around the treatment of CRDs (I've no idea if Helm v3 works better for it). Second, I like the interface and pattern of use.

Listing A.2 shows the script I used to install each version of Knative as it was released. In my script, I rely on the fact that each release of Kourier, Knative Serving, and Kourier comes with YAML suitable for consumption by Kubernetes. Early on I was using raw `kubectl`, but `kapp` gives a much nicer experience overall, because it figures out the ideal order of operations, waits for components to completely load, and so forth.

Listing A.2   install-knative.sh

```
#!/usr/bin/env bash
```
> I always set these three options in my Bash scripts: nounset tells Bash to bomb out if I refer to a variable with no value; pipefail causes
```
set -o nounset
set -o pipefail
set -o errexit
```
> failures in any piped commands to bubble up and fail the script (a truly evil hiding place for bugs). Most of all, errexit causes fast failures in my scripts, rather than letting them run until the end.

```
serving_version='v0.17.1'
eventing_version='v0.17.1'
kourier_version='v0.17.0'
app_name="knative-$serving_version"
```
> Sets versions of Serving, Eventing, and Kourier as variables. Sometimes these are in precise sync, but not always. Defining these variables is convenient for flexibility.

```
# Deploy
kapp deploy \
--app $app_name \
```
> Part of kapp's functionality is to treat multiple Kubernetes resources as a single app. The YAML you provide during a kapp deploy is treated as part of the single app. The --app argument tells kapp which app you're referring to.

```
--yes \
```
> Skips interactive steps. You should only use --yes in a script like this one. At the CLI, it's worth inspecting the nice diffs that kapp calculates before applying.

```
--file "https://github.com/knative/serving/releases/download
  ➥/$serving_version/serving-crds.yaml" \
--file "https://github.com/knative/serving/releases/download
  ➥/$serving_version/serving-core.yaml" \
--file "https://github.com/knative/net-kourier/releases/download
  ➥/$kourier_version/kourier.yaml" \
--file "https://github.com/knative/eventing/releases/download
  ➥/$eventing_version/eventing.yaml"
```

The various YAML files, fetched directly from GitHub. It should be obvious that in a real production environment, you won't do this. But for me, it was convenient.

```
# Update domain
kapp deploy \
--app $app_name \
--yes \
--patch \
```

In my second kapp deploy, I use the --patch option. It tells kapp that you are only patching an existing deployment, rather than overwriting it entirely.

```
--file <(ytt --file code/domain-config-map.yaml
  ➥--file code/values.yaml
  ➥--data-value-yaml ip_address=(kubectl
  ➥--namespace kourier-system
  ➥get service kourier -o
  ➥jsonpath='{.status.loadBalancer.ingress[0].ip}'
  ➥))
```

ytt bakes up some extra configuration that Kourier needs to work.

In the listing, note that Serving is split into two files: `serving-crds.yaml` and `serving-core.yaml`. This is a slight hangover from doing things with `kubectl`, where the order of YAML could cause errors that required applying YAML multiple times. It worked, but was hacky. The split here would improve the chances of things working first time around.

For `kapp`, I don't need to use the split versions, because it calculates the safe order in which things should be applied. But I like the distinction, so I kept it.

Let's dig into the `ytt`/Kourier question a bit more. For Knative to use Kourier as its Ingress controller, I need to do three things. The first is to install Kourier, which I did as part of listing A.2. Then I need to tell Knative to use Kourier as its Ingress controller. Finally, I need to tell Knative what addresses it should receive traffic for. Perhaps zooming in on the `ytt` command will help. Take a peek at the next listing.

Listing A.3   The `ytt` subshell command, prettified

```
ytt \
--file values.yaml \
--file domain-config-map.yaml \
--data-value-yaml ip_address=$(kubectl --namespace kourier-system
➥get service kourier -o
➥jsonpath='{.status.loadBalancer.ingress[0].ip}')
```

values.yaml declares the variables.

A template file for rendering

The IP address where Kourier lives. I then set a variable that's used in the template. There's a modest amount of kubectl magic here.

In listing A.3, the `-o jsonPath` argument is a way of plucking individual fields out of Kubernetes resources without needing to parse any YAML or JSON yourself. My only complaint is that terse embedded mini-languages are like a lightning rod for code golfers.

Listing A.4 and Listing A.5 show the stuff that `ytt` will convert into a real YAML file. Listing A.4 isn't super interesting, so we'll focus on listing A.5.

Listing A.4   values.yaml

```
#@data/values
---
ip_address: '[ERROR! Kourier IP address not provided!]'
```

Listing A.5   domain-config-map.yaml

```
#@ load("@ytt:data", "data")
#@
#@ kourier_data = {
#@    data.values.ip_address + ".nip.io": "",
#@    "nip.io": ""
#@ }
---
apiVersion: v1
kind: ConfigMap
metadata:
  name: config-domain
  namespace: knative-serving
data: #@ kourier_data
---
apiVersion: v1
kind: ConfigMap
metadata:
  name: config-network
  namespace: knative-serving
data:
  ingress.class: kourier.ingress.networking.knative.dev
```

> nip.io performs some DNS magic.

> The top-level nip.io domain added to my little list as part of the DNS dance.

> Here's where I insert my data structure. In a production setting, you can have many domains set here.

> Sets an ingress.class label on knative-serving/config-network. Knative Serving interprets the label to mean "use Kourier for Ingress stuff, thanks."

In listing A.5, I use `nip.io` to perform some DNS magic for me. It's a service that reflects back IP addresses that you've submitted as domain names. For example, if I make a DNS lookup request for `198.51.100.123.nip.io`, the resolved IP address sent back will be `198.51.100.123`. You can use this to send traffic to endpoints for which you haven't configured a domain name. Just promise me that you won't do something silly like rely on this in production.

The IP address I use is injected at the command line. That was the magical part of listing A.3: looking up the IP address of Kourier.

index

W

Y

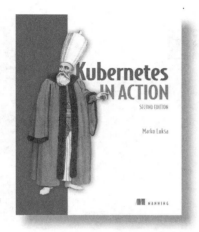

Kubernetes in Action, Second Edition
by Marko Lukša

ISBN 9781617297618
775 pages, $59.99
Summer 2021

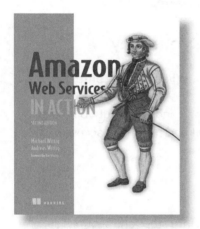

Amazon Web Services in Action, Second Edition
by Michael Wittig and Andreas Wittig
Foreword by Ben Whaley

ISBN 9781617295119
528 pages, $54.99
September 2018

Serverless Architectures on AWS, Second Edition
by Peter Sbarski, Yan Cui, Ajay Nair

ISBN 9781617295423
500 pages, $49.99
April 2021

For ordering information go to www.manning.com

Hands-on projects for learning your way

liveProjects are an exciting way to develop your skills that's just like learning on-the-job.

In a Manning liveProject you tackle a real-world IT challenge and work out your own solutions. To make sure you succeed, you'll get 90 days full and unlimited access to a hand-picked list of Manning book and video resources.

Here's how liveProject works:

- **Achievable milestones.** Each project is broken down into steps and sections so you can keep track of your progress.

- **Collaboration and advice.** Work with other liveProject participants through chat, working groups, and peer project reviews.

- **Compare your results.** See how your work shapes up against an expert implementation by the liveProject's creator.

- **Everything you need to succeed.** Datasets and carefully selected learning resources come bundled with every liveProject.

- **Build your portfolio.** All liveProjects teach skills that are in-demand from industry. When you're finished, you'll have the satisfaction that comes with success and a real project to add to your portfolio.

Explore dozens of data, development, and cloud engineering liveProjects at www.manning.com!